HUNGRY
ROOTS

HUNGRY ROOTS

HOW FOOD COMMUNICATES APPALACHIA'S SEARCH FOR RESILIENCE

Ashli Quesinberry Stokes and
Wendy Atkins-Sayre

THE UNIVERSITY OF
SOUTH CAROLINA PRESS

Published by the University of South Carolina Press
Columbia, South Carolina 29208

uscpress.com

Printed in the United States of America

Library of Congress Cataloging-in-Publication Data
can be found at https://lccn.loc.gov/2023055122

ISBN: 978-1-64336-473-5 (hardcover)
ISBN: 978-1-64336-474-2 (paperback)
ISBN: 978-1-64336-475-9 (ebook)

Grant support provided by the University of Memphis Division of
Research and Innovation, the University of North Carolina Charlotte
College of Humanities, Earth, and Social Sciences, The Fulbright Scholar
Program (Scotland, UK, 2021), and the Institute for Advanced Studies in
the Humanities (IASH) at the University of Edinburgh, Scotland.

To Shawn D. Long, PhD, 1972–2021

Courtesy University of North Carolina at Charlotte.

Shawn, born in Hazard, Kentucky, was one of the most creative, innovative, and joyous leaders we have ever had the pleasure of knowing. He was a colleague and mentor to us both (Ashli was fortunate to work with him on campus and Wendy through the Southern States Communication Association), but also a friend who was always there with a kind word. He taught us a great deal about building community through listening to, and really hearing, what people had to say. His wicked sense of humor and gentle nudging helped all who knew him think more deeply and work together more collaboratively.

Years ago, when the television show *Justified* premiered, called a "backwoods procedural" by the media and set in Shawn's hometown, he sighed, "Ash, don't you wish there were more stories about Appalachia that showed more than our poverty, racism, and substance abuse?" Well, Shawn, this one is for you and the many others who took the time to share their stories with us for this project. *Thank you.* Shawn, and the people whose stories are featured here, recognized the region's flaws and challenges but wanted us to take a closer look, sharing different, and additional, stories. We hope we did so.

CONTENTS

LIST OF ILLUSTRATIONS

Introduction

Why Appalachian Food (Still) Matters

It was May, sunny, dry, and hot. We were standing in the middle of a corn-field in Southern Appalachia, an area surrounding the Blue Ridge mountains that touches Southwest Virginia, Western North Carolina, Eastern Tennessee, and Upstate South Carolina. Our "aha" moment flashed—and the point of our research crystalized, providing insight that helped us recognize the true complexity of the region and its foodways. This experience happened in a part of Appalachia that has historically been dismissed, erased, ignored—the lands of the Eastern Band of the Cherokee Indians (EBCI). We observed how important the regional staple foods–beans, corn, and greens—were as we travelled in and around Cherokee, North Carolina, visiting the Cherokee Indian Nation Mother Town, Kituwah, with its sacred mound and stomp ground, surrounded by land farmed by members of the EBCI. We visited with the lead horticulturalist for the tribal greenhouse who showed us the early growth of heritage apple trees and berry bushes and the sustainable way to harvest ramps, a type of wild onion. We walked the tribal farmland with an elder, who pointed out the poke sallet (a poisonous green that becomes edible through cooking), growing wild on the outskirts of the land. He gifted us corn bead seeds (harvested from a plant that looks like a corn stalk, also known as Job's Tears) to take back home to plant as well as a necklace of his own that featured hand carved bead seeds, carved bones, and a bear tooth. In the local cafe, Granny's Kitchen, recommended by all who we met while in the area, we ate alongside locals (Cherokee Indian and not), area tourists, and Harley riders in town for a big rally, enjoying the macaroni and cheese, stewed apples, greens, and cornbread from the buffet. And we visited in the home of a Cherokee Indian food activist where we were able to watch a traditional "Indian dinner"[1] being made and sat down to enjoy the meal and hear more stories. Although Appalachian food (and the region itself) is often reduced to homogenous, white traditions, this experience served as a reminder that the intermingling of different histories and traditions created a unique area that is frequently misunderstood and overlooked. That intricacy drives this project.

We knew when we undertook this book project that we would spend a great deal of time talking about beans and greens and cornbread. Those food staples of Appalachia were not only first on our mind as residents/ food tourists and researchers, but also appear in histories of the region, in stories told by those we interviewed, and on local cafe and high-end restaurant menus in the region. This time-honored mix of foods reflects the area and speaks to and about the people who live(d) there. In planning our field research and in search of these food experiences, we wanted to be sure to visit many different parts of Southern Appalachia—from tourist-heavy areas to remote mountainous towns, fine restaurants to local cafes, paid tours, festivals, and wandering small town streets. Despite traveling during the global pandemic of 2020–22, we saw plenty of examples of Appalachian foods, sometimes accompanied by images of cartoonish hillbillies or the irascible, Scots-Irish, mountain-dwelling, white man, but often just a part of everyday community meals. We also found these foods featured in bigger cities such as Asheville, North Carolina, where they were served at restaurants with a New South twist and a much larger price tag. Here, the targeted audience was more "hipbilly," trendy and interested in local food, than hillbilly, but the fundamental food messages were the same, regional staples offering diners tastes of tradition and place.

This book is about the foods that have graced the tables of Southern Appalachia for hundreds of years and the stories that the food tells us about the people in that region. We tell food stories that feed into the way Southern Appalachians view themselves as well as the images that people outside of the region have about Southern Appalachians, and, in turn, we examine how these images influence politics and culture. Those food stories include the white, masculine dominant stereotype of the region, but also include the views of people who use the foodways (what Elizabeth Engelhardt defines as "why we eat, what we eat, and what it means") to feed their families and communities at home, in the church, and at community festivals.[2] The stories include the tales of Indigenous people living off foods that came from the land and how their approaches to food blended in with the food traditions of area colonizers. The stories include those of immigrants from parts of Europe and beyond, who came to the region in search of a home, bringing with them their foodways. The stories include the role of Black Appalachians (enslaved and free people of color) in shaping the cuisine of the region, despite a tendency for these skills and traditions to be overlooked in mainstream media. The stories also include newer immigrant communities over time, from Eastern Europeans to Southeast Asians, Mexicans, and many more, making contributions to what constituted traditional Southern Appalachian foods and incorporating foodways from their own backgrounds. And the stories include a modern-day Southern Appalachia that blends many of these traditions together, articulating a more multicultural history as found through the various foods and foodways.

The food of this region reflects, represents, and communicates a message of resilience that is present in the area. Mediated images of Appalachia and even residents who communicate what they think outsiders want to hear continue to portray the area in one way; we challenge those stereotypes, while also acknowledging the intentional messages of uniformity and exclusion, making way for a region that communicates the traditions of one of the oldest and most diverse areas of the United States. Many people we spoke to were hungry for different stories about the mountains. In conversation, they recognized how their food traditions provided roots that help build resilience in a place where that task is often hard, but some also shared with us how much more needed to be done.

To build this argument about how food communicates this search for regional resilience, we rhetorically analyze Appalachian foods and foodways, including the foods themselves as well as the messaging surrounding them, where we critique the ways that food symbolically speaks and evaluate how those messages shape an understanding of the region. Employing this type of rhetorical analysis, accounting for the symbolism of the food, the ways that those symbols circulate through time and space, and the influence that the symbolism has in shaping our understanding of the region and the people, we draw conclusions about the meaning of Appalachia. Before beginning this journey, we explain how Appalachia has often been portrayed and why foodways offer a powerful entry point into interpreting the region, introduce Appalachian food traditions, and explore the various ways that we will account for symbolism through our field research and analysis.

MISUNDERSTANDING APPALACHIA

If you read only mainstream media coverage that often overlooks the region's cultural layers, you might wonder if there is a need for another book about Appalachia, and especially one about its food. Long-running tendencies to characterize the region as deficient increased during and following the 2016 presidential election, with articles telling readers to offer "No Sympathy for the Hillbilly," after the election because "hillbillies are to blame for their troubles."[3] As historian Elizabeth Catte argues in her scathing rebuttal to J. D. Vance's infamous, culture-shaming 2016 book, *Hillbilly Elegy*, this sort of coverage is "melodramatic and strategic" simultaneously, where for more than one hundred and fifty years, the conventional regional narrative presents Appalachia as "a space filled with contradictions that only intelligent outside observers could see and act on."[4]

Indeed, stereotypical media coverage of the region has existed since the term "Appalachia" was used first to describe this area of the United States. Although the economic, social, and cultural development of Appalachia resembles the establishment of other American regions, there is a long history of making the mountains stand apart as a deficient "unified cultural entity" that fuels ongoing perceptions.[5] Scholars argue that during times of national cultural or economic distress, stereotyping increases, as it did in the 2016 presidential election coverage when people saw images of economically depressed Appalachian towns and listened to colorful quips from defiant Trump voters.[6] Symbolic meanings and messages change depending on our cultural or psychological needs and are often reflected in reality television and other types of popular culture outlets. The stable of stereotypes has evolved since then.[7] In 2016, for example, "hillbilly" or "rural white trash" labels were used to support interpretation of voting patterns, remove complexity from group identity, and to despair about the future of the region and the nation. As one reporter warned, for example, "Trump's me-against-everybody combativeness, his refusal to back down . . . are giving the hillbilly class a feeling they haven't had in decades: that they've got a friend at the top."[8] The region was to blame, some argued, for giving regressive-oriented politics more power.

For more than a century, Appalachia has been created, forgotten, and rediscovered for various economic, cultural, and political purposes.[9] Especially following the Civil War, the idea of Appalachia entered the American consciousness, with Appalachian Studies scholars arguing its characteristics come from a "complex intertextual reality" that emerges through writing, not reality.[10] Scholars observe, for example, that Appalachia is an invention, a "creature of the urban imagination," a myth of perpetual otherness created from highly selective interpretations of mountain life.[11] Far from being seen only in nineteenth-century local color travel stories in magazines such as *Harpers, Lippencott's, Appleton's,* and *The Atlantic,* Appalachian stereotypes have long acted as cultural shorthand.[12] Labels of Anglo Saxon racial purity or that of a backwards and isolated people have been used to ground and uphold claims of white ethnic superiority and racism *and* challenge facets of twentieth-century American life such as urbanization, greater reliance on technology, and increased task automation.[13] More recently, visual arts scholar Carissa Massey details how reality television and stock photography featuring rural Appalachians converge to create a discourse loop that reifies this stereotypical imagery, justifies rural poverty as a choice, and provides signs of gender difference and hyper-heterosexuality.[14] Further, reading about Appalachia's troubles ranging from economic desperation following its shift away from coal and furniture industries, its higher rates of premature deaths, or how its declining population is in a "death spiral," makes outsiders feel more secure that their own region is "doing it better."[15]

Although shifting persuasive needs may create these different iterations, the steadfast characteristics of the Southern Appalachian, linked largely (and sometimes erroneously) to the Scots-Irish settlers of the region, have had remarkable staying power, creating a legacy of essentialist and universalistic assumptions.[16] Continuing to perceive Appalachia as primarily populated by white people of Scots-Irish descent ignores its other residents and omits its global influences. This perception stems from a misunderstanding of the region's actual histories.[17] As English scholar Erica Locklear points out, "not all Appalachians were or are Scots-Irish and neither was their food."[18] Rather than learning how Appalachia's growing Latin American and Southeast Asian communities shape its food culture in significant ways, then, visitors to the region's Blue Ridge Parkway see the dominant pioneer version on offer, complete with moonshining, drunken outlaw gift

Figure 1. Hillbilly souvenirs at Tennessee Shine Co., Pigeon Forge, Tennessee. Author photograph.

shop motifs, grist mills, and jokes about having possum for supper.[19] The term "hillbilly" historically referred to Southern Appalachian mountain dwellers primarily of Scots-Irish descent, but ongoing cultural fascination with this stereotype of a group privileges the food and culture of a singular Appalachian community in ways that fuel white American victimization collectively, cultivating suspicion and ostracization of other cultures and their foods within and beyond the region.[20] Instead of demarcating a unified Appalachian culture, Phillip Obermiller and Michael Maloney argue that "more attention should be paid to the multiple heritages Appalachians enjoy and the contemporary identities they are creating."[21]

Some of these ongoing representations present truths about ongoing challenges that Appalachian residents face, but they also reveal what America finds problematic about itself.[22] From the Kennedy and Johnson administrations' War on Poverty to the cinematic legacy of *Deliverance's* North Georgia backwoods hell, to today's television series such as *Buckwild, Appalachian Outlaws,* and *Moonshiners,* featuring poor life choices and often illegal activities, Appalachia is constructed as America's Other, allowing the country to distance itself from its collective problems. In fact, Southern Appalachia suffers from "double otherness" since the South is already maligned in American culture and there is an even greater effort to put Appalachia "in its place."[23] Appalachia scholar Shea Daniels challenges this perceived dichotomy between Appalachia and the rest of America in her study of the region, moving beyond deficit discourse where the region's only music is country, its food paradoxically either down-home or processed, and its population merely majority-white and racist.[24]

Until recently, media discussion of Appalachian food largely reinforced those perceptions of a region in crisis. The notion that our food choices reflect our identities is deep-seated and widely shared across cultures; for Appalachia, its food, like its people, is often presented as crude, primitive, and in need of improvement.[25] Early nineteenth-century local color stories embellished the idea of Appalachians as people who "live on fat bacon, cornbread, and a few vegetables, all cooked in the most unwholesome way."[26] Over the years, high levels of poverty led to problems concerning diet and health, but Appalachian studies scholars work to counteract lingering negative food-related stereotypes that continue to serve as media evidence that Appalachian people suffer particularly from poor food taste and ill health.[27] Contemporary portrayals of the food often reinforce the notion of a backwards region such as, "Appalachia is where the white trash lives . . . Ask the average outsider what Appalachians eat, and they may deliver a similar answer: trash. McNuggets, maybe, or lots of bacon and gravy."[28] Stereotypes of Appalachian children having "Mt. Dew Mouth" from drinking too much of it and the region's people relying heavily on processed, convenience food, and having a predilection for alcohol and drugs remain frequent media themes.[29] If those living outside Appalachia have any ideas about the region's representative food, it will "probably be cornbread and pinto beans. Food that is cheap enough to fill a belly before a day in the coal mines and bland enough to suit the tastes of the Scotch-Irish who settled the area."[30] Despite the growing interest in the region's food, common representations of Appalachian cuisine as "biscuits and gravy, deep fried snacks, and moonshine" continue to fill in the gaps of deficiency stories about the "desperate, jobless white people who still don't regret voting for Trump."[31] Broadening the Appalachian food story has been challenging.

Appalachian food shares similarities with the larger, more well-known Southern food tradition, but praise of and interest in the cuisine is still building. A wide range of scholars such as Angela Cooley, John T. Edge, John Egerton, and others helped detail the history, meaning, and evolution of Southern food outside of misperceptions.[32] A variety of Appalachian writers are similarly engaged in this work, but counteracting a narrative that has been shared broadly since at least the 1930s is difficult.[33] Marcie Cohen Ferris, for example, observes that the US government played a role in shaping a singular Appalachian food narrative, ensuring that tourists encountered a story of "rural isolation, simple rations, and hardworking pioneer families" on their trips down the Blue Ridge Parkway, rather than offering stories about its agricultural diversity, culinary traditions, and a preexisting tourism-oriented economy.[34]

The lingering tendency to view traditional Appalachian foodways as the so-called proof of the steadfast characteristics of the region's people is in keeping with the limited and romanticized perspectives of the food still featured in writing about the region. Stories of rugged Appalachian pioneers were overblown from the start, where even nineteenth-century Appalachians did not always live on food that was "hunted, gardened, and foraged," but the region is portrayed as lost in time, impervious to technological and societal innovation.[35] In popular food writing, Appalachian residents continue to represent "yesterday's people," "who only survive when preserved in an amber crystal of old ways . . . in danger of dying out altogether."[36] This trope operates by wistfully praising those who manage to hang on to the old ways by preparing rustic, and often time-consuming, dishes. These portrayals are problematically nostalgic, especially when complemented by stories of (largely white) Appalachians who rely on grit, skill, and ingenuity to succeed in what is presented as a difficult, hostile region in which to live. Stressing the resiliency of these traditional practices circulates a narrow view of what residents often call Mountain food, ignoring modern developments, innovation, and the culturally evolving nature of the cuisine. Renowned regional cookbook author Ronni Lundy elaborates on this tendency, writing that this style exempts the vibrant contemporary food scenes in Appalachian cities like Asheville, Knoxville, and Chattanooga as aberrations, and ignores the realities of daily contemporary Appalachian life. And it ignores the ways people keep and practice traditions that worked (seed saving, drying, curing, fermenting, cooking in cast iron) while also keeping up with new changes. Meanwhile, we go on growing and eating and keeping on living and evolving culinary ways.[37] In addition to limiting circulation of other, more vibrant and culturally inclusive food stories, distorting Appalachia's full foodways history in nostalgic and narrow ways undergirds claims of white superiority and supremacy. Viewing Appalachians and their food as admirable for their honest, humble qualities has a long, problematic history; by the turn of the twentieth century, reformers and educators emphasized the "simpler," "wholesome cuisine," "prepared by people descended from the 'pure' bloodlines of early Anglo-Saxon settlers."[38] Continuing to revel in these European elements privileges a Caucasian foundation of American culture. Concomitantly, less flattering imagery of white hillbilly food combines with other depictions to entertain and reassure tourists of their superiority over Appalachia residents.[39]

In these ways, some elements of Appalachian folk culture satisfy the nostalgic longings of tourists seeking a return to romantic, pastoral, white-centered lifestyles, reinforce stereotypes, and encourage residents to present the images visitors want to see. Although scholars have largely explored how the contemporary tourism industry perpetuates and reinforces inaccurate and negative cultural identities through everything from the "pioneer" lifestyle design elements of the National Park Service's Blue Ridge Parkway, the rise of hillbilly music, the popularity of comic strips like *Li'l Abner* and *Barney Google and Snuffy Smith,* and the popularity of television shows like the *Beverly Hillbillies,* food's role in this process, for good or ill, has received much less attention.[40] Appalachian scholars examine how the area's handicrafts and music, for example, fulfill visitors' preconceived expectations in ways that also emphasize simplified age-old narratives, but more work is needed to explore how its foodways are also read as authentic, traditional, persistent, racialized, and deficient, often all at once.[41]

APPALACHIAN FOOD TRADITIONS

We arrange food in a hierarchy based on who originally ate it until we reach mullet, gar, possum, and squirrel—the diet of the poor. The food is called trash, and then the people are.

—*Chris Offutt, "Trash Food," Oxford American*

This is the stuff of hunting season, woodland walks, and smokehouses, a truly forest-to-skillet cuisine that requires no formal training, just an instinct for inventively making use of whatever's on hand.

—*Dancing Bear Appalachian Bistro, Townsend, TN*

In these two snippets, we see depictions of Appalachian food that follow expected stereotypical rhetorical contours, serving alternatively as evidence of a region in crisis or romanticizing Appalachians as good, simple, hard-working Americans. Of course, Appalachians are not the only people whose story is delimited through food writing, with the truth about cuisines always being more complex. Food writing, and especially Southern food writing, generally tends to offer romantic, nostalgic depictions of cultures and people, or is so intent on providing scholarly critique that it overlooks the interesting, unique qualities of the cuisine and cooks under analysis.[42] In terms of Appalachian food, this tendency translates into tales of women baking skillet after skillet of cornbread and biscuits to feed their families while lovingly tending to their massive vegetable gardens, filled with exclamations like, "I don't know how she did it!" Conversely, some academic writing reductively views Appalachian women cooks solely as victims of gender oppression, ignoring how some may cook as a hobby or as a way to participate in their communities, for example.[43] To move beyond romantic or disparaging clichés about mountain food while simultaneously appreciating its specific qualities overlooked by the critical glare, this project takes a closer look at the Appalachian food tradition's rise to greater cultural prominence. Beauty and skill are showcased in the cuisine, but similar to other traditions, it must also contend with lack and absence, with cuisine here also reflecting what ingredients cooks have access to and how much.[44] Mountain food represents a wide variety of ingredients, traditions, and practices that benefit from a more complex discussion than is provided through romantic or deficient lenses. This book highlights Appalachian food's themes of resilience to provide this opportunity, challenging glossy images featured by the burgeoning high-end food tourism industry to better reflect the complicated realities of its diverse set of mountain residents and communities.

For instance, in Ashli's Appalachian foodways class, one student, Hunter, from Bryson City, North Carolina, often spoke about how he appreciated learning new details about parts of his food culture that he had either taken for granted or never knew. He proudly wore his "West of Asheville" T-shirt on the last day of class, joking how a local store created it because Bryson City residents often had to explain where they lived using that expression. Growing up less than fifteen minutes from the EBCI's Qualla Boundary, Hunter's class helped emphasize how Cherokee Indian dishes were not always featured in the area's restaurants. He chose to write his final class essay about Cherokee Indian bean bread, also known as broadswords, to learn more about a historically representative Cherokee Indian food that had been used to build "the Cherokee people's sense of community, culture, and care for the land in the Appalachian Mountains." Hunter remembered working at a frybread stand for Bryson City's 4th of July festival but knew even then that it was a controversial food, introduced by the Navajo Indians trying to survive on inadequate government rations. For Hunter, writing about bean bread helped correct the over-emphasis and inaccuracies on frybread in culinary writing about Indigenous peoples. Hunter learned how bean bread became "crucial for the survival of Native Americans in the face of displacement and conflict," and although the food changed over time in response to access to technological equipment advances and ingredients, he wrote it was "a reminder of their culture and ancestry," served at ceremonies and events and able to "maintain its message to the Cherokee people." We, like, Hunter, seek to understand how Appalachian food speaks. A first step is appreciating its variety of foods and cultures.

In contrast to portrayals of mountain food as rustic variations of lingering Scots-Irish and other white ethnic influences, comparable to other defined cuisines, these regional foodways come from a blend of cultures and flavors, and there is no definitive list.[45] Chef Travis Milton calls Appalachia the "New World's first true culinary melting pot."[46] Today's bowl of pinto beans flavored with lard or pork descends from American Indian[47] bean crops, as well as from pigs brought to the lower South in the sixteenth century by the Spanish and from those that the English brought to the upper South in the seventeenth century.[48] European immigrants brought with them their pickling and distilling techniques that led to the creation of chow chow, pickled beans, and moonshine. American Indians contributed by placing a greater emphasis on using corn in their cooking; it is seen in everything from breads, hominy, grits, and distilled spirits, to the use of wild foods such as fish, birds, game, berries, greens, and root vegetables.[49] American Indians also influenced growing practices, including a reliance on the Three Sisters method of planting, where corn, beans, and squash are grown together, and using ingredients in a variety of ways.[50] Dishes such as poke sallet, succotash, and cornbread all have roots in the Cherokee, Seneca, and Iroquois tribes.[51] Cherokee Indians also first foraged for the prized ramp, a wild onion, now a chef favorite that sells for twenty dollars a pound.[52] Nineteenth-century "drovers roads" (a road used to drive livestock) connected Appalachians with Southerners in market towns, where they were introduced to food from African traditions of forcibly enslaved people, such as Hoppin' John, red peas, black sesame seeds, and okra.[53]

Part of the greater pioneer American historical framework, Appalachian food is also grounded in European foodways. British and German traditions, for example, "translated into a meat and starch aesthetic with milk-based sauces, pork and dairy as primary foodstuffs, fermentation and canning as popular preservation techniques, stewing of greens, and other vegetables or fruits as sides."[54] Prior to the Civil War, the mountainous region's abundant and varied landscape led to the production of world-class meats and cheeses from animals grazing on grasses, berries, nuts, and more, thus forming the Ham Belt of Tennessee and Kentucky.[55] German and Italian settlers made sausage and brought other swine-related preparation techniques and related traditions.[56] Similar to other pioneer food traditions, meals were tied closely to the seasons, with the variation in Appalachia coming from regional ingredients.[57] Additionally, biscuits and gravy, stews, chicken and dumplings, pinto beans and cornbread, and home grown produce that is canned or preserved are foods that may be familiar when thinking about Appalachian cuisine. The tradition also features unfamiliar items, not of European origin, unique to the region, including shucky beans, pickled corn, kilt lettuce, and leather britches beans, with dishes using indigenous ingredients like pawpaw, pike, morel mushrooms, and black walnuts.[58] Meat, often pork, was used to flavor dishes rather than being served as a main course, and smoking, was a common way to prepare it.[59] Foraging for produce like muscadine grapes, mushrooms, ramps, poke, sumac, berries, ginseng, and chestnuts is extensive in the region. "Mushroom Man" Alan Muskat continues to demystify the art of mushroom hunting in western North Carolina, supplying nearly four hundred pounds per year to clients including the Biltmore and Grove Park Inn.[60] From the pioneer period and beyond, residents emphasized family labor in tending to farms and gardens, with communities sharing resources, a tendency still seen in the area's large gardens and community canneries.[61] Although Appalachian cuisine continues to reflect these origins, chefs and home cooks alike incorporate influences and techniques from other traditions, so that diners might find their greens braised or avocado served on an egg and cheese biscuit.[62]

Despite incorporating different cultural influences, blending traditions, and evolving along with other types of cuisine, Appalachian food remains characterized generally as simple, frugal, and hearty.[63] Of course, some meals are designed to be filling and nutritious, but are not as cheap or bland as frequently portrayed. For example, Appalachian gardening traditions created hybrid fruits and vegetables designed to maximize taste and yield particular characteristics such as long-keeping squashes or pie apples.[64] Folklorist Lucy Long argues that the Appalachian tendency to embrace regional food practices in their homes over a long time cultivated the perception of a quaint and backwards food tradition in the Mountains.[65] Many of the world's cuisines draw from simple ingredients to create complex, distinctive combinations, however, and Appalachian food preparation certainly follows this pattern. It, too, relies on creating a balance of flavors; the traditional "kilt lettuce" dish mentioned previously, for example, combines the "mix of the umami of the bacon and its grease, the zap of vinegar, the bite of salt and black pepper, and the tang of crisp spring lettuce" to coalesce in a more complex dish.[66] Finally, as with many cuisines, industrialization changed the reliance on traditional ingredients and practices, with the arrival of the coal industry leading to a reduction in appreciation of Appalachia's foodways, thus burying some culinary knowledge and practices.[67] As more people have become interested in food cultures, however, the resiliency of some of these traditions is garnering renewed interest and cultivation.

In addition to possessing the richness acknowledged in other culinary traditions, Appalachian food shares characteristics with more well-known cuisines receiving increased attention. A subset of the larger Southern food canon writ large, some call it the "backbone of Southern cooking."[68] If the South has agricultural conditions that lend themselves to farming, however, with available arable land and temperate winters, Appalachia's harsher landscape features smaller scale farming operations and greater reliance on grazing livestock.[69] Appalachian cuisine is therefore analogous to the larger Southern food tradition, but its shorter growing season, higher altitude, and mountainous terrain, features food preservation, foraged and cultivated crops from the "most biodiverse food shed in North America," and supplemented with the continuing use of game, such as venison, rabbit, quail, and squirrel.[70] Also countering the generalization that Southern food is heavy and fried, Appalachian cuisine features fresh produce, with platters of tomatoes, cucumber slices, sautéed green beans, and corn on the cob frequently on offer.

Appalachian cuisine's use of regional ingredients and emphasis on authentic techniques such as drying, smoking, and preserving make it part of the larger local and heritage food movement that has dominated United States food culture in recent years. Despite a growing nationwide desire to eat more sustainably and locally, pursuing gardening and homesteading, and seeking to connect to authentic food practices or cultures, Appalachian food is not yet embraced as much as the more well-known Southern food traditions.[71] People became interested in Southern food likely because of its ability to offer comfort, nostalgia, and connection for some eaters through its use of traditional foods and practices, and Appalachian food, too, offers these possibilities.[72] Although sixty-two percent of Americans are now considered "food connected consumers," showing genuine interest rather than trendiness, interest in Appalachian food has been slower to develop.[73] Food-obsessed Americans debate hot chicken preparation, argue about ramen, and binge watch cooking shows, but Appalachian food still faces obstacles to becoming a greater part of the conversation about the complexity of American foodways.

MOUNTAIN TOURISM AND
APPALACHIAN FOOD POSSIBILITIES

I resented, and still do resent, being quaint, stimulating, and strange.
It's like being background music for someone else's Technicolor Day-
dreams.

—*Richard Jackson, Henderson County, North Carolina resident*

Far removed from stereotypical images of Appalachians and their "strange"
foods, we sat in the charming Ilda restaurant in tiny Sylva, North Carolina.
The creation of an Italian, Santiago Guzzetti, and Sylva native Crystal Pace,
the eatery met its promise of blending Italian and Appalachian cuisines
as we enjoyed pasta with pesto made of onions and local foraged greens.
Wendy, a vegetarian, passed on an order of Frito Mixto, here served with
frog legs, calamari, and green pepper chow-chow, but we admired the idea
of making the traditional fried Italian appetizer with ingredients residents
would recognize. The cozy dining room was packed with locals and a few
tourists, and the imaginative cocktail list offered an Ilda Old Fashioned, the
usual bourbon combined with Italian Angostura and regionally made ma-
ple-amaro. The menu continued to reflect the blending of the two cultures
for each course, and as we enjoyed the food, we could just as easily imagine
ourselves in New York or Sicily as well as in the heart of the Appalachias.

Although it is disheartening that narrow stereotypes continue while
some other cuisines benefit from more careful attention, another Appalachian story is beginning to emerge through present-day food tourism.
Developments in food-related tourism have helped boost the region's
economy, of course, but these narratives also present different rhetorical
possibilities and consequences for thinking about Appalachian identity.
Indeed, attention to Appalachian food tourism has much to offer the growing cross-disciplinary conversation about tourism, where calls for more
research into the implications of place-making, in particular, continues.[74]
Kristan Poirot and Sam Watson appeal to rhetorical critics to account for
the power of tourism-related rhetoric, explaining, "Simply put, tourism's
undeniable role in contemporary places of memory, especially in the South,
demands a much more robust understanding of tourism as a place-making

technology."[75] Particularly in forms of Appalachian tourism that emphasize white, European origins, the contributions of other cultures are elided; anthropologist Celeste Ray notes how visitors' "emotional investment in a heritage contributes to its celebration and therefore maintenance in public memory."[76] Keeping in mind that a successful tourism industry must sell positive experiences to attract visitors, a rhetorical analysis of Appalachian food helps explain how promotional rhetoric reshapes public identities of places and people in ways that carry significant consequences for the region.

The repercussions of mountain foodways in light of its ascension are varied. In some ways, the potential for foodways tourism to contribute to new perspectives about the region is delimited. As Patrick Huber observes in his work on the hillbilly souvenir, for example, Appalachian tourism turned histories into commodities that "provided these regions with a distinct and marketable identity of authenticity and local color that proved highly profitable" while reinforcing negative stereotypes.[77] Even when travel writers go beyond the usual touristic trinkets in search of a more authentic nature of a given place, however, what they often look for "depends upon, and confirms, those already existing stereotypes."[78] Appalachian folk culture-based tourism also has repercussions for residents, of course. Celebrations of quaint traditions that have been consigned to destruction by the dominant culture means that Mountaineers must either refuse to see themselves in the observer's patronizing terms or remain locked within that limited vision.[79] Since tourism's main product "is the encounter with difference," providing the ability for tourists to see "tantalizing others," it is necessary to not only look at how food-related tourism sells and (re)makes regions, glossing over their complex realities, but to also assess how producers, tourists, and residents alike nevertheless find meaning in touristic representations of Appalachia.[80] As Brenden Martin explains, mountain tourism sometimes reinforces inaccurate cultural images, yet also has the ability to challenge "deeply entrenched elements of regional culture, including racial discrimination and morality."[81] Because food rhetoric also contributes to nation and region building, with forms of embodied rhetoric (dining experiences, festivals, etc.) cultivating new knowledge about places, the role of Appalachia's food within its tourism industry calls for a closer look.

Increasing interest in the cuisine has led to what has been called a move-ment, revolution, or moment for mountain food.[82] As Ronni Lundy puts it, "Appalachia has not gotten the attention it deserves, and now it is begin-ning."[83] There have been at least two Appalachian food summits that de-bated the future of the cuisine. The Southern Foodways Alliance devoted an issue of its quarterly magazine, *Gravy,* to the mountain South and focused its summer symposium on the region in 2018. Ronni Lundy published *Vict-uals,* an award-winning and sweeping account of the region's recipes and stories, an edited anthology took a detailed look at a variety of Appalachian cooks, eaters, and food traditions, and a new book explores literary repre-sentations of the region at the table, and many festivals, dinners, and mar-kets now feature the cuisine.[84] There is a lot to talk about. A recent USDA Census of Agriculture report, for example, explains that direct farm sales in Appalachia grew three times as fast compared to the rest of the country, with Appalachians spending more per capita on those sales.[85] The Appala-chian Regional Commission (ARC) created a website called "Bon Appetit Appalachia," where residents and visitors alike can learn about area restau-rants, markets, wineries, breweries, and more. State tourism boards devote website sections to their Appalachian regions, with, for example, Virginia's "Heart of Appalachia" page guiding those interested in finding Appalachian products. Chefs, such as Travis Milton, open new restaurants to highlight the region's food in new and familiar ways, and restaurants like The Shack, in Staunton, Virginia, and Over Yonder in Valle Crucis, North Carolina, highlight Appalachian dishes.

In economic terms, this interest in types of craft agriculture, farming, and food-related tourism is seen as a way to create economic diversification for Appalachia not imposed by external forces, such as the once-dominant coal industry of the area.[86] Some journalists claim that reviving heirloom apple orchards to make award-winning ciders, harvesting Appalachian salt, rehabilitating old sorghum mills, supporting specialty meat processors, and visiting agritourism efforts are the region's best hopes for addressing its myriad challenges. These observers contend that through food industries and tourism, Appalachia is entering into a "new, more optimistic era; that a resurgence in local farming, coupled with renewed interest in traditional Appalachian foodways, could help steer the region toward an environmen-tally and economically sustainable post-coal future."[87] Chef Milton, for example, helped develop an 800-acre property, Nicewonder Farm, its restaurants using the products from its gardens and heritage breed animals.[88] Proponents see restaurants as driving other parts of tourism businesses while also convincing former residents to return and bring "real and creative capital back to Appalachia" as they revitalize the region's endangered foodways.[89]

Some, however, advise caution in viewing foodways as a regional solution to economic challenges, worrying this latest cycle of interest in Appalachian food-based tourism risks becoming yet another example of an extractive economy, where profits benefit everyone except those who live there. One scholar notes that ninety percent of the property rich in resources is owned by outside corporations.[90] As one chef warns, "If I open an Appalachian restaurant in Richmond, what benefit is it to the Appalachian region other than seeing the word 'Appalachian' appearing in an article or magazine?"[91] Similarly, the luxury resorts, upscale restaurants, and wineries that have opened in the area sometimes sell the typical story of Appalachia without supporting fairly their employees or supplementing local economies. Others worry that food-related businesses must be viewed as part of an approach to address regional concerns; as Lundy cautions, food is not the only solution, and is only a "piece of what you have to weave a larger net around."[92] To wit, some of the claims of a so-called new food economy fall back on another familiar trope—the determined Appalachian pioneer who makes good despite the odds, successfully pulling himself up by his bootstraps. If we hear about those succeeding through a mountain food version of the grit and determination story, what role do changes in regional food and tourism policy need to play? Scholars argue that in areas where tourism dominates, areas lose a sense of community and self-sufficiency, but when part of a diversified local economy, tourism brings important benefits to communities.[93] Awareness about Appalachian food and investment possibilities is clearly growing, but from a rhetorical perspective, it is crucial to understand all of the messages that Appalachian food sends to contribute to the conversation about which ones are beneficial, which are problematic, and which land somewhere in between. In particular, the celebration of certain Appalachian foods must be viewed cautiously. As Elizabeth Engelhardt warns, this increasingly popular quest for "authenticity, forgotten origins, and obscure knowledge" tends to "over-privilege a small subset of available food practices and cultures in the South," where, for instance, visitors seek out hot fried chicken, Benton's bacon, and hidden moonshine stills, and "almost everything has been pickled, preserved, or smoked once again," rather than being appreciated on its own terms.[94] We see an emphasis on trendiness, too, when moonshine is mixed in cocktails that sell for twenty dollars, when food is served in cast iron vessels, and hipsters open biscuit joints in Asheville.

Similarly, the development of a new Appalachian cuisine may be counterproductive in expressing contemporary Appalachian identity, as we will further explore in chapter 4. In places like Asheville and other food tourism hotspots with upscale restaurants, thriving craft beer scenes, and easy access to wineries and food tours, diners enjoy "fancied up" Appalachian dishes "using expensive ingredients, demanding culinary techniques, or highly trained chefs."[95] Within a new Appalachian cuisine, for example, diners might enjoy "North Carolina Mountain Trout with Herb Beurre Blanc with an appetizer of fried bean cakes" or "Appalachian polenta," a version of traditional slow cooked grits.[96] These new Appalachian dishes tend to celebrate food made in a specific place with distinctive ingredients rather than featuring local produce or reflecting the culinary heritage of the area, complicating claims of new food-based identities. Simply calling grits Appalachian polenta, does not value a regional food on its own terms.[97] Viewed in this way, the new Appalachian cuisine is not so new and shares more of the same story. Italian pasta is revered for its combination of flour, water, and masterful preparation techniques but mountain sausage gravy is not, seemingly requiring translation or improvements for acceptance.

Still, the enthusiasm for food-based tourism may intervene in stereotypical Appalachian personae as it helps move the region's economy forward. The renewed curiosity about the cuisine reflects a different image back onto Appalachians that recovers lost histories and provides different stories.[98] As one chef concurs about the need to learn these new stories, "you have to understand what it's like to grow up with derogatory portrayals of the region in your face as part of everyday life . . . even through hokey trinkets (in gift shops or around state parks) we were telling a story about who we are to the outside world . . . we're also selling that story to ourselves about how much we value our own cultural assets."[99] If the culinary elite is now able to "wear their backwoods badges without irony, without camp, without poking fun at mountain people" drawing from traditional Appalachian techniques to create new dishes, food serves as a new *topos* (topics or commonplaces) for considering Appalachians.[100] Chefs draw from traditional practices like the use of shuck beans, which are specific to the region and feature cooking with dried, dehydrated beans originally meant to last through the winter, to create dishes where the beans are smoked or pureed into a sauce. This pull from tradition creates something new, suggesting how food rhetoric might offer intriguing directions for Appalachian identity.[101] Even new Appalachian food takes on qualities that have been viewed negatively "as evidence of backwardness or Otherness" in different directions, tapping into consumer desires to connect to the land and to the previous pre- or anti-industrial lifestyles of their ancestors. Appalachians are redefined, desired, or envied, the featured dishes suggesting "ideals that all Americans should be striving for—a utopia, almost, of local, place-based food communities tied to the natural cycles of resources and seasons."[102] Through the emergence of a new Appalachian cuisine, instead of being seen as problem people, Appalachians were, in fact, "living properly all along."[103]

Any of these descriptions may serve simply as types of culinary tourism marketing, but the rhetorical implications are more significant. Whether they celebrate traditional ingredients, play into a trend, or proclaim the merits of a new Appalachian cuisine, embedded in all these discussions about Appalachian food lie judgements about the people who cook it, create it, grow it, sell it, or eat it. The language choices tell a new story, the same old story, or serve as pieces of a larger story, but they all call for more exploration. Further, there are more presentations of Appalachian food than those summarized here waiting to be discovered. The rise of Appalachian food allows scholars to assess whether, and how, this attention provides the region with new ways to think about itself and for others to understand it. Both have implications for individual agency, relationship building, and decisions about food and tourism policies, inside the region and out. We employ rhetorical fieldwork and analysis to help explain why Appalachian food still matters, perhaps now more than ever.

RHETORICALLY INTERROGATING THE REGION

As rhetoricians, we are interested in the communicative power of food and the messages circulated about food. Our previous book, *Consuming*

Identity: The Role of Food in Redefining the South, provided the basis for exploring how food is rhetorical, or symbolic and persuasive, arguing that the kind of food we choose to eat and serve sends particular messages. Southerners use food choices to help build individual identities, using food to tell stories and share memories and messages that connect different backgrounds, to describe how they view themselves and others, and to read situations (e.g., formal or informal). Undertaking rhetorical fieldwork (explained more in-depth later in the chapter), we gathered and analyzed hundreds of texts to explain how food creates the cultural ties and divisions that help make us who we are. These messages offer a significant and meaningful way to open up conversations among different groups of Southerners. Analyzing how people share and celebrate stories about Southern food illustrates how they are sometimes able to focus on finding similar histories and traditions, despite the racial, gender, socioeconomic, and other divisions that have plagued and continue to haunt the South.

If that project contributed to a growing conversation about *food* in communication studies scholarship and brought attention to *communication* in the food studies discipline, this book builds on our initial arguments to offer new insight for both areas. There is still a pressing need to explore the idea of Appalachia, asking "what problem it solves and whose interests— intellectual as well as practical—it serves."[104] For rhetoricians, work on Appalachia underscores why food must continue to be considered an important example of contemporary rhetorical activity, as it provides additional ways to consider a variety of disciplinary conversations, including those surrounding methodology, regionalism, identity, and race, just to name a few. Simultaneously, we see contributions to food studies and Appalachian studies alike through our focus on food's communicative elements. Rhetorical studies' emphasis on persuasive symbols and strategies complements the oral histories, literary analyses, and folkloric approaches frequently found in food studies, for example.[105] Looking at how Appalachia is communicated through food allows the discussion to move beyond shaming residents and trivializing their problems.[106] By juxtaposing these opposing depictions of how traditional and contemporary foods of the area are portrayed with ones that reflect more of the range of people's food experiences, the usual story about Appalachia gains much needed complexity. As historical scholars Sara Wood and Malinda Lowery point out, examining food's role in shaping a region requires a focus "not only on origins, but exchange."[107] Lowery refers to how American Indian food evolved while also maintaining traditions and preferences, but her observations apply to a variety of other Appalachian cultures as well. Layers of cultural exchange occurred before Europeans settled in the region. Similar to the mountain range that defines the area geographically, different gradations have built upon one another, creating rich and diverse cultures. We rhetorically analyze its food to better account for them, outside of stereotypes.

To get Appalachia "less wrong," we agree with scholars who caution against uncritical celebrations of a region or its people.[108] Clinging only to positive characterizations does not encourage the region to grow or change.[109] Instead, it is necessary to look closer at how discussions about Appalachia's food sometimes perpetuate, as well as counter, stereotypes that an entire region is deficient in order to generate new conversations. Clearly, we agree with those trying to complicate the narrative that Appalachia is more racist, more backwards, and just more problematic than other parts of America, but we also need to acknowledge and critique the circulated messages that do, in fact, support these deficiency claims. For at least the last five years, messages about Appalachian food have multiplied. Certainly, celebration of new chefs and restaurants, new techniques and products, time-honored traditions, and non-white and non-male Appalachian food voices have become more commonplace. Simultaneously, however, Appalachian food continues to symbolize the region's white ethnic racism, nationalism, poverty, and ignorance. Journalist Amy Rogers notes that "everything is a food story," and our research supports the idea that foods speak volumes about culture.[110]

Although American Indian, African, Jewish, German, French Huguenot, Welsh, English, Swiss, Slavic, Eastern European, and other groups all shaped Appalachia, from its food, music, and storytelling to its agricultural and building practices, this multicultural legacy is frequently left out of the conversation.[111] Indeed, despite two decades of scholarship debunking notions that the Scots-Irish were the primary drivers of Appalachian culture and a wealth of research into the area's myriad cultural migration and influences, mythologies of homogeneity and isolation remain. Although economists, American studies scholars, literary critics, sociologists, political scientists and more trace the implications of this tendency to ignore Appalachia's multifaceted cultural influences, we need to understand more about how the rhetoric of Appalachian food contributes to these stereotypes while also helping to free the region from them. Other disciplines and scholars explore food and meaning, such as interdisciplinary scholar Psyche Williams-Forson's analysis of African American food photographs, literature scholar Doris Witt's examination of representations of soul food, Jennifer Jensen Wallach's history of Black foodways, and American Culture Professor Rafia Zafar's illumination of African American history through a variety of food texts, among others.[112] As Stephanie Houston Grey writes, however, due to the symbolic nature of food, rhetoricians are uniquely positioned to contribute to the interdisciplinary conversation, offering a "rich set of innovative analytic frames" that help in "unwinding the multiple messages about food and its meaning."[113] We join those in other disciplines explaining the relationship between Appalachian stereotypes, identity, and culture by using a rhetorical lens to explore how the perimeters of Appalachian identities have been established and are reiterated.[114]

Rhetoric of Food and Foodways

The rhetoric of foodways has motivated a growing body of literature, showing the significance of this important cultural symbol. Studies in the rhetoric of food examine messages in a wide variety of contexts and purposes—scholars explore food's relationship to identity, depictions of food in cultures, the relationship between food, regions, and nations, food and cultural myths, food sovereignty movements, the role of food in shaping our lived experiences, and issues of production.[115] Scholarship in this area also analyzes messages about food to show how people form attitudes and take action, respond to injustices, understand the effects of particular representations, and use these representations to reinforce societal expectations.[116] Rhetoricians explain how even seemingly mundane texts about food shed light on gender roles, workplace relationships, ideas about parenthood, identity and stereotype construction, and cultural and economic anxiety.[117] Some rhetorical scholars further turn their attention to the South, and Appalachia in particular, looking at issues such as taste and authenticity erasing complex and problematic regional histories and food movements overlooking types of "traditional localism" such as canning, gardening, and hunting that have comprised regional culture for hundreds of years.[118]

Broader Southern food culture, for example, sometimes erases race or continues racist practices, where tendencies toward nostalgia in white-authored Southern food cookbooks reflect unrealistic and underinformed racial histories of the region. The infamous *Charleston Receipts* cookbook, for example, has sold more than 100,000 copies, its copy written in dialect and lacking attribution of the African American women who actually created many of its featured recipes.[119] This problem is particularly acute in media coverage about Appalachian cuisine, with its numerous tales about (white) Grandma's cast-iron corned beef and cabbage removing echoes of other diverse histories and perspectives.[120]

A rhetorical reading of food also provides a particularly strong entry point into a study of the rhetorical shaping of the region. Approaching Appalachian foodways rhetorically, and not as chefs, reporters, or restaurant critics, helps us embrace the region's complications, "not sinking into the easiness of the expected, the stereotypical, or the narrowly seductive adventure" that reading about the region's foods sometimes promotes.[121] It is important to us, too, to use our academic training not only to reach scholars but also to serve as a resource for those working to represent the Mountains in more varied and inclusive ways. To do so, we explore how Appalachians themselves use food to shape their identities and cultures while tracing how and why certain perceptions continue to circulate. We also seek to be mindful in using the language that is preferred by different Appalachian communities, where, for example, some say they are from the "Mountains" rather than hailing from the more academic sounding "Appalachia." We will traverse the region, both literally and figuratively, as both a regional insider (Ashli, born, raised, and living in the region until after college) and an outsider (Wendy, born and raised in Texas, but having lived in several Appalachian states), but both as critics looking for deeper meaning in the symbols of Appalachian food. Indeed, exploring Appalachian food rhetoric not only tells us more about what the region means as a whole today, but it gives us new ways to talk about the area.

Our study of the region also accounts for a variety of perspectives and representations. We seek the intriguing food stories Appalachians share, and there are many. Like others working in food studies, though, we contend that it is necessary to move beyond nostalgic memories about food while also honoring stories that may not act as forms of scholarly critique but serve an important personal or community-building roles.[122] Rhetoric gives us the tools to do both. As Abby Dubisar and Kathleen Hunt summarize about rhetoric's contribution to the larger food studies discipline, "Food, like rhetoric, transverses the boundaries between public and private, individual and community, nature and culture, imbricating democracy, ethics, and social justice."[123] If that sounds like a tall order, focusing on food's communicative power in Appalachia examines these questions on a human, humane, and approachable scale. Appalachia encompasses a large geographical region, but its people are eager to talk about how food shapes their experience in significant ways, especially when they are able to tell the stories themselves rather than have others tell it for them.[124] In this spirit, we let Appalachians guide this book. We share their stories and messages, analyzing the rhetoric of Appalachian food to explain why these stereotypes endure and detailing how Appalachians respond to them in ways that shape their identities.

We complement Appalachian and food studies scholarship exploring these questions of identity in the face of cultural change; in the process, we contend that disciplinary conversations about variations in regional identity must continue. Some argue that academic discussions of Southern identity, for example, are too sentimental, ahistorical, and based on outdated theoretical conceptions about the American South that ignore cultural difference.[125] These scholars assert that it is writing *about* Southern identity that *creates* notions of that identity. English scholar Scott Romine, in particular, believes commodifying Southern food through writing creates a region that fails to fully consider race and class inequities.[126] Here, discussions of Southern identity sometimes veer into uncritical celebrations that appropriate and profit from the creativity and labor of Black cooks, for example. Superficial calls for diversity and inclusion fail to challenge the "systemic racism that continues to disadvantage people of color" and "flatter (largely white and upper class) Southern readers and donors."[127] Part of the mission of this book is to elevate and complicate the variety of ethnic and racial contributions to Appalachian food, but our findings suggest that symbolic communication about food constitutes Appalachian identity.[128] Some Appalachians continue to enjoy cornbread and pinto beans and talk about the importance of that dish in their families and communities.[129] Rather than seeing the dish as only a celebration of white European ethnicity (which ignores how other ethnic and racial groups prepare and eat these foods), analyzing the interplay of traditional and contemporary foods within Appalachia destabilizes the monolithic story of its past while also suggesting who its people are and can come to be. To wit, the corn in the cornbread needs attention to highlight American Indian contributions to the Appalachian food story, while the bean links the region to other cultures similarly relying on legumes. Food cultures move; they migrate. We need to share more of these food stories instead of assuming people are familiar with their nuances.

Rhetorical Fieldwork

To account for these regional mindsets, we turn to the residents and the region itself as a source for texts. Historically, rhetorical criticism has analyzed written or visual symbols to understand their persuasive potential. Although rhetorical critics have examined different symbolic meanings of the variety of food practices that create food culture, rhetorical fieldwork helps better understand the relationship between food and identity. Studying traditional rhetorical texts such as restaurant websites, farm tour brochures, and menus demonstrates how food and ingredients are valued and encouraged to be understood by diners in particular ways. Examining alternative texts gathered using *in situ* methods, such as photos, sound recordings, interviews, assessment of space and place, and the like, suggests how people receive, adopt, adapt, and circulate these identity-shaping experiences. Fieldwork helps explore how one type of text influences another and suggests how people's preconceptions guide the meanings that are generated.[130]

Since writing our first book, grounded in rhetorical field-based research, the rhetorical discipline has seen an increasing amount of scholarship that develops an understanding of rhetorical fieldwork. The method of collecting texts in the field goes by many names—"rhetorical ethnography," in situ rhetoric, "critical rhetorical ethnography," "rhetorical fieldwork," "field rhetoric," and "rhetorical field methods."[131] All of the scholars who have envisioned this type of research explain a need to account for the everyday, ordinary symbolism that is often missing from analysis of more traditional written texts. Rhetorical fieldwork scholars argue that attention to the "vernacular voices that are often undocumented" is made possible through

Figure 2. Observing alternative texts while conducting fieldwork, Hendersonville, North Carolina. Author photograph.

observation in the field, providing access to "rhetoric that resists dominant structures" and amplifying marginalized voices.[132] Because there are no filters on these messages—unedited, obtained despite differing power structures and without having to pay to gain access to the public—field research provides what feels like raw access to a community, learning how texts and lived experiences combine to create significant meaning, but also allowing for a more meaningful interaction between the researcher and others.[133]

Food studies scholars argue that being there, analyzing the food experience itself, along with the "stuff" of cooking and eating, like "cast-iron skillets, beaten biscuit machines, canning jars," and more "all bear meaning" and should be considered.[134] Rhetoric's goal of trying to "experience rhetorical action as it unfolds," applying immersive participant observation, privileges these meaning-laden experiences.[135] As we have previously argued, it is possible to understand more about the relationship between food and identity by accounting for "the sight, smell, touch, and taste of the food that begins the experience . . . the conversations that are happening over the food and with the wait staff, the photographs hanging on the walls, the music playing in the background, and the neighborhood that contains the restaurant."[136]

Through field research, we also investigate how people's lived experiences contribute to discourses circulating in Appalachia, where previously, circulation largely addressed written or visual texts. Especially since there is a growing contrast between the rhetoric of Appalachian cuisine that is celebrated in some of the region's tourism efforts (visible in its fine dining restaurants and resorts) and the everyday lives of its residents, fieldwork reveals where these different types of messages connect, divide, and differ for individuals. As Appalachian scholar Ronald Eller puts it, we need to do more than "slay false images;" we use food to expand the picture of Appalachians through their foods.[137] Using fieldwork methodology helps move beyond long-dominant media representations of Appalachian food culture to explore how newly emerging depictions of the area suggest different possibilities for identities that not only appeal to residents but offer new regional perspectives.

Fieldwork counterbalances portrayals of Appalachian food with everyday experiences of people in the region—the home canners, local diners, farmers selling their produce, grocery store offerings, and more. Along with others who employ rhetorical fieldwork, however, we recognize that we bring our own backgrounds, identities, and perceptions to the field and that those experiences may interfere with attempts to fully capture a site's meaning; we attempt to be reflexive in approaching our positioning in the field and to be aware of perceived power differences.[138] For example, considering that we are two white women with Southern accents, there is a chance that we are perceived as insiders even though both of us live outside of the region. Nevertheless, we agree that the field-based approach helps locate the commonplaces of Southern Appalachian cultures and how they shape life in the region.

Rhetorical fieldwork also helps to explore whether or not a rhetorical shift in Appalachian identity is taking root beyond the walls of places like

The Grove Park Inn, Blackberry Farm, or other resorts and restaurants featured in the culinary media. Asking Appalachians about what is being done to their grits and cornmeal as they circulate through resort menus, hot restaurants, and "it" breweries in the region is important; in doing so, we assess the implications of trendiness for other food cultures. For example, Blackberry Farm's $25 ramp pesto suggests an entirely different message than a homemade Ball jar of blackberry jam gifted to someone who stops by your home. Neither is necessarily more valuable than the other, but they do share different stories about who their producers and consumers are. You might think about the person who took the time to make and share a jar of jam with you when you spread it on your toast; conversely, putting a jar of Blackberry Farm's ramp pesto on your cheese board suggests insider knowledge about a trendy Appalachian ingredient as well as the disposable income to buy it.

Although we explore this contrast in Southern Appalachia's Blue Ridge Mountain area, food studies in general benefits from separating media hype from how people use food to express their identities and relationships with others.[139] Undertaking rhetorical fieldwork to do this work provides a comprehensive analysis of these messages by visiting, talking with, and experiencing as much of the Blue Ridge area's food-related experiences as possible. We describe our encounters with foodways at various regional festivals. We study the area's luxury resorts and restaurants and follow that experience with eating at local restaurants and talking with their owners, staff, and customers. We eat at the many food trucks and stands scattered throughout the mountains, and we find that their messages are quite different from what you might hear after ordering a tofu taco in Asheville at a food truck rally. These varied foodways have a lot to say. What they say about the region matters, because it reflects the Appalachia people think they know, the Appalachia they do not, and the Appalachia people hope it can be.

As we explore the stories of those who bring new cultures to the region and take Appalachian culture to other places, focusing on questions of migration helps to re-historicize Appalachia with an analysis of *all* who live there. Migration looks at the meaning of belonging across borders, nations, and languages. Highlighting how the region's culture is influenced by migration from its earliest European settlement, we attend to myths about the

Scots-Irish origination of Appalachian culture, providing a fuller assessment of the variety of cultures influencing the region historically and today. We need to know more, for example, about American Indian influences in creating Appalachian cuisine that move beyond early iterations to include current expressions; similarly, we appreciate how the food of new residents from Latin America and Southeast Asia alters Appalachia's landscape.[140] Using food to better understand the myths and realities of historical and contemporary Appalachian identities has implications for regionalism, nationalism, and globalism and is in line with the current direction of rhetorical scholarship that attends more closely to the structures that support whiteness.[141]

WHY *SOUTHERN* APPALACHIA?

To undertake this study of Appalachian identities and foodways, we zero in on one portion of the region. Appalachian boundaries are contested, but if understood geographically as a 205,000-square-mile region that follows the spine of the Appalachian Mountains from southern New York to northern Mississippi, that is 1,000 miles of different traditions and people, making the task of capturing Appalachian rhetorical characteristics difficult.[142] Work has begun to make this process manageable; in 2009, the Appalachian Regional Commission (ARC) revised its classification of Appalachian subregions sharing relatively homogenous characteristics (topography, demographics, and economics) into smaller parts to better reflect these sub-regional differences. We focus largely on the Blue Ridge or Mountain South, what the ARC calls the South-Central region, allowing us to explore Appalachian food's commonalities and contrasts. While this smaller Blue Ridge sub-region shares characteristics with other parts of the massive region, its geography and cultural characteristics make for distinctive rhetorical work.[143] These contrasts play an active role in creating the two versions of the Appalachian story frequently seen today—poor, white, fat, dumb Appalachia, and hopeful, diverse, progressive Appalachia. Specifically, to emphasize the stories that exist outside of this false binary, we examine the rhetoric surrounding the residents, producers, consumers, and tourists in the sixty-county region that is roughly within 100 miles of Asheville, North Carolina.[144]

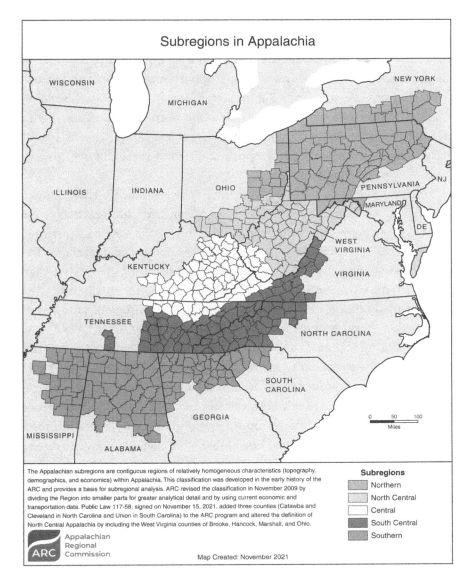

Figure 3. Appalachian Regional Commission Subregions Map.
Graphic provided by Appalachian Regional Commission, November 2009.

By drawing a boundary around this Blue Ridge sub-region, we risk omitting some stories and messages, but conducting fieldwork encompassing Southwest Virginia, North Carolina's High Country and Asheville's leisure industries, the Knoxville area's tourist mainstays of Gatlinburg/ Sevierville/Pigeon Forge, the Eastern Band of the Cherokee Nation's North Carolina boundary, Appalachian communities in South Carolina, and into the surrounding areas, provides a ripe opportunity to contrast touristic messages from everyday ones. Taking Asheville as the center of this region, as others do, offers a great deal of contrast between more urban and rural areas and economically advantaged/disadvantaged areas. It is a fruitful place to begin to think about the push and pull of these different expressions of Appalachian identity.[145]

Deeply immersing ourselves into Blue Ridge foodways rhetoric, particularly given Appalachia's overall size and myriad cultures, makes our findings more precise and better able to account for the wealth of rhetorical activity here. As we discussed previously, scholars warn against claims that Appalachia is comprised of one culture with one set of identifying characteristics; indeed, even the region's boundaries are perpetually contested. By focusing on the stories of how residents of this sub-region eat today, we avoid making these generalizations. Doing so also resists the trap of nostalgic food writing that tends to "romanticize the shuck beans and fried dried apple pies to the exclusion of the rest of the table."[146] We investigate how a specific group of Appalachians eat and talk about eating, acknowledging that their diet, like that of other Americans, relies on a mix of convenience, restaurant, and local and home foods. Southern Studies scholar Elizabeth Engelhardt warns that analyzing how individuals' diets are comprised from these different elements is difficult to study because it must bridge eating myths and daily realities, yet better represents "how people actually eat, historically and into the present."[147]

A ROADMAP FOR OUR JOURNEY

Given this task of rhetorically exploring the Southern Appalachia region, we take readers on a journey through the food and drinking establishments that allow for a deeper assessment of Southern Appalachian food culture, exploring meals provided by churches, dinners at luxury restaurants and resorts, snacks purchased at the area's music, wine, community, and other festivals, and community food care initiatives, stopping at various locations to listen to food stories.

We provide an in-depth analysis of the variety of rhetorical messages used to articulate Appalachian foodways, the consequences to shaping new forms of identity, and the possibilities of these identities to create new ways to think and talk about the region. Working from a rhetorical theory of resilience, we explore various aspects of Appalachian foodways. Discussions of resilience have become ubiquitous since the start of the pandemic, although Appalachian resilience has long been a topic in the region. Resilience as a rhetorical framing tool can be problematic, but we also explore the ways that resilience can make positive change.

We explore how the dominance of Scots-Irish cultural markers still seen in Appalachia have become unmoored from the region's complex history of cultural influences, tracing ideas about food and migration to explore the privileged white European narratives that remain. Awarded a Fulbright grant, Ashli traveled to Scotland to explore how the Ulster Scots mythology gained traction in defining the region in ways that continue today. Back in the Blue Ridge, we investigate the rhetorical legacy of this mystique by exploring food culture experiences that embrace the Scots-Irish persona, such as the famous Highland Festival held each July on Grandfather Mountain.

We also account for the most stereotypical Appalachian foodway, turning our attention to Southern Appalachian drinking culture and moonshine more specifically. We analyze symbols surrounding the moonshine and liquor industries, exploring how they fuel local economies while simultaneously reinforcing beliefs in the drunken, hypermasculine, irascible Mountaineer and influencing public memory surrounding Appalachia. We also look at alternative narratives surrounding moonshine that provide a more productive message of resilience.

Exploring the role of tourism in developing regional identity, we delve into how food tourism might best speak a message of resilience and interrogate the types of identifications these experiences offer travelers and residents.[148] Tourism centered on resilience works to create understanding and connections between travelers and residents, altering the relationship to the region. We explore travel experiences that fail to make those connections fully, as well as examples of tourism that succeeds in doing so.

Finally, we explore initiatives that use food to sustain communities sometimes faced with a severe lack of resources. By looking more closely at place-bound food activism, we share a less circulated Mountain story.[149] We consider the ability of all these different types of rhetorical food activities to intervene in the region's future. Here we attend to how ideas about region are critical to both rhetorical and Appalachian studies; we conclude by illustrating how our research emphasizes why regionalism has become an important component of twenty first-century American identity.[150] As others also point out, the region should be viewed as constructed by many voices with different concerns; from this standpoint, Appalachia becomes more than just a regional topic, with its rhetoric significant in parsing how regions are created despite their geographical location.[151] We thus write complexity back into the region's story, offering several versions of a food-influenced Appalachian future. Come along with us to learn what tastes of Mountain food offer for the region, for rhetoric, and for an understanding of resilience.

Chapter 1

Regional Resilience in Appalachian Foodways

In the summer of 2022, Kentucky faced severe flooding that killed at least 37 people and left many residents homeless. The photographs and videos of the destruction, highlighted in national newspapers and news shows, not only demonstrated the sad state of the region in responding to the emergency, but also framed this situation in a larger and longer discussion of the many failures of Appalachia. The floods, media outlets argued, were caused by environmental degradation due to poor land protection and an opportunistic coal industry that runs rampant under poor local government control. Even the places that Appalachians chose to live were to blame—scattered houses in remote areas and in flood plains.[1] Although Kentucky represents Central Appalachia, the exact location is rarely spelled out or differentiated in national headlines—Appalachia is mainly viewed as one large indistinct struggling region. The stories explain that the area's problems are yet another example of longstanding issues with poverty, infrastructure, and extreme levels of opioid addiction that define the region.[2] All of these struggles "make solutions extremely difficult" and are frequently blamed for driving out much of the population and causing a 'brain drain.'"[3] Appalachia and its residents are cursed, these stories often conclude—as we pointed out in the introduction.

And yet, despite the story that is told *ad infinitum,* the region thrives in many ways, maintaining a booming tourist industry and receiving accolades for its arts, food, and lodging.[4] There is another story to tell about Appalachia that centers the narrative on the resilience of the region. For example, our travels to a "Feastival" dinner, planned as part of the 2019 Mountains of Music Homecoming, allowed us to learn more about Southwest Virginia's tourism efforts. At the dinner, we heard about efforts to revitalize Marion, the eager entrepreneur proudly telling us about the renovation of the old General Francis Hotel and creation of its restaurants and cocktail bar. Although we missed the social hour at the remodeled Wayne C. Henderson School of Appalachian Arts, designed to preserve and promote Mountain culture, we were able to enjoy bluegrass music and traditional dancers in the newly renovated Lincoln Theatre, decorated with large painted panels featuring frontier days in the area. The next day, we met with the son of Villa Appalachia's new winery owners, Heyward, who was excited to tell us about his dry Italian style wines made with Virginia grapes. Firm in his belief that residents and visitors alike were looking for something beyond the sweet muscadine wines common throughout the region, he provided us with tastings of a complex Sangiovese wine and two of his own unique blends. Later, our eyes widened when we saw the scale of a family friend's home-canning operation; Jewel's shelves were loaded with neat row upon row of jars. After just two days, along with gifts of canned ruby-hued beets, pickles, and jam, we left with an appreciation of how hospitality is extended to strangers in Southern Appalachian food culture and a better understanding of how this region, despite its flaws and obstacles, remains resilient. The stories of Appalachian areas revitalizing and flourishing are abundant.

It is true, however, that amidst messages of welcome, possibility, and optimism, we also saw evidence of struggle and discord. As one employee told us at another winery, she quit working at a nearby upscale resort because management positions were few and far between for locals. One industry professional later emphasized the divide between some long-term residents and the tourism industry, noting that "it's still pretty segregated . . . the people who live here don't purvey or consume the tourism food side."[5] Seventy percent of the visitors to her business were tourists, she said, with the rest consisting of residents bringing friends and family who were visiting. She cautioned that while Southwest Virginia held untapped resources that could develop the region's food-based tourism economy, there was also "ugliness, and hatred, and discrimination, and violence, really" that could thwart these efforts. Curious about one resort that she pointed to as particularly emblematic of these attitudes, we decided to drive by. Outside a small Western-themed resort offering a saloon and weekly fish fry, we noted two Confederate flags and an enormous banner that warned: "If you vote LIBERAL you are trespassing PLEASE LEAVE." Despite efforts to remove it, this resort remains as a site on the "Artisan Trail" promoted by the state's tourism office. Driving away, we thought about the very different messages we had received about who was welcome to experience these forms of Southern Appalachian food tourism and who was not. Over a lunch of bean and ham soup, biscuits, and poundcake at a local cafe, decorated with a hand sewn quilt and an American flag, we talked more about the two different forms of Appalachia tourists could experience in as many afternoons—one open, hopeful, and resilient, the other closed, hateful, and clinging to a past they never want to see end. Being resilient, after all, is also about conserving and maintaining the ways of the past. When people travel through and eat out in what the media continues to lump together as "Trump Country," a monolithically rural, Far-Right bastion, they experience both.[6] Which message dominates has implications for the region's identity, its economy, its reputation, and for cultivating relationships between its people. There is a need to study resilience in this context, not only to better understand the region and its people, but also to learn how a message of resilience develops. In particular, we want to develop an understanding of how Appalachian foodways both reflect and construct messages of resilience.

Responding to recent scholarship calling for more nuanced discussions about the South and Southern identities, this study of Appalachia provides an entry point into exploring the true complexity (both good and bad) of the South.[7] Letting these traditional images of Appalachia stand in for the region ignores and silences its diverse voices, defaulting to assumptions about the region based on whiteness and poverty. As rhetorical scholars Patricia Davis, Brandon Inabinet, Christina Moss, and Carolyn Walcott explain, constantly "defining the regional outlook, culture, and voice as white" not only downplays other Southern communities, but also risks "preserving the colonizing nation as virtuous," ignoring larger structural barriers.[8] In fact, the broader story of Southern Appalachia presents an image of regional resilience that goes beyond Scots-Irish hillbilly outlaws making do in the backwoods of the mountains. Foodways, more than any other rhetorical text, reflect the diversity of the region and challenge this understanding.

Appalachian foodways may contribute to negative characterizations of the region that we have outlined, but if we look closer, it also articulates a stronger region and people. Consequently, in this chapter we explore the rhetorical meaning of Appalachian foodways, arguing that critical analysis of those foodways shows a region built on rhetorics that cultivate and reflect regional resilience. Specifically, our analysis locates three significant food-based messages of resilience that shape an understanding of the region—a foodway that strengthens the region by preserving and resurrecting different iterations of its food traditions and practices, fortifies its communities through food care, and offers a much broader narrative about the region, melding stories together and making it possible for more people to see themselves reflected in Southern Appalachian stories. At the heart of these iterations of resilience messages is community—an emphasis on coming together to survive and thrive. We also recognize that resilience can be used to burden individuals and prevent larger structural change. Multiple uses of resilience are accounted for in this chapter to broaden our understanding of a term that has taken on increasing significance in recent years. We develop this argument by first exploring resilience and circulation, explaining how rhetorical circulation works with food, before exploring how Appalachian food traditions constitute a resilient region that challenges some of the old narratives but continues to reify familiar damaging stories.

CONSTITUTING AND CIRCULATING APPALACHIAN RESILIENCE

Stemming from the Latin *resilire* (to "leap back"), resilience is one of the great figures of speech, referring to withstanding or recovering from adversity and possessing strength "in the face of a grave threat," the ability to respond to events with "stoicism," and "toughness," and often with emphasis on building community strength for dealing with long-term challenges.[9] Resilience has gained academic steam in recent years, but especially since it has become a hallmark of our historical and rhetorical moment. From the COVID-19 pandemic to questions of climate change, calls for increasing resiliency are pervasive. Resilience is often related conceptually to adaptation and adaptability, but scholars contend that the term has also taken on a "heightened (and in some ways suspicious) sense of vulnerability and responsibility more than opportunity."[10] Indeed, some argue that the rise of resilience rhetorics is ascendant with the "rise of the global [R]ight, economic nationalism, and global deregulation" that characterizes contemporary society.[11] Being on what many would consider to be the losing side of existing privilege structures such as socioeconomic status, race, and gender makes enacting resilience processes increasingly important but difficult.[12] Rhetoricians are particularly interested in the characterizations of resilience, calling for examinations of the dialectic between change and stability and security and vulnerability.[13] To wit, they pinpoint how cultivating popular conceptions of resilience as a tool or skillset echo American bootstrap logics that privilege the role of the individual rather than the problematic or oppressive systems that require it. To envision better, more responsive conceptions of resilience requires moving beyond individual deficiencies of character, class, or custom to highlight how inequality is symptomatic of structural problems and lack of social equality.[14] Resilient populations may recover from damage, but people in precarious circumstances become an insufficiently resilient group, and scapegoated, at times, for their inability to bounce back and contribute to society.[15] Increasing notions of community shape a more constructive understanding of resilience because it shifts the focus back to larger social structures.

In light of the critiques of resilience, considering alternative settings for resilient rhetoric such as Appalachian food rhetoric, where food is used to demarcate, praise, and demonize individuals and communities in the region, may yield a deeper understanding of the concept. Rather than trying to understand resilience rhetoric abstractly, we join scholars who call for a more localized, delimited examination that "contextualizes and problematizes specific sites and practices of resilience discourse."[16] In some places, resilience in Appalachia might be tied to place, emphasizing particular triumphs over tragedy, while in others, appealing to communal memory embedded in traditions, rites and local policies, is key to building resilience.[17] Attending to these different expressions of resilience in the region's food rhetoric provides contextualized and specific ways to consider the region as well as the ability to appreciate the consequences of what these constructions mean for those who live in, or care about, the area. Our research provides many examples where resiliency is a discourse of possibility, security, and an acknowledgement of value and meaning, but also identifies how it is often expressed in ways that are limiting, problematic, and stymie meaningful change. Examining the ins and outs of resilience rhetorics in Southern Appalachian food helps identify what this discourse does in the region, the publics it constitutes, and the points of intervention it offers, thereby contributing to a broader understanding of the overall resilience *topos*.[18]

Notions of resilience expressed through foodways are constrained and shaped by discourse in particular ways and result in observable consequences and outcomes—they are constitutive, contributing to regional identities.[19] As a discourse, food also creates identificatory experiences, where eating, ordering, and talking about food together contributes to the formation of our identities, or how we understand who we are, including whether or not we perceive ourselves as resilient. Tracing uses of metaphor, narrative, or anecdote in food rhetoric, for example, and exploring how people identify with each other through food preferences, similar language use, images, ideas, and more, helps us understand how they may develop a shared sense of identity that drives possibilities for building up or thwarting regional resilience.[20]

From a constitutive viewpoint, it matters how people discuss Appalachian food. Conversations centered around food help shape how residents understand themselves and contribute to how others consider the region; food sometimes reinforces negative stereotypes of backwards mountaineers or privileges white voices, but these conversations also offer opportunities for residents themselves to sketch the contours of Appalachian identity and to circulate alternative messages.[21] As food scholars Kathleen LeBesco and Peter Naccarato argue, circulating representations of food have the potential to reinforce and transgress specific ideologies.[22] All messages compete for audience attention. The texts that circulate most effectively, flowing throughout culture, become carriers of public consciousness, framing people's understanding and memory of events and cultures.[23] Since publics are constituted through the "reflexive circulation of discourse," as Appalachian food messages circulate, their meaning may shift, with individuals forming different perceptions and also motivating people to act in particular ways.[24] Rhetorical scholars are increasingly interested in understanding the outcomes of identifying with a message; exploring how resilience is constituted in unconventional rhetorical Appalachian food texts helps account for how claims about food *do* rhetorical work.[25]

Rhetorically analyzing food, accounting for how these messages shift and change as they flow throughout Appalachian culture, better explains how resilience is constituted in regionally specific ways. Communicative elements move through time and space, with texts taking on new meanings that create different identifications as they circulate, flowing "unanchored, around and through our daily lives" where rhetoric not only transports ideas, but also creates meaning as it moves along, working to "interpolate and sustain the people."[26] As messages move and shift, they beget communities, repurpose texts, create institutions and roles, and provide new public vocabularies.[27] The more any rhetorical device circulates, whether through analogies, arguments, images, or tropes, the public "begins to articulate, and thus recirculate, the language political and media actors use to discuss events," although some messages circulate more easily than others.[28] By extension, this idea helps explain how Appalachian food became characterized in familiar patterns, from trash food, to bland, hearty fare, to the way food should be. Consequently, paying close attention to food texts that circulate suggests how Appalachian resilience is constructed/constituted, including among residents who bolster and contest these swirling messages themselves.

Appalachians continue to be surrounded by imagery featuring moonshining outlaws and stories about MaMaw's cornbread, but they also experience a landscape filled with taco trucks, East Asian vegetables at the farmers' market, and Latin Takis snacks lined up beside nabs (the regional name for a type of cracker snack) and boiled peanuts at the gas station. Appalachian regional identity is generated through intersections between external and internal forces, where identity is shaped as new cultures and practices brush up against long-running traditions. As Dwight Billings and Ann Kingsolver put it in their work on the region, "culture transcends localities but also resides in places and is worked up in new ways there."[29] Appalachian studies scholar Emily Satterwhite addresses this tension, for example, noting how best-selling fiction set in Appalachia portrays the region as a distinctive place and offers feelings of belonging, even as people move away.[30] Geography scholars, too, argue there is "substantial evidence," that persistent regional identities in Appalachia are connected to the mountain range itself.[31] Investigations of identity must consider how people change as they retain these traditional cultural and regional markers. When discussing Lumbee identity, historian Malinda Lowery points out, for example, "Indians *change*, like everyone else, but we remain Indians. We remain Indians because instead of doing things the 'original' way, we do things the *appropriate* way, which is to say, we share, we remember, we retain our dignity, despite the stereotypes."[32] Identity flexes and shifts, then, retaining recognizable qualities as new demographics, economics, and cultural practices mix in.

APPALACHIAN FOODWAYS AND ITERATIONS OF RESILIENCE

Fieldwork visits to multiple areas of Southern Appalachia illustrated that resilience was a significant *topos* in contemporary food rhetoric. *Topoi* are central to rhetorical invention, referring to the recurrent themes, patterns of reference, and images that people use to generate discourse.[33] Viewed creatively, *topoi* are a source for the development of new ideas and conversations, serving as a helpful "method for discovering things to say about a specific topic."[34] Uncovering the *topoi* that emerge from Appalachian foodways discussions illustrates rhetorical messages that offer new possibilities for regional identities, thus encouraging new perspectives or dialogue. Circulating *topoi,* for example, might challenge received claims about culinary authenticity and provenance rooted in whiteness that is entrenched in discussions about Appalachian food. When recipes are credited to particular people and families rather than to chefs or cultural traditions, they provide their writers with credibility because they have value within their particular cultural group, favoring different, more inclusive kinds of authenticity and provenance.[35] Similarly, when cooks alter recipes, they act subversively, making a recipe their own and claiming authority over a dish, showcasing the power of rhetorical invention as recipes morph. As foodways change and expand, then, new *topoi* arise, highlighting not only how "authentic culinary knowledge is circulated rather than fixed" but also how conversations about food challenge perceptions about authority and expertise.[36] Cookbooks circulate these new *topoi,* but fieldwork also uncovers other locations of inventional opportunities. It is not surprising to locate ongoing uses of resiliency rhetorics in these regional foodways. Whether it is seen in activities such as canning, putting up vegetables to last through the winter, drying fruits to use later in pies, or continuing to rely on folkloric planting advice, Appalachians are frequently lauded for being resilient—practical, prepared, and able to weather the storm, through their foodways.

Although resiliency rhetoric is increasingly seen throughout contemporary discourse in general, in discussions about Appalachian resilience it is often connected to the area's food.[37] As one chef commented at a fundraising dinner, for example, "Appalachians are resilient, we're not afraid to fuse our old traditions with new traditions. We can't let some of these old traditions go, but we can celebrate them in new ways."[38] Other chefs argue that the media story about the region's cuisine should be "one about strength and resilience, rather than shame."[39] In Appalachia, resilience discourse circulates in three key *topoi*—preservation, fortification, and melding.

There are also limitations to this message, however. Resiliency *topoi* offer a range of messages that influence an understanding of the region, challenging the white-dominant myth present in the region, but also bolstering that narrative. Rhetorical symbols and messages are read through our own experiences and beliefs, so it is possible to have multiple interpretations depending on who is listening and experiencing the messages. Being inherently conservative, resiliency messages often emphasize moving *back* to a past state (rebounding, replenishing), preserving what hegemonic groups might see as important, and emphasizing individual accountability. The limitations of the *topos,* consequently, also informs this analysis.

Preserve

to keep alive or in existence; make lasting
to keep safe from harm or injury; protect or spare
to treat food in a particular way so that it can be kept for a long time
   without going bad

Preservation is the first characteristic of resilience found in Appalachian foodways.[40] Although restoring traditions is not always necessary, there is an element of protection in resilience, guarding that which is deemed to be important. While resilience can be connected to discouraging change, preservation can also be used to create clearer connections by establishing common ground. Constitutive messages are grounded in commonalities that occasionally need to be rescued or resuscitated in order to make connections possible. In this case, Appalachian foodways serve as the connecting ingredient and celebrating shared food traditions is one significant *topos* used for regional identity and community-building. Despite longstanding food traditions in the region, modernized society can change expectations, habits, and processes. It is easier to run to a grocery store for a can of beans than to labor through all the steps of canning your own goods. Whether people participate in those traditions or merely see them enacted by others, traditional foodways function to constitute a whole, joining people together in a common experience.

Although Appalachian food stereotypes might be built on images of lower-quality ingredients and basic techniques, much of that perception is misplaced, coming from poverty-shaming and a desire to use Mountain food as a reminder of how much "better" other regional cuisines (and therefore their people) are. Despite the dismissal of these food traditions by some they continue to be symbolic of the region. As one Appalachian chef notes in a *Humanities* interview, "Our history here was made by survivalists . . . It's centered around pickling, preserving, curing, making things last and stretching them. The heart of Appalachian dishes is about preserving history and ensuring that these concepts and recipes don't get lost or forgotten."[41] The reliance on local ingredients was driven by the need to sustain families through gardening and preservation since they were often long distances from grocery stores and had less money to buy convenience items. As one interviewee explained about her desire to incorporate this part of the Appalachian cuisine tradition into her restaurant, "You know, growing up 45 minutes outside of town, you run out of something, you can't just run into town and grab it. You really gotta think on your feet and be able to make everything from scratch in your house."[42] Preservation is both about tradition and fulfilling a practical need. The push for survival that is often a part of the Appalachian foodways story does not mean that the food is lacking in creativity, though. Resilience is reflected through foods showing creativity in terms of growing and selecting ingredients but also inspires innovation in flavors and techniques. As Chef Travis Milton points out, "This [Appalachian food] is not a still photo as much as anyone wants to make it that, this cuisine has been an ever-changing thing . . . that to me is just sheer brilliance and looking back on the things that she [his grandmother] was able to do and the things that she cooked from her garden just to sustain us and her family were on par with some of the stuff that I was working [on] with chefs . . . "[43] Milton argues for disrupting the circulating messages that question the worth of Appalachian foodways. Far from being a food defined by poverty and making do, many Appalachian foods are just as complex as other lauded cuisines.

These traditional foodways are also an important part of the regional definition. Driving into the area, it is not difficult to find historical replicas of grist mills displaying the arduous process of creating a central ingredient in the regional food—corn. Area museums and festivals feature sorghum and apple butter–making demonstrations. Magazine articles speak romantically about the region's historically significant harvested, homegrown, and preserved ingredients such as salt, ham, pinto beans, melons, and berries and note the purity of Appalachian cooking.[44] Although much of the region's foodways have emerged out of necessity, those creations have often been praised based on their innovation.

Canning, for example, has been a staple of the region for many years and continues to thrive. Local stores, tourist-focused businesses, and even high-end shops often feature rows of locally made goods (or, at the very least, products designed to look homemade). Southerners have "dried, salted, pickled, potted, canned, jellied, or otherwise preserved every kind of food," as John Egerton writes, and those efforts not only provided sustenance, but also allowed home cooks (generally women) to create a more efficient kitchen as techniques improved.[45] Beyond filling the pantry, however, these foods have grown to become a preference. As Abingdon, Virginia food truck owners, one the son of Pakistani immigrants and the other a native Virginian, explain about naming their business the Packalachian to meld Appalachian and Pakistani food cultures, "Canning is a part of life in this area . . . The process that began out of necessity for this region turns out to be one of the biggest contributors to Southwest Virginia's comfort food reputation . . . It makes it real. It gives it that taste of home. That taste that's really hard to do."[46] Recognizing the importance of home canning in symbolizing the region changes the message about *why* Appalachians continue to embrace that tradition.

We saw many examples of canning throughout our travels, but two instances were more memorable. In one, we were invited in to see a family friend's canning collection. Although we knew of Jewel Spencer's food preservation skills, and visited her for this reason, we were not fully prepared to see how extensive her collection was. We walked into her canning shed and were faced with row after row of every variety of reused glass jars imaginable, all filled with home-grown goods—several varieties of beans, peas, cucumbers, beets, jams and jellies, tomatoes, and more. Jewel was clearly

Figure 4. Jewel Spencer's canned goods shelves,
Southwestern Virginia. Author photograph.

proud of her recognized status as a skilled canner, but also pointed out that these kinds of foods were just expected, with women passing along instructions for future wives so that they could "recreate mom's food." And, as is often the case, Jewel was generous with her creations, sharing them with family and friends, arguing that "no one should leave empty handed."[47] We were very happy to drive away with a cooler filled with sandwiches, potato salad, and canned goods of our choosing.

Likewise, our visit with Tyson, a Cherokee Indian food activist in Cherokee, North Carolina, brought us face to face with his extensive collection of canned goods made from produce not only grown on local Cherokee Indian land, but that highlight vital parts of Cherokee Indian food traditions.[48] Years earlier, he realized that many of the Cherokee Indian foodways were dying off with the elders and he made it part of his mission to preserve and share those foods and techniques. Knowing that there was no way to find many of the traditional ingredients in the local stores, he worked with other Cherokee people to plant and harvest and forage for the traditional ingredients, while also finding a way to share those goods with others. Sochan, bear lettuce, leather britches, poke, hen of the woods mushrooms, and ramps all made their way into many of the dishes he was trying to preserve. Canning made some of this process easier and he was happy to do so, turning a section of his house into a pantry that stored rows of jars. Laughing at a previous interview with environmental activists when they asked about permaculture (sustainable growing techniques), he joked, "Permaculture? I *am* permaculture!" Importantly, Tyson circulates the Cherokee Indian experience into discussions about Appalachian foodways resilience.

This type of food preservation work is not only an example of community care, but also a demonstration of a food process that is central to this region, providing an innovative way to provide nourishment. As one interviewee reflected about canning's decline in some areas, "people are busy and older folks are tired," but there are efforts to preserve the tradition's importance. In Carroll County, Virginia, anyone can use the community cannery—they are not required to have experience, are provided with an on-site specialist to guide each step, and are encouraged to can anything they please from meat to fresh vegetables. Symbolically, this food tradition speaks a message of resilience from many locations, private and public.

Sorghum provides a different example of preservation in the region, especially as it has been recognized for its environmental sustainability in recent years; the grain is tolerant of drought and poor soil quality and adaptable to a changing climate.[49] Renewed interest today is also a result of its high fiber, gluten free, "hillbilly umami," qualities, its syrup containing a nutty, grassy, sweetness that chefs and foodie-related media are rediscovering.[50] Preserving sorghum cultivation is appealing for these reasons, but media discussion tends to follow a common pattern. We hear more about dishes that became essential in regional cooking such as stack cakes, gingerbread, and fried apple pies, the use of sorghum syrup on biscuits, or the increasing number of sorghum culinary products that are emerging, but less about how different Appalachian communities continue to process the grain to preserve their culture. Indeed, as Glenn Roberts (founder of Anson Mills, a company that collects, grows, and sells heirloom grains) told us, there's more to sorghum's story than is typically printed, and part of it involves the crop's role in the African American community.[51] Indeed, as Black culinary historian Michael Twitty warns, renewed interest in sorghum risks omitting its role in sustaining the African diaspora and its foodways: "I wanted ways to kind of reclaim sorghum. Sorghum has recently become a boutique ingredient. But you don't really often hear the story of how it is an African cultigen. That's very important to me."[52] It is a fascinating journey.

Originating in Africa as a fundamental crop, sorghum traveled to Asia, then to the Middle East, and records suggest it was grown in America as early as the 1700s.[53] Others argue that African families have grown sorghum in the South since the 1600s, although poor record keeping makes it difficult to document.[54] Records do suggest that when the Portuguese first arrived on the African West Coast in the 1480s, they observed native Africans baking sorghum, millet, and rice in open fires. When enslaved people were trafficked to Virginia in 1619, grain sorghums came too. Called guinea corn, chicken corn, and broom corn, African Americans made porridge and griddle cakes with the ingredient.[55] Similar to other grains, processing sorghum was often a rural community affair, where access to one mill saw groups of African Americans working together to crush the stalks for syrup, but, typically, poor historical accounts overlook sorghum's role in forming the fabric of enslaved African American Appalachian communities.[56] For instance, white slaveowners forcibly brought enslaved Africans to the Great Smoky Mountains (also known as the Smokies) around 1790, but their skills in running the area's sorghum mills are largely unknown.[57]

Today, however, there are increased efforts in preserving the story of the grain's importance in African American communities and in reintroducing people to this other side of the story. African American chefs and farmers who grow sorghum or cook, bake, and brew with it preserve its legacy. Southern craft brewers using red sorghum from Africa in special release beers offer a "sense of recovery, of gaining what's lost."[58] As African American filmmaker Atinuke Akintola Diver points out, in the process of making a documentary about Black craft brewers, she found out her grandmother brewed butta kutu, an African fermented drink made of sorghum, leading her to realize that when craft brewers use these ingredients, they "feel and sense a connection to the ingredients that their forebears would have used, and integrated into their practices."[59] Similarly, when a shipment of white

African sorghum is sent to Gullah farmers working to make it a staple in the American diet again, they are offering dishes 300 years in the making.[60] TrueLove's African diaspora seed collection also offers sorghum seeds to help preserve this part of its culinary history within the Appalachian culinary narrative.[61] As culinary historian Jessica Harris explains about the value of Black Americans using food to connect the dots of their histories, "It's about a real desire to know one's background: where one might be from, what one's ancestors might have eaten."[62]

Ultimately, what we discovered through our fieldwork illustrates how the resiliency *topos* stressing preservation has several positive rhetorical consequences, including using food traditions to define communities, cultivate empathy, and shift the narrative from traditional foodways being used out of desperation and toward a purposeful embracing of historical ways of life. These types of resiliency messages help people cope individually and move forward, but they also collectively prepare communities to combat vulnerabilities to come.[63] At the same time, the process of preservation assumes that there is something worth saving and that others view it in the same way; that is not always the case. Some restaurant owners, for example, claim that Appalachian food can be a turn off for tourists and residents alike. They commonly discussed resistance to change and a "closed off" mentality. In describing that resistance, Joe Reagan, chef of Sisters' Restaurant at the historic Martha Washington Inn and Spa in Abingdon, Virginia, explains: "It just feels like a lot of meat and potatoes. Even if I'm using ramps and some really intricate techniques to do things or whatever, some people might just say, well, my grandmother used to make me eat ramps and I hate them. I just want a burger or something like that. Sometimes it's hard to get people to open up here. I think the younger generation is going to help us out."[64] Even within the region, different presentations of Appalachian food or ingredients face resistance from some residents. Overall, the idea of clinging to the past for the sake of preservation alone can have negative consequences since those actions are more about maintaining the status quo. Arguing for the continued veneration of the Confederate flag as a symbol of the South, for example, does not help establish resilient communities that are inclusive. Despite limitations to the resiliency *topos,* multiple meanings of resilience are always at play and the strengthening aspect of this idea should not be overlooked.

Fortify

to make strong; impart strength or vigor to" "to strengthen mentally
    or morally
practice of deliberately increasing the content of one or more micro-
    nutrients . . . in a food . . . to improve the nutritional quality of the
    food supply and provide a public health benefit

Fortification, or making the preserved stronger, is the second characteristic of resilience.[65] Preserving foodways not only celebrates and renews traditions but also strengthens communities by highlighting consubstantiality. The *telos* (or ultimate end) of constitutive rhetoric is action and themes focused on strengthening the built community through Appalachia's resilient food messages serve as an example of symbolism that provides an impetus for change. Given the material challenges that Southern Appalachia often faces (both social and environmental), regional foodways reflect the ways that Appalachians create connections to survive and thrive to fortify their community. Food can weave together regions, histories, and people through circulation and merging of traditions. It can also be a part of community care, emphasizing the commonalties among groups and highlighting those connections. Community-focused strength is a significant part of regional identification and Appalachian foodways demonstrate this type of resilience.

Although Appalachian foods are much more diverse than what is often portrayed, beans served with cornbread is considered a main dish of the region. The dish is often viewed as poor, white food, but pulls from many different food traditions. As David Anderson, horticulture operations supervisor for the Eastern Band of the Cherokee Indians (EBCI) points out, American Indian tribes have been growing and eating beans and corn dishes long before Europeans arrived, but even the beans these ancient communities use hailed originally from South America.[66] Once adopted into North America, Cherokee Indians and other Native peoples would dry beans and raise corn to grind into meal seasonally, growing them alongside squash as part of the familiar Three Sisters planting method. Today, although the Midwest is the largest producer of pinto beans and they are found throughout the United States, Appalachians continue to identify

Figure 5. Beans and cornbread at Bush's Beans Visitor Center,
Chestnut Hill, Tennessee. Author photograph.

this meal with "home," a dish about survival, family legacy, and ritual.[67] At Bush's Beans Visitor's Center in Chestnut Hill, Tennessee, they are celebrated as a symbol of the Great Smoky Mountains, where visitors can learn about the company's long history, walk through a giant bean can, and read about the global connections that beans create. Despite more creative dishes on offer in the on-site restaurant, diners continue to order a simple plate of beans and cornbread. Not only are these foods bound to the region through history and culture, they provide abundant food options that are also economical and environmentally friendly, serving as "the nutritionally perfect food."[68] Symbolically, the two continue to help care for Appalachian communities but remain symbolic of them as well. They are served in small cafes throughout the region and form a backdrop as residents catch up during the lunch hour.

The humble dish continues to serve a variety of important roles, but often its significance in caring for and fortifying one Southern Appalachian community is less well known. One role is community-building more broadly. Each October, the EBCI hosts the Cherokee Indian Fair to attract tourists, serving traditional foods at vendor stands by those connected to the community, but the celebration also plays an important role in fortifying community identity. Cornbread and beans continue to be a critical part of the core purpose of the Fair which remains the same after a century— "to bring the communities together to celebrate Cherokee culture and traditions."[69] Visiting the 110th Annual Fair at lunchtime on a Friday, the predominant visitors were people from the seven small Cherokee Indian/ Qualla Boundary[70] communities—workers with company identification badges visiting traditional Cherokee Indian food vendors, chatting with employees that included family members and friends, reconnecting at the Fair. People chatted across the outdoor tables, discussing what they would order and from whom. One family arrived from out of town to buy tickets for the meal; the father and his children were enrolled EBCI members and were admitted free while the mother paid the entrance fee. We watched the family walk through the exhibit hall, the father pointing out particular vegetables and fruits honored with blue ribbons to the children, also connecting the family to its cultural traditions. Before the lunch rush, the opening ceremony for the Fair's Veterans Day helped families catch up over a buffet meal, volunteers in EBCI T-shirts circulating to chat and hand out iced tea refills, coffee, and dessert. Although seemingly the only people in the room without a tribal connection, we were handed coffee to enjoy, and intentionally included in the celebration. But beans and cornbread anchored the Fair. Veterans and their families could enjoy them from the buffet, order them from vendors as part of a traditional Indian Dinner, or buy traditional bean bread, soft cornmeal dough studded with brown beans and wrapped in a small foil package. All were ordered enthusiastically, fortifying community reconnection and identity. Another role that this food tradition serves is direct care through fundraising, where beans are often featured. The night before the Appalachian Food Summit in Berea, Kentucky, the organization hosted a "pay as you can" community bean supper; later, outside Chattanooga, the community of South Pittsburg, Tennessee, sold the dish to raise funds to help revitalize their town.

There are other ways that communities use food to renew identity and fortify residents. Some community festivals centered on regional foods serve as vital sources of community care. Hillsville, Virginia, located in

Southwestern Virginia Carroll County, for example, is classified by the Appalachian Regional Commission as a transitional economy, meaning that it has somewhat more economic resources than its distressed or at risk neighbors, but continues to face challenges as its dominant industries have closed or relocated. Antique and hobby stores dot the once bustling Main Street, but many are shuttered. Local churches organize food pantries, their small congregations raising an impressive $20,000 to feed residents in need; at the twice per month food pantry at the Hillsville Presbyterian church, supported by Feeding Southwest Virginia, the pantry is at capacity.

Despite challenges, the Friends of Hillsville (Virginia) group, largely made up of volunteers, works to preserve and enhance this small town, offering events such as the Historic Hillsville Chili Shootout, Halloween events, live bands, canned food drives, and the like. Held in conjunction with the county's Pumpkin Festival, the courthouse square was bustling on a sunny October afternoon as guests arrived for the Chili Shootout. Similar to what we had observed in Cherokee, North Carolina, local residents were clearly in attendance, greeting each other over cornhole competitions, pumpkin cannon and apple slingshots, food trucks, and high school clubs holding bake sales to fund their activities. The Taco Bout food truck was popular; its owners worked feverishly to keep up with the line. Local businesses sponsored the Shootout teams who decorated their booths elaborately. Guests could purchase tasting wrist bands for five dollars and vote in the People's Choice awards. The organizers also clearly put effort into recruiting judges (professional chefs), reading the chefs' biographies carefully to highlight their expertise. There were surprisingly large cash awards for winning chilis, but the organizers also pointedly selected the best cornbread, the best salsa, the best decorated booth, awarding as many community members as possible. It was a small-town festival, to be sure, but it was more, too. Food was used to bring residents back into a disused and depressed downtown, demonstrating to guests that people would attend, perhaps encouraging further economic development of the town. While Ashli was walking later on a rural road to take in the fall scenery and admiring seasonal decorations, a woman (who owned the decorations, incidentally) stopped her car to chat with her. Ashli immediately recognized the woman's voice as the event's MC. She asked if Ashli had gone to the Shootout and other questions—Where was she from? Who were her people? Would she please tell others about what was happening again in Hillsville? "I'm Leanna Surratt," she said, "pleased to meet you, and please come back."

In the end, the work put into strengthening communities through food is a significant part of the resilience message. Feelings of community— preserving common traditions—only go so far to sustain a region and its people. Using those preserved traditions to then fortify the community, however, emphasizes the need for communal work. It is roots-based work, empowering individuals by highlighting the regional power of fighting against common constraints. At the same time, the danger of this kind of message is that a dependence on communal solutions does not necessarily address institutional weaknesses and barriers. Resilience messages can also be used to place blame on individuals and to encourage a contested "pull oneself up by the bootstraps" mentality. Regional connection and even community-based outlets (e.g., garden-based food offerings and restaurants with pay-as-you-can options) for socioeconomically challenged residents does nothing to secure employment options with fair pay and health options for those individuals. Ideally, though, the emphasis on community redirects the focus of rhetoric from individuals being on their own in confronting their problems and toward the importance of group efforts.

Meld

to merge; blend
the physical acts of cutting or blending . . . that generate tastes and
    smells that weren't there before

Thus far, the themes of preservation and fortification are primarily focused on an internal, region-based audience.[71] That is, there needs to be a sense of community before its members are motivated to work toward strengthening it. The third characteristic of resilience in Appalachian foodways rhetoric is melding or combining multiple parts to make a stronger whole. Given the ways that Appalachia is influenced by outside perspectives and rhetoric, it is critical to consider the ways that the region can offer a more complex and complete image to those outside of the region. In this case, the Appalachian turn to emphasizing the diversity of the region's history, people, and foodways—melding traditions—provides a rhetorically powerful message. Melding might mean taking the old and making it new again through change and altered narratives surrounding Mountain food, but might also involve merging foodways, cultures, traditions together to better reflect (and feed) the region. While combining elements together can potentially undermine some cultures, histories, and perspectives, amplifying some while silencing others, a more resilient approach finds strength in diverse traditions and uses that multiplicity to create something new. Many contemporary discussions of Appalachia, for example, highlight the diversity of the residents and, therefore, the cultural influences inherent to the region. Despite the range of people who settled and moved to the region over time and influenced Appalachia's food culture, Americans tend to know more about the region's European roots than its African or American Indian ones. As one chef complained, "We were the first melting pot in America. I mean, this has been an ever-evolving thing and it's been probably one of the most pliable cuisines in the South . . . it's just ever shifting and ever changing out of need and what you have."[72] A closer look at these traditions reveals cultural richness as well as communities influencing one another through circulation. Appalachian food is as "much about flows, friction, and fraction" as it is about "consensus and cultural wholes, with different groups contributing to the culinary tradition."[73] Because they have been left out of the dominant narrative, the perspectives of Latinx, Southeast Asian, Eastern European, American Indian, and African American cultures must be shared more broadly, weaving more of these stories into the region's narratives and developing more awareness of its multicultural layers. This emphasis highlights Appalachian adaption while also challenging continued circulation of white dominant ideology, a move that rhetorical scholars argue shifts away from privileging larger national narratives and accounts for local racial formations and identities. As Meta Carstarphan and Kathleen Welch argue, "the work of resisting racism and constructing decolonized antiracist alternatives ultimately begins at home."[74]

Examples of rhetorical work that highlight diversity and adaptation in the region through its foodways are abundant. Celebrated Appalachian chef Ashleigh Shanti has centered much of her work on spotlighting African influences and adaptations in Appalachian foodways and embracing the role that African Americans have played in the food stories of the region. As Shanti notes, "one of the reasons for coming here [to Asheville] was to pay homage to the women who have been here. When I'm stumped or lacking inspiration, I think about what my grandmothers would make and how they cooked."[75] Shanti draws from past traditions but does so to highlight these overlooked stories rather than repeating the all-too familiar narratives about how white women in Appalachia cook. Although she has now moved on from her position as head chef at Asheville's Benne on Eagle, she left behind a mark of her presence on the kitchen walls—"Beside her name, she wrote 'sankofa,' a word borrowed from the Akan Tribe in Ghana. Typically illustrated by a bird plucking a seed or egg from its back, it means 'go back and get it'"[76] This chef, and others like her, find meaning in reclaiming—connecting—the food legacies that came from diverse cultures and communities that helped shape Appalachia. Although the origins in this case were connected to the painful history of enslavement, this type of action highlights cultural connections and histories that have been forgotten (in many cases, intentionally) and circulates a different message about African connections to Appalachia.

Similarly, Tennessee whiskey giant Jack Daniel's recent efforts to acknowledge Nathan (Nearest) Green, a formerly enslaved man who taught Jack Daniel how to make whiskey, also shows the process of broadening the narrative. Fawn Weaver's experience at the distillery motivated her to pressure the company to share Green's story, and by extension, the inextricably entwined history of slavery and whiskey-making. When the Brown-Forman Corporation eventually named Nearest Green, not Jack Daniel, as its first master distiller, circulation of his and other stories challenged the tale of American whiskey as a "whites-only affair, about Scots-Irish settlers who brought Old World distilling knowledge to the frontier states."[77] Weaver eventually founded the Uncle Nearest distillery where she, Green's descendants, and other company leaders have shifted the industry in important ways. As Weaver explains, "It was our job to make sure that people understood that what they were doing when they bought a glass or bottle of Uncle Nearest was not simply to sip on the whiskey. We need them to tell the story. We need for the first African American master distiller—his name—to be forever known and honored, the same way that Jack Daniel and Johnny Walker and Jim Beam have been known and honored for 150 years."[78] It is an old story, but one that is only now being circulated more widely. Tennessee whiskey is unique, Weaver explains, because of the filtration process through sugar maple charcoal, a technique that she argues was introduced in the United States by enslaved people.[79] Although a claim unique to Weaver, this is the story that is frequently repeated in mediated discussions about the regional technique since Uncle Nearest whiskey emerged. Enlarging the story of whiskey, as Weaver does, adds an important new thread to the Appalachian story and we will continue to explore this in chapter 3.

Historical interdependence between different cultural groups in the region also shows the region adapting, and this type of interchange between different communities continues today. The neighborhood Greek-owned diner, various Mexican restaurants, and new sushi spots found across Appalachia also carve out their own stories in contemporary mountain communities. American Indians and African Americans shared planting techniques and introduced new crops as mountain communities developed, and the region's food continues to offer dishes that combine different histories and cultures in intriguing ways to eaters. Leticia Ruiz, chef/owner of the Mexican and American restaurant El Rincon in Blowing Rock, North Carolina, speaks to this mutually constitutive interplay, offering country breakfasts and full Mexican and American lunches and dinners every day at her restaurant, telling us "You can eat cornbread with pinto beans, you can eat tortillas with pinto beans, it's kind of why I decided to make the menu Mexican and American. Because to me, it hooked me together."[80] The chef/restaurant owner takes evident pride in offering dishes reflective of both Mexican and American "real home cooking." Her food and the way she talks about it contribute to a different way of thinking about foodways of the region.

In fact, regional food-based experiences offer a particularly strong way to change circulated perceptions about Appalachian resistance among tourists and residents alike. A stroll down Main Street in Abingdon, Virginia, offers visitors the chance to eat in a restaurant built in 1799 and still serving familiar fare, but it also encourages them to enjoy a craft beer, sample cold pressed raw juice, or talk with a variety of vendors at its thriving farmer's market. One cold December morning found us sampling Eastern European baked goods like *burek* at the market before warming up with locally roasted coffee at The Girl and the Raven cafe, its mission to support local farmers. Visiting Abingdon might also find you at the previously mentioned Packalachian food truck. The owners see their work as doing more than just offering another tasty food option, explaining: "Our dialogue kind of focuses on, 'Hey. You love where you live, but guess what?' There's this other country that has all these same, very similar agrarian ideals and roots that have so many different types of flavors and we're going to combine them and you're going to start to realize like, 'We were all from the same thing and we're all eating the same food.'"[81] Similarly, Karmen, who owns a Middle Eastern–inspired bakery, uses food to introduce new cultures to her Blacksburg, Virginia community: "I want to do something like a little Mediterranean, little Arabic. So, we use Rosewater and pistachio a lot on desserts and syrups. When you take a bite from this, you know, I make it with love . . . I never copy anyone. I create my own recipe and introduce my culture on this."[82] All of the elements of the food and food experiences, with the diversity of the flavors and the experiences circulating a different story of the region, emphasize the way that Appalachian food has been changed by the melding of cultural influences.

While these examples of efforts to bring more traditions and flavors into play were readily evident, we also noticed acknowledgement of the work that remained to make the region's communities more inclusive as we traveled through the region and talked to Appalachians. Several restaurant owners and employees, for example, noted that there was more that they could do to build a more diverse, inclusive community, and one that is culturally aware. As Christina from Gillie's in Blacksburg put it, "I think we [Gillie's] will always be a hub for anyone who is seeking out culture and just safe spaces for minorities and for people who are being disenfranchised."[83] Indeed, heading down the mountain on Highway 52 into Mt. Airy, North Carolina, we passed produce stands flying "Trump, Guns, and God" and "White Lives Matter" flags, stopping into one of the many small establishments deemed charming for their traditional Appalachian or nostalgic American diner type food, surrounded by walls framed with white memorabilia (signed Andy Griffith photos, old images of white only football teams). It's hard to imagine a person of color feeling welcome or comfortable eating the 1954 Dairy Center's famous ground steak sandwich in this space, with only white patrons there the day we visited. Some of tiny Marion, North Carolina's, Main Street eateries proudly flew Pride flags and made a point to acknowledge that everyone was welcome, but parts of Southern Appalachia could be experienced by tourists as supportive only of "traditional" lifestyles. Despite travel writing emphasizing welcoming messages (as one advertisement claims, a traveler will "experience Southern hospitality that most believe has been forgotten and warm welcomes that remind you of home"), not all travelers experience the same kind of welcome and there is clearly more work that can be done.[84] Nevertheless, the message of melding in Appalachian food rhetoric allows for a more inclusive and accurate depiction of the region, providing opportunities for outsiders to hear a counternarrative to the kinds of stories and images more frequently circulated.

IMPLICATIONS OF RESILIENCE *TOPOI*

Paying attention to the rhetorical messages that challenge the images of Appalachia as a helpless or defiant, white, conservative region provides some guidance for locating alternative narratives, demonstrated by Appalachian foodways. Specifically, this analysis shows that food speaks in multiple ways, circulating ideas and perceptions, influencing identification, and shaping regional identity. Because rhetoric serves a constitutive function, forming, reifying, and reforming the way we see ourselves and others, examining Appalachian foodways serves as a means of understanding this regional identity. Constitutive messages reach us through all the senses and channels of communication; we are shaped by the imagery, language, and larger narratives that appear in the media, in conversations, on roadside political signs, and also through our food. The identities and ideas that are formed are then circulated, eventually working their way into a general understanding of the region. Attention to those messages is crucial to understanding cultures, but especially in trying to understand how Appalachian culture continues to identify with the past while simultaneously pushing forward into a differently defined region. As we will continue to explore in the remaining chapters, Appalachian food is key to creating the image of resilience that shapes the region and that should become a central component to the narrative. Beyond the implications on Appalachian image, however, we complete this chapter by exploring limitations to key characteristics of the resilience *topos* before exploring what makes this version of resilience rhetoric—that based on Appalachian foodways—different.

Resilience, more broadly, has become a large part of the post-pandemic narrative. As with the case of Appalachian foodways, this descriptor can be used to bolster a community, but can also harm individuals and create a framework for a lack of systemic action. An emphasis on self-reliance, for example, calls into question the worth of those who are not perceived as resilient and rewards those who are. This bootstrap mentality can then be weaponized to further marginalize those who are not able pull themselves up—those who are dependent on other entities, whether government or charity. Appeals to self-reliance or self-sufficiency, too, often feature individual and personal responsibility rather than acknowledging and confronting systems of inequality in Appalachia and elsewhere.[85] As philosophy scholar Robin James notes, resilience often follows a specific logic where damage is incited, the individual who manages to overcome is rewarded and highlighted, and their own resilience boosts society's reliance but normalizes toxicity and decay.[86] That is, if resilience becomes a psychological or ecological trait that certain individuals or communities possess, or is understood as an idealized stable place that people return to (that may have never existed in the first place), those who do not, or cannot, meet these criteria remain vulnerable.[87] Similarly, when Appalachian people are constituted as vulnerable but able to bounce back through their foodways and other practices, this normative response precludes other ways of thinking about their challenges.[88] As rhetoricians Nathan Stormer and Bridie McGreavy aptly point out, vulnerability may stimulate adaptation, but if it becomes a continuous experience, addressing a group as resilient breeds the political distrust that is endemic in the region.[89] Conceptualizing resilience as merely coping in order to reduce vulnerability or to provide a false sense of control merely heightens this distrust.[90]

Not only does this emphasis on individual resiliency not solve problems but also there may be a tendency to discourage change. After all, part of resilience is bouncing *back* or going backwards to a starting point. This move back to normal does not motivate or reward new approaches to problem-solving nor does it emphasize learning limits, avoiding precarious futures, or enabling more democratic and sustainable solutions.[91] In their work on the rhetoric of food charters, Philippa Spoel and Colleen Derkatch argue that the enactment of resilience as self-reliance "largely re-inscribes a static hegemonic discourse" that is unable to provide new ways to become resilient.[92] These scholars write about how resilience discourse operates in particular contexts, but collectively emphasize how it sits in a dialectical tension that straddles the line between the positive or productive (as in encouraging particular rhetorical behaviors and choices) and conservative or problematic qualities (as in maintaining the status quo or the inability to address regional issues).

Although there is potential to use the resiliency *topos* to cause damage, those concerns diminish when community becomes a focus of the narrative. Community, in fact, seems to be a central part of Appalachian foodways rhetoric, emphasizing change that benefits individuals and communities alike. Each of the characteristics of resilience that we identify —preservation, fortification, and melding—depends on community. Preservation is dependent upon a previous creation by others. Fortification assumes a need to strengthen a community and a collective to work toward this goal. Melding connects multiple communities and traditions together, creating a stronger whole. In each element, resilience involves others and is crafted based on relationships. Resilience, in other words, should be recognized for its role in forging and fortifying community despite rhetorical limitations. Critically, a focus on community helps conceive of resilience as stemming from adaptability and sustainability, acting *with,* rather than on, recalcitrant problematic systems and structures, helping develop rhetorical capacities and potentialities.[93] Southern Appalachians have long been aware of the myriad challenges that face them, sometimes working together as a community to drive change within systems often stacked against them.

Resilience's complexity matches the characteristics of the region in an insightful way, exposing a core part of Appalachians. One of the primary concerns about rhetorical messaging surrounding Appalachia is the centering of a white narrative; the many examples of resilience circulated in rhetoric within/about the region serve to both reinforce and contest that narrative. The resilience *topos* can be read as a reluctance to change or to leave behind what has historically defined the region's past, embracing the tired story of white Mountain America. At the same time, other variations of this *topos*—the ones we analyze here—highlight a version of the culture that celebrates preservation of food traditions to create community, fortification of community through food, and melding food stories that undermine dominant narratives. Appalachian food acts symbolically to demonstrate how to speak, but also—more importantly—how to *enact* resilience, with each part of the resilience narrative laying out components of the argument and the connected actions. Each step has its challenges, its own barriers; at each step, there is a possibility for the resilience message to fail. As rhetorical circulation scholar Caitlin Bruce warns, the power of messages in changing the conversation can get lost, "becoming another stop on the trolley tour," a failure in "interpretation, misreadings, and potentially inevitable commodification."[94] This concern is particularly relevant in a food tourism context, when messages might be interpreted differently, from taste, to sight, to discussion. Changing how we think about resilience does not remove all the real problems that the region continues to face, but it does recognize the importance of much of the work, often unrecognized or acknowledged, that is happening in Appalachia to strengthen the region through traditions. With the resilience framework in mind, we now turn to those specific Appalachian stories that demonstrate preservation, fortification, and melding.

Chapter 2

Dualchas, Connection, and Food Migration in Appalachia's Culinary Tradition

According to family lore and supported by a detailed genealogical chart, Jenny Wiley is Ashli's great-grandmother six times removed. For a book seeking to expand the narrative of Southern Appalachia through foodways, this kind of historical family tidbit is troubling. Readers may be unfamiliar with Wiley's story, which has more than twenty variations, but they all feature the same key elements. On the 1789 Virginia frontier, her cabin was mistaken for that of another man who was said to have killed two American Indians. Looking for revenge, a group comprised of several different tribal members murdered Wiley's brother and her three children, taking pregnant Jenny Wiley into captivity along with her one-year-old son. Trying to escape the settler's search party, Jenny's pace slowed the fleeing group, so they killed the young child and eventually the prematurely delivered baby. In captivity for months, Wiley supposedly taught her captors weaving skills and learned a bit of their language, ultimately escaping and reuniting with her husband. Beginning life again in Kentucky, Wiley became an enduring symbol of courageousness and resilience, with numerous websites, a yearly festival, and a theatre still dedicated to her. As the Jenny Wiley Festival webpage puts it, she represents the mythic enduring Appalachian persona—"the people that settled this land had to be strong, mustering a force as mighty as the rocks jutting out of the ground. Jenny Wiley embodies the spirit of our landscape and the strength of heart it took to survive here."[1] The American Indians who defended their resources and land also influenced the character of the region, but we tend to know much less about their stories.

Rather, stories like Jenny Wiley's, largely handed down orally from generation to generation and filled with inaccuracies and glorifications, continue to privilege European-American, and frequently Scots-Irish, narratives about Appalachian culture. Wiley's marriage to a Scots-Irish immigrant and her ability to escape, reunite with her husband, and begin a new family is celebrated as astonishing. These captivity stories, loosely recalled and passed along with vague historical accounts, contain elements of horror and romance and a lack of historical research, where savage attackers die in an eye for an eye settler justice.[2] Their legacies feed Scots-Irish and greater Appalachian pioneer mythologies, with their tales of survival and resiliency impressing ancestors and fueling regional pride among those who feel represented by the narratives.

Wendy also wrangled with her own family stories in the middle of researching this book. Her father had always passed along stories of their family moving from Tennessee to Texas. What she heard for all those years were tales of ancestors migrating from England and eventually establishing a life in a sparsely populated mountainous region, navigating the Civil War landscape, establishing businesses that served their communities, and building churches and congregations. And, while those stories are true, some of the specifics had faded away. In her brief genealogical research, she quickly found evidence of enslaved people being willed to family members, tales of family homes being "shot up" by Cherokee Indians, and the Trail of Tears running straight through the small town that she had heard so much about—Tellico Plains, Tennessee. Wendy began this project feeling like an outsider, someone who grew up far from Appalachia and without a connection other than enjoying regular visits. But, her ancestors, too, had been a part of the region's story, contributing to its traditions—good and bad—as well as its problems. This past rumbled in her head as we continued our research journey.

These two examples that glorify greater European settlement in Appalachia are not limited to family stories, with tourism, specifically culinary tourism, helping to create this echo chamber of inaccurate, outdated, and white dominant rhetoric. As we have previously explained, despite growing acknowledgement of the variety of cultures that developed Southern Appalachian cuisine, some popular culinary tourism writing continues to privilege Scots-Irish and other white ethnic ancestral histories. This coverage tends to evoke nostalgic, romantic perceptions of place that link descendants and visitors to a problematically idealized past or highlights the so-called insular, peculiar nature of its food, drink, or culinary festivals.[3] Scholars explore the role of heritage tourism in creating and challenging these mythologies, both in the United States and Scotland, but food's contributions in forming these perceptions has been underexplored.[4] By attending to regional migration patterns, rhetorically analyzing messages about migration, or the movement of people, crops, and goods, it becomes easier to see how these culinary tourism narratives are created in ways that privilege particular stories, values, and peoples. We underscore historical readings that offer alternative stories about the foods and the values associated with them, seeking more reflective and representative understandings of the region's cultural influences. We trace stories of four grains, oats, barley, corn, and sorghum, from Scotland to the Appalachian Mountains to argue that their histories offer messages of cultural adaptation alongside ones supporting narratives about the region's white settler heritage. Closer attention to messages about regional migration helps highlight how certain foods and practices became Appalachian in harmful ways that do not reflect the region's complicated cultural interdependence, with messages preserving food traditions but also cultural misunderstandings.[5] Tracing the migration of these grains locates messages of possibility that emphasize different connections between land, people, and culture. The stories present opportunities to shape how tourists experience the region and its perception in the public imagination.

To add to the conversation about heritage tourism, we first highlight how Scotland and its Appalachian descendants are rhetorical inventions. We then examine the relationship between migration and heritage/culinary tourism, exploring how tourist experiences appear to privilege one Appalachian imaginary amid numerous rhetorical possibilities. Developing a theoretical framework drawn from interdisciplinary scholarship about migration and the rhetorical uses of "*dualchas*," a Gaelic term meaning tradition, heritage, culture, and character, we then analyze three food examples based on fieldwork in Scotland and Appalachia, illustrating how migration shapes the experiences tourists are offered.[6] That is, we illustrate how much of contemporary culinary tourism echoes origin stories, reverberating in Appalachia hundreds of years later and informing so-called hillbilly experiences (preserving the wrong kinds of narratives), but also provides alternative experiences that may change how a tourist perceives the region (preserving tradition while being cognizant of different perspectives). Rhetorically analyzing these grains with migration as a framework emphasizes Appalachian culinary tourism as an unfolding process, rather than as a never changing product to consume, where new meanings circulate and re-circulate. To begin to dismantle Appalachian food tourism's static borders, we first discuss how regions are invented in ways that tourism solidifies.

MIGRATION AND THE INVENTION OF APPALACHIAN CULINARY TOURISM

The critical regionalism rhetorical project with which our research aligns seeks to disrupt the narratives of a place in order to reconsider whose ancestors count as members, centering different voices.[7] Definitionally, regions are invented and unstable entities that do not contain uniform identities and perspectives.[8] Indeed, created in the 1960s as part of the American federal government's War on Poverty's, the federal and state partnership known as the Appalachian Regional Commission shows how the very creation of Appalachia's boundaries was an inventive process, with government officials arguing over which states and counties should be included for funding, regardless of their proximity to the mountain range.[9] Examining the ongoing romanticization of Scotland as a nation for hundreds of years is useful in appreciating how Appalachia, too, was invented as a place symbolic of values that serve particular rhetorical ends. Similar to Appalachia's trajectory, tourists could find in Highland Scotland "the primitive virtues that the modern world seemed to have destroyed."[10] In enjoying views of the "high, rugged, green hills" and "solitude, the romance and wild loveliness," they could ignore how landowners' forced eviction of tenants created this vision.[11] Highland imagery distinguished Scotland from England. Later, stories about peculiar white mountain folk did the same for other parts of America, but both tendencies erase the possibility for other stories to shape their futures.

But what happens when we take a closer look at these origin stories? The Scots-Irish may have been the largest ethnic group who settled on North Carolina's mountain frontier but claims about their influence on

Appalachian culture begin to fall apart when learning the group sometimes called the "people with no name" do not share a single national identity nor clear ethnic boundary markers. The term Scot only came into usage as a way to identify the fusion of Lowland and Highland Scots living in Ulster, Ireland; these people were already migrants before arriving in the United States years later.[12] These permeable ethnic boundaries make it difficult to attribute elements of material culture to the Scots-Irish, much less make claims about their influence on Southern Appalachia's cultural values or personalities. Nevertheless, as some scholars contend, Americans with Scots-Irish ancestry number around 23 million, including Cherokee Indians and African Americans who claim this background. We should examine why tourists want to connect with this murky past. Scots-Irish scholar Christina Wilson argues that the group has a "highly malleable" narrative that provides a number of constructions of ethnic identity; these stories have a legacy in shaping the Appalachia that residents and tourists alike experience today.[13]

Heritage–Legacy Tourism and Culinary Connections

Scholars investigate the pull towards the rhetorical invention of particular places through heritage and legacy tourism experiences, and more recently, culinary ones.[14] Through heritage tourism, visitors seek to find their roots, connect with ancestors, and reinforce their self-identities, seeking experiences that they believe "authentically represent the stories and people of the past and present," which are often sustained through nostalgia.[15] Traveling to the homeland of Scotland or to events like the Grandfather Games, then, heritage tourism pilgrims in search of ancestral clanscapes connect with religious, secular, and familial traditions and values, simultaneously creating Scotland and Appalachia in this image. Often, seductive, experiential performative elements encourage commodification, especially concerning notions of authenticity.[16] Scottish-American tourists may recognize that their Burns Nights Suppers[17] are staged, while Blue Ridge tourists in search of their own Appalachian heritage also know that women in pioneer costume, serving platters of biscuits, are part of the performance.

Nevertheless, these practices reinforce what are assumed to be authentic and traditional parts of the culture that are then replicated. Exploring migration enhances heritage tourism scholarship because the desire to claim voluntary ethnicity and identity remains strong and helps remake the past, privileging some food experiences.[18] Indeed, among those tourists able to claim or ascribe membership and who feel communion with other community members, feelings of unity may drive territorial behaviors when boundaries are threatened.[19] Gathered "in exile" on the "Scotland-like" Grandfather Mountain, for example, Scottish-American tourists "evoke the ties of kinship, faith, identity, and community," but the Games also "remind people to consciously stand together as a group apart."[20] Whether critiqued for their staged or nostalgic elements, or presented as authentic places, cuisine is a significant part of these heritage tourism experiences.[21]

Though underexplored rhetorically, culinary tourism, often described as the "intentional, exploratory participation in the foodways of another," is significant in shaping tourists' perceptions of regions and peoples.[22] As tourists search for what they deem to be authentic food, locals may reflect back what visitors want to see, "eliminating from the photo that which is not pleasurable to consume" and divorcing culinary experiences from histories and context.[23] Highlighting migration patterns in culinary heritage tourism shows how some traditional foods and foodways have been overlooked but also helps resurrect obsolete recipes and revitalize culturally significant foodways.[24] Indeed, in both Scotland and Southern Appalachia, fieldwork experiences ranging from casual (Scotland's sausage roll on the go and pintos for lunch in Eastern Tennessee) to fine dining (Tom Kitchin's Michelin-starred Scottish restaurant or six course farm dinners in North Carolina), provided sounds, sights, tastes, and smells that reinforced but also challenged typical stories tourists encounter.

Redrawing the Borders of Mountain Food through Migration

Migration theoretical frameworks consider how people and their cultures shift through time, disrupting stereotypes accumulated by certain versions of social history.[25] Long focused on the experiences of male migrants crossing borders for work or escaping political persecution, migration scholarship generally reconsiders cultural development and highlights narratives that are less well known in shaping culture by unpacking relationships between whiteness, gender, heterosexuality, and other identity components.

While eating at Benne on Eagle in Asheville or selecting foods from the buffet at Granny's Kitchen in Cherokee, North Carolina, culinary tourists might notice African and Cherokee Indian Appalachian food influences, for example, but an emphasis on migration helps highlight these narratives. The legacy of Appalachia's settlement patterns provides opportunities to explore regional narratives about who belongs, simultaneously identifying persuasive arguments and strategies that offer different possibilities for membership.[26]

Migration narratives reveal how Appalachian borders gradually became rhetorically established, influencing public vocabulary, exposing how cultural narrative inclusion is regulated, and highlighting the ways that this regulation can fortify borders in harmful ways.[27] Attention to migration also uncovers how the movement of people creates these blended cultural landscapes and stories, offering a perfect place to see the process of mutual influence and to assess its rhetorical force. As food scholar Akhil Gupta explains, attention to the movement of foods and cuisines is particularly needed because "perhaps no other area of social life demonstrates the hybridity of cultural encounters as thoroughly as the preparation, display, and consumption of food."[28] Food and migration scholarship generally examines how migrants' food traditions are maintained and adapted to new cultural settings, focusing on how immigrants worldwide who become the so called other cope through food practices, examining how food maintains ethnic identity and challenges colonizing discourses, and assessing how notions of immigrant cooking reinforces cultural hierarchies.[29] Exploring culinary migration thus shows how food is used to affirm and challenge cultural borders. Foods brought into dominant cultures through migration are sometimes viewed suspiciously as potentially "poisonous intake" or, conversely, to falsely signal multicultural acceptance.[30] Still, the inclusion of an immigrant culture's foods is not always superficial, slowly changing the components of a region's cultural geography. Rather than telling stories about its isolation, emphasizing the dynamic, fluid, complex nature of Appalachia's cultural borders shifts hierarchies, with interweaving migration continually reshaping what it means to be Appalachian, where taco trucks are as much a part of the local foodscape as "meat and threes," where diners choose a meat entree and three sides as a meal.

TRACING MIGRATION'S INFLUENCE ON APPALACHIAN
FOOD THROUGH THREE INGREDIENTS

Tracing the circulation and exchange of texts (in this case, food) as they pass from one culture and language to another, creating new connections, is particularly germane to understanding the legacy of Appalachian migration. Although Appalachian food is often connected to notions of Scots-Irish or white ethnic European traditions, the American expressions of these dishes are not direct translations using the same techniques or even the same ingredients. Desires to maintain or mark ethnic boundaries through food may remain, with some traditions taking on moral responsibility and obligation, but cultural expression shifts as dishes migrate. Some Appalachian tourists may feel they are experiencing history through eating foods that can be traced back to the waves of Scots-Irish and other European immigrants in the eighteenth century, but dishes important in Appalachia and America alike linked to Scots-Irish emigrants exemplify adaptation, not duplication. Over time, oatcakes became pancakes and breads, scones became biscuits, bonny clabber became cottage cheese, meat pies became pot pies, Scotch broth became soup, and the use of the potato (itself introduced to the Irish by Sir Walter Raleigh in 1565) became widespread. Modification and adaptation are crucial—traditional griddle-cooked oatcakes gave way to cakes made of corn while Cherokee people were also imparting knowledge about processing corn into grits. Spanish-brought pork replaced British mutton as a preferred meat, and the beans that were a mainstay for American Indians became an adapted favorite of the Scots-Irish and English.[31] This complexity is simplified in many tourist experiences that continue to privilege the legacy of isolated, back-country Scots-Irish people barely getting by, but tracing culinary adaptation appreciates how some of these narratives have become more tellable than others.[32]

Exploring the movement of cereal crops into Southern Appalachia is particularly helpful in underscoring the push and pull between tradition and adaptation that more fully characterizes Appalachian cuisine. Sorghum, rye, barley, oats, and wheat are still indispensable and universal to many cultures and in the colonizing ventures that brought them to America, where even children today sing adapted versions of English and Scots-Irish folk songs asking, "Do you or I or anyone know how oats and beans and barley grow?"[33] The legacy of these crops may be evident, but their origins are so anchored to the past that many claims about them are a matter of conjecture and debate.[34] Along with the uniquely (Native) American corn, cereals play important roles in Appalachian cuisine that deserve another look. These landraces, plant species that adapt over time to local environmental conditions, represent agricultural heritage as well as genetic biodiversity; they are again prized in the local grain movement in Appalachia and the greater South for their nutrition, flavor, and ability to reconnect to culinary traditions.[35] By exploring the movement of these grains through particular culinary adaptations, assessing how they draw on particular elements of *dualchas* (appeals to tradition, heritage, culture, and character), we appreciate the alternative ways that the borders of Appalachian cuisine might have been constructed differently. Tourists visiting Scotland are still offered fried mars bars, haggis, and whisky[36] while Southern Appalachian tourists feast on biscuits, gravy, and moonshine, despite how many foods have moved beyond these mythological ones.

Constructing the Rhetorical Foundations of Tradition through Oats

Tradition is a powerful component of *dualchas,* and cultures tend to imbue discussions about foodways with this idea. Oats highlight how cultures value and guard tradition through food, yet evolve, connected to the past but drawing from it to adapt and meld.[37] Indeed, no oats are indigenous to the United States, but they trace an enduring path across the Atlantic.[38] Despite the gradual domination of the corn crop in the Appalachian diet, oats are "steeped in the agricultural history" of the United States, reminding us that Appalachian, and more broadly, American, culinary history partially originated on other soils.[39] Because of different growing conditions, Scots-Irish settlers adapted the practice of cooking oat breads on a griddle, and then corn gradually replaced the use of oats.[40] Still, oat varieties bred for "peaty, marshy soils" in Scotland grew in the South's wetter areas, including in North Carolina, with some landrace varieties collectable as late as a decade ago.[41] A number of Appalachian oat recipes descend from Scottish ones, including porridges, oatmeal bread, and oatmeal cookies.[42] Although indirect because of different growing conditions in Southern Appalachia, tracing oat consumption from Scotland to their Appalachian adaptations, particularly into corn-based dishes, uncovers a biological profile that echoes rhetorically. Heritage tourists take boxes of Walkers Shortbread back to the States, but they should also tuck some oatcakes into their luggage for a deeper taste of the connections between Scottish and Appalachian culture.

Indeed, after spending a day at a state-of-the-art Scottish oat product factory and talking to its now retired executive director, touring a 100-year-old oat mill in the Scottish Borders, and experiencing how oats represented a fundamental part of the Scottish diet, the discussion of oats illuminated the relationship between tradition and adaptation that characterizes both Scottish and Southern Appalachian cuisines. Ashli traveled to Scotland to research the Scottish roots and mythology of Southern Appalachian food, where messages about oats located themes of connection and ingenuity in the two cuisines often similarly maligned. Both diets are characterized as bland, heavy, unwholesome, and even bizarre, making the most of inhospitable landscapes and harsh climates, prizing self-sufficiency, and subsisting on frugal, largely meatless dishes. Both incorporate dried beans, peas, and cereals, supplemented with milk, cheese, and butter, and, over time, became associated with fried, heavy, or otherwise unhealthy foods.[43] Both are keen to use traditional foods to create healthier communities and more positive media representations; as one Scottish food writer complains, "Scotland has to start showing the world that our traditional diet is actually teeming with wonderfully healthy stuff."[44] Oats, "so synonymous with Scottishness," help illustrate how traditional foods also serve as sources of inventive rhetorical connection that do more than guard against change.[45]

People do still eat biscuits and gravy in the Mountains; similarly, some fieldwork experiences did exemplify how foods connect people to traditional culinary and cultural identities and provide familiarity, comfort, and connection as cultures change. Throughout Scotland, for example, some forms of culinary tourism remain "powerfully locked in the past," with images of tradition, history, and rurality portraying the country as a place where "time almost seems to stop for a while to rest," in its shops, restaurants, and souvenir food products.[46] Despite the country's movement toward a progressive, agriculturally sustainable nation, the ongoing reliance on oats symbolizes how cultures use foods to fortify and maintain appeals to tradition.[47] Oats are one of Scotland's oldest surviving crops, with oatcakes eaten regularly since at least the Middle Ages.[48] Visiting Nairns, an almost 50-million-pound business that produces 1 million oatcakes per

Figure 6. Nairn's Contemporary Oat products,
Edinburgh, Scotland. Author photograph.

day, former president Gavin Love emphasized their historical importance, outlining ancient culinary practices and painting a picture of agricultural, rural Scotland, with self-reliant warriors, rocky peaks, grazing sheep, and prized family recipes. As Love explained, tradition was crucial to Nairns's success: ". . . in an age where most of our foods have lost their authentic flavor we are proud to carry on our Scottish tradition of making cakes using modern equipment but using traditional ingredients to make a product which would still be recognized by our ancestors."[49] From the subtle glimpse of tartan embedded within Scottish hills on the packaging, to the slogan on the box, "We've been baking in Scotland with pride and imagination since 1896," people connect with traditional Scotland through their consumption.

Oats also symbolized familiarity and comfort, visible in family-owned cafes serving oatcakes alongside traditional red lentil soup and at places like the House of Bruar, where tourists encounter an array of oatcakes in its traditional Scottish food hall. Tourists might notice the struggle between the old and new as they pass through Scottish Border towns ruined economically when wool fabric factories ceased production, but traditional culinary experiences push these struggles into the background. Visiting a 100-year-old oat mill, climbing winding stairwells with worn iron handrails, walking across time-smoothed hardwood floors, and listening to the deafening roar of the Willy Wonka–style assortment of manufacturing equipment, it could be 1821 or 2021, with oats always produced in the comforting, familiar way. For tourists and residents alike, oats help center traditional, familiar Scottish foodways. In the way that Appalachian cooks talk about cornbread preferences, people told us how they liked a "bit of sweetness," or "crispness (though not brittleness)," but they were all variations of the same recipe, forming an omnipresent cultural background and preserving traditions.

Oats may offer a taste of Scotland's past and appeal to traditional values and cultural identity, but their culture-wide foundation also functions as a site of rhetorical invention regarding Scotland's culinary significance and national identity. Featured at cultural events and festivals, and showcased alongside award-winning Scottish cheeses, venison, and produce, oats represent all that is grown, reared, or sustainably made in Scotland.[50] Oats "sustained Scots for centuries," but among Nairns' oat product development and marketing teams and Michelin-starred chefs alike, they represented nutrition, possibility, and versatility, with one chef explaining, "if you think of them like another grain, as you would buckwheat or barley, you can see all sorts of uses."[51] Similarly, Bosse, a Swedish immigrant farmer, celebrated his efforts in growing landraces, including oats, to feed the population more healthfully and sustainably. Enrolled in Bosse Dahlgren and his wife's, Wendy Barrie, high demand Scottish Food Studio cookery courses, tourists share crackers made from their rye and oatcakes spread with Scottish cheese, learning how growing traditional grains reclaims Scottish agricultural heritage following Brexit.

Exploring these flexible appeals to tradition through oats provided several parallels to the use of grains in Appalachian cooking, where they similarly venerate the past and suggest resistance to change yet provide room for interpretation and adaptation. At massive pancake houses throughout the region, some Appalachian culinary tourism experiences emphasize how white ancestors combined cornmeal with a few other ingredients to bake on a fire in a hidden mountain log cabin, but Scottish fieldwork

Figure 7. Oatcakes and sustainable Scottish food products,
Edinburgh, Scotland. Author photograph.

emphasized there's more to it than that. Passed down from Scots-Irish ancestors cooking oats on a griddle but actually rooted in Cherokee Indian foodways, cornbread, for example, symbolizes how culinary (and cultural) traditions similarly shift, melding cultural behaviors together. Cornbread is Appalachia's oatcake—easy, quick, cheap, and simpler than biscuits; like the Scots, early Appalachian settlers would have grown everything they needed to make cornbread. Now universally American, cornbread is the food of Appalachia's people, recipes endlessly adaptable, forgiving, and widespread. Back in the Appalachian foothills, tourists can experience traditional grains in ways that similarly guard the old ways while embracing the new. Out investigating North Carolina wineries one weekend, the authors stumbled upon Linney's Water Mill, built in 1790 and one of the few fully operational North Carolina cornmeal mills remaining. We walked the worn floors with owner Billy "Smiley" Linney, who offered us a tour on the spot as he was closing up for the night, cornmeal swirling in the air and covering the floor. He showed us how the corn was milled and how he and his family tie the bags to sell to tourists. The grain was different, but the experience of tradition was the same. But then, Smiley proudly told us how the cornmeal won awards at the "Foodie Oscars" in New York and that Oprah overnighted their cornmeal to her chefs for creating modern dishes, no doubt. The next day in Brevard, a tourist mecca, we ate Jimmy Red gluten-free grits, recently saved from extinction by Marsh Hen Mill, served with roasted vegetables, egg, and basil sauce at a cafe in a part of town undergoing new development. We had come full circle. Tracing oats' migration and adaptation emphasized how tradition not only frames negative, stagnant, conservative qualities that prevent change, but also fuels innovation. The grain's journey into Appalachia's corn dishes suggests that circulating stories overlook how migration shapes its culture, where culinary tourists seeking only to connect to tradition miss out on richer stories that signal change and adaptation. Many Scots are hungry for new uses of old ingredients and Southern Appalachians make more than just cornbread with their cornmeal. Continuing the story of corn also helps recenter the role of tradition in other overlooked culinary stories, showing how it evolves, melds, and fuels cultural resilience.

Corn and Cherokee Indian Cultural Survival

Culture makes up another element of *dualchas* appeals, and no ingredient symbolizes Cherokee Indian culture more than corn. Specifically, focusing on corn's migration privileges the seminal, often overlooked role of the Cherokee Nation in creating Appalachian food cultures and highlighting the expressions of resilience that inform them, countering the pioneer tourist trap image of the region and people.[52] Stories about corn's significance in Southern Appalachia must extend beyond those featuring cornbread and grits, or risk continuing their teleological march toward *The Beverly Hillbillies* Jethro stereotypes, servers always dressed in overalls, brandishing a skillet of cornbread just off the Blue Ridge Parkway. For example, adaptation of indigenous cornmeal created a stable of dishes that eventually became ubiquitous on America's tables, including corn pone, johnnycakes, ashcakes, hoecakes, and corn dodgers.[53] These dishes tell us less about Indigenous people than about the European settlers dependent on them, however. Corn is significant in Indigenous identities, "the center of (Native) diets and their cultural and spiritual lives," symbolizing a "deep, almost symbiotic relationship" that shifts away from tracing colonial American cuisine.[54] Cultivated for more than 9,000 years in Mexico and beyond, corn highlights food's role in the rhetoric of Cherokee Indian cultural survival, moving beyond the problematic culinary writing tendency of keeping Indigenous histories detached from their modern translations.

Conducting fieldwork in Cherokee, North Carolina, we saw this thread of tying meaningful traditions to ongoing expressions of culture and values, and not just the Scots-Irish version. Unfortunately, tourists may have to look past the pioneer-themed parkway stops and produce stands, but there are food tourism experiences that offer stories of connection and cultural expression if you know how and where to look. As David Anderson, the Jessie Owle Dugan Native Plant & Greenhouse Horticultural Specialist, told us, for example, all Cherokee people are said to descend from seven clans bringing their soils to create a mound that was still visible (if you knew what you were looking for) in the middle of a cornfield.

This spirit of interconnectedness was evident in the Tribe's general approach to sharing agricultural resources, but is particularly pronounced in corn stories, where they allow tribal members to define the past in their own terms while highlighting how the crop cultivates their collective contemporary resilience and survival. For example, we were invited to the home of the Cherokee Indian food activist mentioned earlier, Tyson Sampson, who, alongside two elders, conducted an online cooking demonstration for a group of Oklahoma Western Band Cherokee Indians who no longer had access to many of the ingredients available in Southern Appalachia. Here, corn took on a deeper cultural significance than what is typically offered through the touristic gaze on Othered people featured in the town's gift stores and experiences. The group cooked lye dumplings (made with cornmeal) flavored with broccoli sprouts and ramp salt, streaked pork meat, and October beans (similar to pintos). Fortunate to sit down and partake of that feast once the camera turned off, we shared beans and greens and cornbread (well, lye dumplings). These were not served alongside stereotypical trinkets, but by Cherokee Indians who celebrate and preserve their matrilineal and earth-based traditions through the offerings, highlighting their role in Appalachian foodways, and strengthening their community by sharing these foodways. Curious tourists may not have the opportunity to eat with tribal elders. They are, however, able to visit places such as the Long Family Farm, reclaimed by tribal members in 2015, its owners named North Carolina small farmers of the year in 2019, or Qualla

Figure 8. Presenting to the Western Band of the Cherokee Indians about traditional recipes, Cherokee, North Carolina. Author photograph.

Java Cafe, a Cherokee Indian-owned coffee shop downtown serving up signature drinks named after Cherokee Indian icons. These experiences offer the opportunity to learn how their purchases contribute to and reflect Cherokee Indian Appalachian history.

Months later, with people locked down during COVID-19, there was a boom in food-related digital media programming and virtual tourism more broadly. Pre-pandemic, culinary tourism stressed *in situ* experiences, but spatially unbound, digital tourism disrupts this paradigm while also echoing some of its practices.[55] This type of programming often privileges the white European tourist gaze but can also circulate different cultural stories and values. For instance, one episode of the Magnolia Network's "From the Source" about corn in Southern Appalachia cuisine resisted appropriating Cherokee Indian values and culture.[56] On camera, Amy Walker, an almost 80-year-old Cherokee Indian Elder Woman whom we shared a meal with, teaches Katie Button, a white chef with restaurants throughout Southern Appalachia, about corn's significance among First Nations people. Filmed in Kituwah, the Cherokee Indian name for the settlement we visited months before, as well as the house where we had helped the group cook, Katie learns how corn connects people to their Cherokee Indian identities and values. Gently correcting Katie as she helps process Amy's corn grown for cornmeal and hominy, Amy remarks, "My roots got taken away from

me, I felt like a tumbleweed," until she returned to farm Kituwah's corn-
fields, where corn revealed her ancestral ties: "I am a Cherokee woman . . .
I identify with corn, what we call Selu, the corn mother, this is me." The
camera zoomed in closely on her eyes, she confronts the lens, connecting
corn to cultural survival: "I do what I can to preserve the culture of the
seven generations that came before me. I share, I think we have to be it, to
do it, to express it." Additional Cherokee Indian instructors teach Katie to
make chestnut bread, consisting of cornmeal, chestnuts and other ingredients, the group praising her for making "perfect, present-like packages,"
true to the historical version.[57]

The episode then privileges a more typical white Appalachian culinary
perspective as the group prepares a shared meal. Katie asks if she can cook
for the group, using corn and other traditional Cherokee Indian ingredients
such as wild greens and mushrooms, but notes how she "doesn't really cook
with corn" and uses garlic instead of onions, which are more traditional in
Cherokee Indian food culture. Cherokee Indian names for the ingredients
flash on the screen while Katie cooks in their kitchen, in essence taking
over the space. Amy is seated, watching instead of cooking. Sitting together
on the porch to eat, though, the narrative again stresses the role of corn for
the Cherokee people, not the chef. Kate's side dish of skinned corn with
wild greens (*kanohena nole wanegidv*) is served with a stew of beans, corns,
and black walnuts (*sudasedi*), October beans (from Amy's garden) dried,
then re-hydrated and braised to make leather britches (common all over
the Blue Ridge); and, finally, chestnut bread (*tili disu selu*). Onita Bush,
another Elder Woman, blesses the food while the group says to Katie, ". . .
we just wanted you to understand why we do what we do as First Nations/
Indigenous people."

The episode might be read as relying on a white European tourist gaze,
with a white chef modifying a Cherokee Indian ingredient, yet watching
the group learn and eat together, a strong sense of cultural reclamation and
preservation emerges. Writing about Cherokee Indian foods often emphasizes lack and sadness, highlighting the loss of land, agency, and heritage,
but here, there is defiance, resilience, and determination. Katie remarks,
"corn may be everywhere," but the show places its origin in Appalachian
food as firmly Cherokee Indian.[58] These digital culinary tourism experiences do not provide the same *in situ* experience for visitors as eating at

the Cherokee Indian Fair or visiting its Native American Brewing's Tap and Grill, co-owned by the granddaughter of one of the EBCI's last recorded medicine men, but they do circulate alternative cultural food narratives. Of course, a variety of political and socioeconomic factors influence how effectively these stories challenge the images peddled by the predominant tourist industry, but digital and analog experiences alike offer Cherokee people forms of cultural production and reproduction that help negotiate power imbalances and strengthen community.[59]

Barley and the Heritage of Whisky Experience

Dualchas is also created through appeals to heritage, and whisky tourism is full of those, often preserving and circulating stories of old that fortify parts of Appalachia that have been intentionally left behind. From the beginning, mythology surrounded whisky's history, but it too symbolizes how cultural values are reflected and circulated through food and drink tourism rhetoric. Stemming from the Gaelic *"usage beatha,"* meaning "water of life," debates about whisky's origin and evolution continue. European monks arriving in Scotland between 1100 and 1300 used barley, yeast, and water for distilling, while the Scots-Irish who brought it later to America preferred using corn and rye.[60] But in Scotland and the United States alike, tales of illicit stills and crafty bootleggers romanticize its past. The settlers' hatred of the British excise tax, the colonist's Whiskey Rebellion, and subsequent changes in liquor laws developed the moonshining and bootlegging industries throughout Appalachia, with both countries passing laws to curtail the practice in the 1800s.[61] America's first moonshine, Scotsman William Laird's applejack brandy, created in 1698 as a substitute for Scottish whisky, was supposedly enjoyed by George Washington; meanwhile, at The Glenlivet in the Scottish Highlands, tourists of today learn how founder George Smith hid from customs officers to perfect a craft that echoes in today's 12-year-old Illicit Still single malt. Such mythologies continue to influence how whisky is promoted and consumed, particularly through experiential appeals to heritage that underlie culinary tourism in both places.[62] After conducting fieldwork in Scotland and Southern Appalachia, we contend that tourists experiencing the heritage of whisky, particularly through its places and practices, may participate in a shared sense of enjoyment and expertise that sometimes serves divisive ends.

Indeed, the ability to experience whisky, participating in time-honored rituals of place, knits groups of tourists together, more confident in their shared knowledge and appreciation of the craft. The group experience is rhetorically significant in tourism generally, with "immersive, sensory-laden, emotion-provoking" elements creating a meaningful shared experience.[63] This approach is central to whisky tourism. As one distiller explains, there is a strong experiential pull when drinking whisky in a specific place, and "alcohol has always been an expression of people and place. When you drink something crafted by hand, it's like the distiller is sharing a particular sensation or experience with you."[64] On tours and in tasting rooms, the experience of place figures importantly. Guests are often presented with samples where, together, they taste how elements of place are expressed, such as the flavor of a particular apple at Holman's applejack distillery in the Blue Ridge, or the notes of dried grass and local bluebell flowers in the whisky at Glenkinchie in the Scottish Lowlands. On another tour, one guest exclaimed, "It's like an ad for Scotland!" at the conclusion of the introductory video featuring a typically Scottish sense of place with copper stills, miles of coastline, green glens, and pure mountain water.[65] At Copper Barrel Moonshine distillery in the North Carolina foothills, we learned why the region's own well water was important and that the phrase "Wilkes County" was stamped onto every bottle to emphasize its water source as well as how "people know moonshine here."[66] Promoting these senses of place reinforces who claims whisky's heritage but situates groups together to experience their importance.

It is this experience of place that collectively connects tourists to history and heritage, whether real or imagined. At the Grandfather Mountain Highland Games, for example, group experiences surrounding whisky emphasized the importance of place in tightening connections to Scottish ancestry and deepening cultural pride, thus creating a sense of community that might not have previously existed. At a group whisky tasting, with the sound of bagpipes playing in the background, our guide, Andrew, took us to Scotland, calling on what whisky expert Blair Bowman calls whisky's distinctive participatory element, where "the simple act of sipping a whisky in Tokyo can transport the drinker to Islay in an instant."[67] Our guide created what he called "olfactory hallucinations," activating senses of smell to spark memories of Scotland and relive any past experiences with the country.

Figure 9. Whisky tasting at the Grandfather Highland Games,
Grandfather Mountain, North Carolina. Author photograph.

Careful to note connections between the minerality of the water used in Glenmorangie's North Highland distillery and that used in Kentucky's bourbon industry, Andrew also drew on taste parallels between the use of smoke (peat or charred barrels) in creating whisky in either place. These sensory elements of place tied the two larger whisky regions together, as well as the assembled group.

Whisky embodies more than just terroir, or the soil and ingredients used, in informing a sense of place, however. By participating in the distilling process, visitors gain further confidence in their expertise, better able to speak whisky's distinct language, and become part of a special, knowledgeable group. Before our tasting in The Macallan's Distillery, for instance, we learned how barrel construction influenced what we would sample. We watched a video of craftsmen meticulously forging Scottish whisky casks from Spanish and American oak, sharing in learning about the importance of each step. Later, at the Scotch Whisky Experience, an animated ghost of a former distiller narrated the history of the distilling process as our ride in whisky barrel-shaped cars proceeded. Ending up in a replica of an 1880s-style sample room, we were encouraged to taste the differences in the way that a master distiller might. Although careful to present whisky as accessible, tours often associated the drink with time-honored, unchanging practices and (frequently male) expertise that they are taught to embody. Tours send a clear message that guests are now better equipped to appreciate and share how whisky is meant to be enjoyed. They are now part of the process—whisky experts.

Although many distillery tours privilege the importance of the past, some reinvent history to encourage new interpretations and appeals that offer different types of shared experience, melding together cultural influences. At Edinburgh's newly opened Johnnie Walker Princes Street, guides sought to explode myths about the stuffy origins and presentation about Scotch as a drink and Scotland in general. Guests were encouraged to put their own spin on its tradition, with Scotland's elements of place providing for endless high-quality variations of its national drink. Encouraged to garnish our personalized cocktails with neatly and beautifully arranged candied ginger, dried lemon peels, and rose petals, whisky became modern, young, and accessible, not outdated, or elitist, requiring special knowledge to enjoy. Absent were lessons about nosing whisky, replaced with loose guidance that violated expected norms and unspoken communicative rules. Back in North Carolina at Copper Barrel distillery, our "Spirit Guide" similarly emphasized how we could use a wide variety of juices, garnishes, and combinations to craft a moonshine cocktail that was just our style. In shared whisky tourism experiences, these messages build from history to adapt it to the present echoed throughout.

Whisky tourism thus often draws on a place's heritage to bring people together in a shared experience, but these connections risk fueling more problematic expressions of voluntary group identity. At the Grandfather Games, for instance, after listening to Scottish folk music, trying Scottish foods, and watching Highland dance competitions and sheep herding, we visited a tent where a group of Scottish descendants' friendly conversation about the long-running tradition of holding the Games on Grandfather Mountain took a much darker turn. Offered a dram by the host, the shared sense of community and expertise cultivated earlier at the whisky tasting became dominated by white supremacist membership claims. Some argue that the processes of memorialization and celebration evident at Southern Highland Games allow tourists to connect to their Scottish ethnic origins,

Figure 10. Customizing whisky cocktails at the Johnnie Walker Experience, Edinburgh, Scotland. Author photograph.

claiming identities rooted in Scotland's history and traditions rather than from their relationship to slavery and Jim Crow.[68] These narratives have encouraged some white Southerners to distance themselves from the actual historical past and embrace a more comfortable version of history. Parallels between the fall of the Old South and the defeat of the Highland Scots were used to claim white victimhood and rewrite racial histories. Perhaps due to whisky's reserve-lowering properties, sharing drams of whisky facilitated appeals to heritage that tightened ethnic and racial cultural borders. The white, male "head of the family" complained about how African Americans in his North Carolina hometown were "making such a big deal" about reclaiming a contested public space to build a monument, furious at the protests against racial injustice springing up following the death of George Floyd.[69] In this tent, symbolic linkages to the defeat of the Highland Scots played a role in reconstructing public memory surrounding Jim Crow–era division of public space. Whisky-fueled conversation encouraged cultural separatism and racial hierarchies. Other attendees challenged his argument, but racism bubbled under the surface of the weekend's celebrations of voluntary identity and was visible in some of the iconography. The entwined American and Scottish flags, tartan shops, and Scottish food stalls took on additional meaning when adjacent to "don't tread on me" T-shirts, Confederate flags, and All Lives Matter stickers for sale. Rather than drawing from a shared heritage created by migration patterns to disrupt narratives about racist, redneck hillbillies, drinking whisky confirmed symbolic connections and fueled a heritage of hate, in this case.

TRACING FOOD TRADITIONS

Today's Appalachian tourist experiences echo practices brought here long ago and preserve traditions. Exploring crop migration also provides insight into the types of audiences that tourism constructs through appeals to *dualchas* and their consequences, not only for the visitor, but for those who care about these messages. This framework thus also provides opportunities for melding traditions. Analysis of Appalachian culinary tourism experiences reveal how food and drink are deeply rhetorical, able to fortify and change perceptions about regions and their residents. Lingering connections to real and imagined historical roots simultaneously inform stereotypes about the isolated, racist, backward Mountaineer or draw from history to offer *different* notions about Appalachia's traditions, heritage, character, and culture. Tracing oats from Scotland into the mountain diet locates messages of comfort, connection, and allegiance to time-honored cultural values and beliefs, but also excavates ones of ingenuity, invention, and creativity that are downplayed in many tourism experiences today. Enduring legacies of corn highlight how foods fuel cultural preservation and community, forming a character of resistance, resilience, and strength that was always there, but not always discussed in tourism literature. Barley celebrates elements of place and develops shared senses of expertise that connect, as well as divide, the tourists who experience them. Tracing food traditions highlights how cultures adapt to survive and reflect new influences but, as seen in the whisky fieldwork, these adaptations do not necessarily reach a positive teleological end. Tracing the migratory patterns of other foods might also emphasize division, not connection, in culinary tourism opportunities.

Nevertheless, the ability of culinary tourism to draw from contested pasts to reinforce or justify beliefs and values underscores the importance of offering different experiences connected to those histories. Some culinary tourism experiences drawn from Scots-Irish mythology will continue to fuel regional perceptions of a backwards, isolated culture resistant to change, but other experiences embrace openness, adaptation, and innovation that meld traditions together. Carolina Ground, Anson Mills, and Farm and Sparrow replant staple crops brought by immigrants to recenter history for culinary expression and agricultural rejuvenation, offering products that return to their roots to provide deeper flavors, more variety, and improved, more sustainable, nutrition. Eating at Southern Appalachian restaurants that celebrate this diverse history, tourists enjoy biscuits that aren't mass produced vehicles for fatty meats or edible vehicles of culinary claims of authenticity, but experience flavors that thread the agricultural past with the culinary present that show its ongoing evolution, melding traditions and flavors together. As Chef Travis Milton emphasizes, "This [Appalachian food] is not a still photo as much as anyone wants to make it that, this cuisine has been an ever-changing thing . . . there's a lot more layers to what we do here."[70] Culinary tourism has been explored for its impact on changing a culture's foods and foodways, but this chapter illustrates how it helps change the perception of people, too.[71]

Exploring the role of migration in the rhetoric of culinary tourism is important because it builds different public vocabularies and offers additional types of belonging, even for those who aren't tourists. Rather than providing experiences in keeping with outdated expectations, new interpretations help reduce the distance between the audience and the producer, making the Other more familiar. Some travel experiences merely feed into a narrow understanding of the region, keeping power hierarchies in place and the Other safely apart; when tourists sip strawberry moonshine on a rustic faux porch, they consume the past in an easy, distanced way. Of course, even culinary tourism that challenges regional tropes through more careful presentations is not necessarily capable of changing people's perceptions of regions; some tourists only want to try new foods, not change their viewpoints. Still, learning about new ingredients might open up a conversation or offer historically marginalized groups "refreshingly honest" and "transforming" experiences.[72] Culinary historian Michael Twitty's garden in Williamsburg, for example, notes the imprint of enslaved people on America's landscape, emphasizing the "visceral impact of slavery and the unyielding influence of the African American horticultural tradition."[73] These "landscapes of resistance" carry the seeds of rhetorical significance: "I don't pretend that everybody that comes [to Yorktown] is coming there to hear us talk about vegetables. But I hope that we change people's perspectives in a positive way."[74] Creating more of these types of experiences decenters whiteness in culinary tourism because when tourists are able to visit a place with its broader history in mind, a different message may be more apparent. There is work to be done in Southern Appalachia to offer more opportunities that motivate this type of thinking.

Nevertheless, the possibility of culinary tourism experiences in generating conversation calls for more rhetorical attention. Tourism observers note that there is a palpable hunger for more representative heritage tourism experiences. We have illustrated how culinary tourism, *in situ* or digitally, can offer powerful moments of connection and cultural recognition by appealing to *dualchas*. Importantly, though, *in situ* culinary tourism plays a different, significant rhetorical role in engaging tourists at a visceral, sensory immersive level, whether they are dining at the Hatfield and McCoy dinner show or learning about traditional Appalachian agriculture when attending a dinner on a local farm.[75] Embodied experiences provide opportunities for personal identification as well as for transgression, making analysis of culinary experiences that offer more and different connections to Appalachia crucial.[76] As Phaedra Pezzullo writes, some travel fosters more significant interactions between travelers and tourists, creating an opportunity for "outsiders to travel in order to *be present* and, perhaps more importantly, *to feel present*."[77] The consumption of traditional grains in new contexts provides opportunities for tourists to reconnect to cultural values that have been overlooked or downplayed. The estimated market for Scottish heritage/ancestral tourism may be 50 million people, but we must attend to those experiences that offer connection to those of different Appalachian ancestry.[78] We should continue to examine how culinary tourism offers additional opportunities for representation, and what work these texts do in constituting a new sense of belonging to Appalachia. Embodied culinary experiences may offer connections to Appalachia, and this place is rich in them. Understanding food tourism rhetoric also helps explain the rhetorical nature of regions, where experiential tourism creates "territorialized heritage narratives" that reinforce or challenge typical regional stories.[79] Although grappling with experiences that more accurately depict the influences of migration patterns in Appalachian culinary culture may be "complicated and painful," they are valuable because "they open up space" for tourists to taste history more honestly.[80] To continue to complicate notions of the Appalachian region, analyses of culinary food tourism go beyond the linguistic, offering the opportunity to consume how these boundaries are created, maintained, or destroyed.[81]

Chapter 3

Moonshine Mythologies in Appalachian Public Memory

Walking through downtown Pigeon Forge, we knew we were not likely to find carefully refined, nuanced stories of Appalachian life. Home to Dollywood, hillbilly themed dinner theaters, and miniature golf courses, the town attracts millions of visitors each year who are often seeking out experiences they think reflect the region's culture and character. At the tasting rooms of Tennessee Shine Company and Old Forge Distillery, we saw much of what we expected—mason jars of multi-colored and flavored moonshine, spaces mimicking backwoods shacks, hillbilly souvenirs. These portrayals make some Appalachians cringe. Yet, many others are thankful for the tourist dollars and all that the income brings to the region.[1] After all, the moonshine industry in Southern Appalachia is booming, with 500-plus distilleries in North Carolina and with Virginia's distilleries contributing $163 million to the state's economy.[2] Distilleries such as Ole Smoky, Sugarlands Distilling Co., Tennessee Shine Co., Call Family Distilleries, and Copper Barrel not only produce massive amounts of (the now legal) moonshine but also play major roles in the region's tourism industry; Ole Smoky alone pulls in 4 million visitors per year, "more than all the distilleries in Scotland, and more than the distilleries on the bourbon trail in Kentucky."[3] Travelers make their way to moonshine and whiskey[4] showrooms in large tourist areas such as Gatlinburg and Pigeon Forge, Tennessee, but also smaller towns like Dalton, Georgia, and Wilkesboro, North Carolina, to get a taste of the concoctions.

Wanting to top off the whiskey/moonshine experience several months later, we planned to start our day at the Uncle Nearest Distillery in rural Shelbyville, Tennessee, and end the day at the Ole Smoky Distillery in the heart of uber-touristy Gatlinburg, Tennessee. Uncle Nearest, as we explored in an earlier chapter, breaks away from the typical touristy stories of recipes

Figure 11. Banana Pudding Moonshine at Ole Smoky,
Gatlinburg, Tennessee. Author photograph.

handed down between (white) relatives. Nearest Green is the first recognized Black distiller in the region and the family histories shared in the distillery highlight a very different story. As we began walking into the former horse barn-turned-welcome center, we noticed that the tourists arriving with us were primarily African American, that the portraits that lined the entry hallway featured Black family members, and that the placards told a different version of the whiskey story, blending the Scots-Irish customs frequently told at other Southern Appalachian distilleries with stories of forcibly enslaved people bringing distilling techniques with them from Africa. We left Uncle Nearest and drove through rolling land dotted with horse farms and slowly made the trek to "Appalachian Disney World"— Sevierville, Pigeon Forge, and Gatlinburg. Arriving late in the evening, we drove along the central corridor, noting the neon signs and billboards for the moonshine/whiskey experience that was more familiar to us in this region. We slowly made our way in a tourist-congested downtown Gatlinburg, to the Ole Smoky distillery and storefront. There, visitors wander through the open distillery area, with signs explaining the process, while making their way to the store. Outside, rows of people in rocking chairs listening to a lively overall-wearing, banjo- and fiddle-playing band on stage. Inside, we found the same neon-colored liquid in mason jars that we had noted at other moonshine outlets. Although the roots of the stories told through the Uncle Nearest and Ole Smoky experiences were similar (focusing on cultural traditions and histories, celebrating rural America, lauding the importance of Appalachian ingredients), the tone was vastly different, and as we drove on through the winding Smoky Mountain roadways, those stark differences lingered in our minds. A few days later, the feeling intensified, as we drove through Highlands, North Carolina, on our way back home. Little did we know that Highlands claims to be the site of the "Moccasin Wars," a fight between Moccasin, Georgia, moonshiners and Highlands residents after those moonshiners were arrested and jailed by revenuers. As the story goes, a standoff ensued and the moonshiners blocked the road into town. The legend's details are murky, but clearly moonshine plays a significant role in the region's history, on display, literally, through a marker in the middle of Main Street.

Although not immediately apparent, the Southern Appalachian moonshine and whiskey narratives explored thus far include themes of rhetorical resilience, strengthening the region through preservation of tradition, fortification of community, and a melding of cultural foodways. Although moonshine's history is complex, we know that early settlers re-created the liquor for many reasons, but partially to reconnect with the drink traditions that they knew best.[5] Southern Appalachians were also innovative with moonshine production, creating "shine" (a nickname used to refer to moonship) to sustain their families and communities when in need of a steady income. Still, the story of moonshine—and alcohol more broadly—is often written off as the story of backwards, barefoot hillbillies making their illegal hooch up in the woods. As Emelie Peine and Kai Schafft write, "It is no coincidence that the cartoon image of the hillbilly that is marketed to tourists in the T-shirt shops and souvenir stands of east Tennessee almost always carries a jug marked with the triple Xs that denote alcoholic content, and that the Tennessee state song 'Rocky Top' has two verses referring to moonshine."[6] Images of moonshine distillers ultimately became "a symbol of what was wrong with Appalachia," earning ridicule from outsiders and disdain from some Appalachians.[7] Simultaneously, whiskey and moonshine serve as signs of creativity and ingenuity, a regional metonym, with moonshine documentary filmmaker David Weintraub contending, "everything you know about moonshine is wrong."[8]

This chapter adds nuance to our understanding of the meaning of moonshine and whiskey public memories in the Blue Ridge Mountains, accounting for their history, their role in producing messages of resilience, and the problems and possibilities that their narratives bring to the region. Contemporary rhetorical work surrounding distilling plays a vital, but varied, role in creating and reinforcing Southern Appalachian public memory that serves multiple purposes. Just in the past 100 years since the 18th Amendment, also known as the Prohibition Amendment, went into effect, moonshine symbolizes a simpler, yet appealing and slightly illicit American past, where imbibing allows enthusiasts to "flirt with danger," while drinking their "faux country" 'shine, now flavored with raspberries, doughnuts, and even Moon Pies, likely to the horror of their ancestral distillers.[9] More contemporary moonshine and tourism industry narratives broadly present a conflicting version of the region. Mainstream moonshine memories feed into regional resiliency stories, for example, but come at the expense of glamorizing a white, masculine, impoverished, law-breaking culture, creating limited and unproductive roles for Appalachians and eliminating and silencing other historical voices. At the same time, alternative narratives provide a compelling story of resilience of tradition, regions, and people that creates a more productive role for Appalachians. We briefly explore regional moonshine and whiskey history before analyzing the public memories created through the typical and alternative moonshine narratives. These everyday rhetorical reflections of public memory significantly shape regions and identities, influencing the way that Appalachians and outsiders view the area. This case study offers an example of public memory interventions and the potential for creating more nuanced images of cultural traditions.

HISTORY OF MOONSHINE AND WHISKEY
IN SOUTHERN APPALACHIA

The advertisements for moonshine distilleries often lure people in with the idea of experiencing an authentic part of Appalachian history, learning about family histories and recipes while sipping the forbidden and gazing at the fast cars of the past. As Southern foodways writer John T. Edge explains about moonshine's renewed appeal, it's a "hip flask accessory for authenticity seekers," whereby taking a sip of the no longer illicit spirits is more about participating in a story "embedded in the moonshining mystique" rather than drinking quality spirits.[10] Part of the experience is to imagine life off the grid, up in the mountains, experiencing lawlessness and a devil may care attitude. Alcohol certainly helps craft the experience, but moonshine in particular sells that image of the region, with moonshiners continually portrayed as "crazed and backward, romantic and rowdy" in popular images since the late 1800s.[11] "Moonshine," journalist Erin Carson writes, "whose name is often attributed to distillers working in secrecy through the night, has gone mainstream."[12] Although the tourist-focused messages make it seem as if everyone who lives in Appalachia has a still in the backyard and a muscle car to outrun the law while hauling the goods, moonshine and whiskey have a much longer history in the region, as discussed in chapter 2.

That history, in fact, is vital to understanding the region. In the forward to historian Joseph Earl Dabney's *Mountain Spirits,* he notes, "The making, the drinking, and the marketing of corn whiskey are deeply enmeshed in the rural and pioneer Southern mystique, much more deeply than perhaps many Southern social historians have been aware. The fiery beverage has been rooted in the lives of the people in the Appalachian South for over two-and-a-quarter centuries—and long before that in the lives of their ancestors in England, Scotland, and Ireland."[13] Clearly, cultural connections to whiskey and moonshine make both important parts of the foodways story. Whiskey was also a central component of regional hospitality, serving as a welcoming drink in homes as well as at community gatherings. Moreover, moonshine was used as a home remedy for any number of ailments, despite a lack of medical support for the claims.[14] As Charles Thompson sees it, whiskey was a key part of Appalachian culture: "Many a song paid tribute to its transformative power. To most it was considered a God-given right."[15]

Beyond those cultural roots, however, the production of alcohol also served a role that was specific to the region, creating an industry that provided a means for survival in impoverished areas and demonstrating characteristics of ingenuity and innovation through foodways that we have explored throughout this book. In an area that has continually been plagued by economic hardship, moonshine production allowed the people who lived on that land to survive and even thrive in some cases. As Daniel Pierce writes, moonshine provided "cash in a generally cash-poor society" and allowed farmers to pay "their tax bills, mortgages, and store bills; bought shoes and school books for their children and new land or homes for themselves; started businesses; and realized genuine benefits from their 'ill-gotten' gains"[16] By the early nineteenth century, more than four million gallons were being exported annually, bringing in significant incomes to the region.[17] Peine and Schafft explain that "moonshining constituted both an economic foundation and a cultural currency that was predicated on a shared understanding of the need for secrecy, and also a surreptitious pride in the community's own resourcefulness . . . One horse could haul ten times more value on its back in whiskey than in corn."[18] Moonshine provided a way for Appalachians to take care of themselves and their community, and that independence became a point of pride, despite changes in American society that made distilling taboo. As Thompson writes, "That sweat money made liquor bosses rich, but it also bought and preserved small farms, keeping people out of the mills and mines and on their own land for a generation or two longer, leaving people some independence to determine their own directions and to change their families' futures."[19] And, of course, economic stability brings with it the possibility for stronger communities that allow the region to grow, as a whole.[20] Economic growth comes with costs, but the pursuit of illegal moonshine sales motivated Appalachians to embrace it, whether directly involved or not.

Moonshine and whiskey production also demonstrated an innovation in production, using land resources that were abundantly available and the difficult, often dangerous work required to distill the liquor. *The Foxfire Book,* a collection of essays venerating Appalachian traditions, calls moonshining "a fine art," carefully describing the complicated process, arguing, "By any standards, moonshining has to be counted as one of the most fascinating mountain endeavors."[21] The work that went into making moonshine was not consistent with its typical lackadaisical image, with men lazing around the porch and strumming a banjo while waiting for the production to be complete; instead, moonshining was "hard work and required complex strategies for sales networking and clever means of transport."[22] Creating the instruments that would make distilling possible, securing the ingredients, going through the intense steps of distillation, all while worrying about being discovered by authorities demonstrates an ingenuity and dedication that strays from the parodied image of moonshiners.[23]

The popular portrayal of moonshiners also does not recognize the diverse history of the spirit. In fact, moonshine is not even unique to North America, with the word tracing back to the British Isles, dating back to the 1400s. Globally, the ingredients change to adapt to the land and people, crafting "every imaginable fermentable foodstuff into illegal booze."[24] A variety of Indigenous peoples also contributed to the North American story of whiskey, with early versions made primarily using indigenous grain, or what early Scots-Irish Appalachians called "Indian corn."[25] After being introduced to liquor by Europeans, Cherokee Indians began to produce fermented liquor, initially using it for rituals and medicine. The United States government then attempted to regulate Cherokee Indian production, leading to "one of the first ways in which the Cherokees asserted their nationalism."[26] The Scots-Irish connection demonstrates cultural migration, but the traditions continued to change as they were influenced by other cultures. The American story of whiskey and moonshine, like many Southern foods, tragically also has ties to enslaved people. As culinary historian Michael Twitty explains it, "American slaves had their own traditions of alcohol production, going back to the corn beer and fruit spirits of West Africa, and many Africans made alcohol illicitly while in slavery."[27] These connections to enslavement have not been fully folded into the whiskey and moonshine story, but as Southern foodways research continues to uncover forgotten histories, additional links to African culture may emerge. "Slavery and whiskey," *New York Times* journalist Clay Risen writes, "were inextricably entwined. Enslaved men not only made up the bulk of the distilling labor force, but they often played crucial skilled roles in the whiskey-making process."[28] Women were also frequently left out of the history of Southern moonshine, despite being an important part of the distilling process.[29] In short, moonshine is not unique to Appalachia and the production is certainly not limited to white men, but the often-circulated public memory surrounding moonshine does not reflect this history.

Given the role that moonshine plays in so many characteristics of Appalachian culture, the shift to viewing distilling in a negative light is perplexing. Indeed, it took an organized effort to criminalize the production and make the process taboo. In the 1870s and '80s, moonshiners were

still portrayed by many "as heroic symbols of defiance of federal authority."[30] In the early 1900s, however, prohibition of distillation and sales in
the region changed an important way of life for many Appalachians who
had grown used to ready access to moonshine and other liquors, as well
as the economic benefits that grew alongside those creations. As historian
Bruce Stewart argues, this reform represented a major turning point for the
region.[31] Whereas before, moonshiners were viewed as community entrepreneurs, Prohibition brought with it a portrayal of distillers as corrupt,
amoral, and even violent. Whiskey makers were portrayed as being a significant part of the societal problem that was sketched out in Prohibition campaigns by government agencies as well as community-based organizations.
Eleven years after the end of the Civil War, whiskey-making was declared
illegal and this change "made a product of presidents and missionaries into
the contraband of criminals."[32] The move to criminalize distilling was heavily rhetorical, shaping the way that outsiders viewed the Appalachian liveli-
hood through language centered on illegality and sin.

Beyond Prohibition, public campaigns to undermine the role of moonshine in Appalachian culture continued. Perhaps most symbolic of this
type of work was a 1967 pamphlet, "The Incredible Moonshine Menace,"
published by Licensed Beverage Industries, Inc.[33] The front cover tells the
reader that moonshine is a "Destroyer of Health and Life," a "Breeder of
Crime and Corruption," and a "Colossal Tax Swindle," while including a
"salute to the moonshine fighters," that is, the Internal Revenue Bureau's
Alcohol and Tobacco Tax Division, and implores "Every American" to join
in the "war on these callous criminals."[34] Arguing that the "old stereotyped
moonshiner—barefoot, awkward and amusing—went out with the buggy
whip," the authors used the pamphlet to demonstrate that moonshine had
become a big business in the region and brought with it crime, seediness,
and sin.[35] Over time, then, the image of moonshine, distilling more broadly,
and the Appalachians who were involved in the enterprise shifted from accepted to vilified in some circles.

Although the portrayal of moonshine varies, it is not surprising that the
history of moonshine and whiskey is frequently invoked in public reflections about mountain culture, whether in travel literature, at a tourist spot
along the highway, or in businesses within the region that target travelers.
Much of the modern role of moonshine and whiskey in the region is bound

up with popular images and memories. Given the rhetorical work that goes into creating regions, it becomes important to account for these everyday portrayals of Appalachians and the influence that the rhetoric has on those inside and outside of the region.[36] Stereotypical moonshine narratives make the region and the people easier to dismiss as inconsequential and victims of their own creations but also has a larger impact on how we view Southern identities, including race, class, and gender.

PUBLIC MEMORY AND REGIONAL IDENTITY

Public memory is both the memory of publics and the publicness of memory, influencing much of what we remember about historical events through the way we discuss and visually portray history, creating "multiple, diverse, mutable, and competing accounts of events."[37] Because rhetorical work in this area focuses on texts that are public, not appearing in private conversations, much of the research explores more formal types of rhetoric, public memorials, and similar sites.[38] But public memory research also accounts for the more transient and fleeting sites of memory, including media and other types of popular culture.[39] As Chandra Ann Maldonado argues, public memory scholarship must focus more attention on "nondominant historical narratives" using various methodologies that allow for gathering more texts and more diverse texts.[40] For example, Maldonado suggests that public memory scholars should account for aspects of stories that fall outside of official historical reflections, including the voices of "individuals/visitors who bring their own experiences into the commemorative space as extensions of those memory networks within the commemorative situations."[41] Similarly, John Bodnar explains that public memory is formed through both expressions of "cultural leaders or authorities," as well as "vernacular culture," that represents a wider swath of individuals.[42] Rhetorical scholarship recognizes that public reflection on texts makes the work more accurate, because "memory and commemorative work does not exist within the vacuum of academic discourse; they are public discourses that continue to shape the way that we live."[43] Including reactions to these narratives helps uncover public memory's impact. To that end, we analyze both the official, corporatized narratives of moonshine as well as the more vernacular—moving beyond the larger corporations and to the ways that alternative narratives stemming from smaller distillery spaces, their owners/distillers, and community members discuss moonshine. Both approaches contribute to circulating memories.

Public memory serves different rhetorical functions, but most relevant to this consideration of Appalachian remembering is the role that it plays in influencing regional identity. The narratives that are articulated through various texts ultimately form a "construction that forwards an at least momentarily definitive articulation of the group," allowing for a sense of connection and belonging.[44] What public memory scholarship must do, Carole Blair, Greg Dickinson, and Brian Ott argue, is determine the endpoint of these identities—what groups they create, what narratives they uphold, and so forth.[45]

Significantly, many scholars point out that whiteness is an assumed part of public memory and is often not explicitly discussed unless it is directly relevant to the narrative. Although misrepresentations of race in narratives are also damaging, it can be equally problematic to leave out details that may lead people to read history in a different way. As John Lynch and Mary Stuckey explain, "Public memory is a competition because it involves the creation of meaning about the past."[46] In other words, our memory of history is formed as we embrace some aspects of the narrative while also choosing to ignore (or not be exposed to) other facets. Because the narrative surrounding past events is often centered on white men, other perspectives are often omitted. Whiteness, G. Mitchell Reyes argues, serves as the "invisible hand of official public memory."[47] That is especially true in the South where, "whiteness has historically served as the default identification associated with the term 'southerner,'" Patricia Davis points out.[48] Indeed, as Erica Locklear observes, discussions of corn in Appalachia became linked to white Southern moonshiners rather than with the cultural importance of the crop within its Cherokee Indian communities.[49] Tourism and popular culture—some "official" and some "vernacular" voices—contribute to these "white washed" stories of the South, serving as a "constitutive component of memory environments" and influencing readings of Southern narratives.[50]

Erasure also occurs with socioeconomic status; stories are largely told and remembered devoid of class experience, generally omitting details of economic struggle unless they serve the narrative. Moonshine history, however, provides an exception to the dismissal of class. In many public iterations of the history, stories of poor Appalachians are included as an important element of the memory. In most cases, however, poverty is both a motivator for the distilling and a defining characteristic of Appalachians. The inclusion of class markers is mainly used to sell the region to outsiders; tourists, those with the means to visit the area, buy the products, and take those poverty stories back to their friends and family, while laughing about the hillbilly mystique. The consequences of that narrative are complex, with benefits stemming from the tourist economy, but also damages to the region as it continues to be portrayed as a caricature, thereby opening the door for continued Southern stereotypes that harm all Southerners.

Because public memory is constitutive, creating an inviting role for individuals through the narratives, it creates a sense of community and shapes a worldview, thus potentially wielding rhetorical power if used in certain ways.[51] Public memory research accounts for not only what is included in memory but also what is excluded. The rest of this chapter will look more closely at the public memory messages that are developed through moonshine narratives, paying attention to both contemporary mainstream and alternative versions.

PLAYING ON APPALACHIAN STEREOTYPES

Studies that explore the foodways of Appalachia without attending to moonshine omit an important part of its culture. As we travelled across the region, especially in areas that target more tourist traffic, we began to realize that dismissing the role of moonshine in the story of Southern Appalachia would be a mistake. Moonshine offers the ability for Southern Appalachians to resurrect the sense of entrepreneurship and pride in producing a now wildly successful product but also the opportunity for tourists to engage with part of the South they may once have mocked, but now find valuable. Moonshine and other spirits have emerged as instruments of their drinkers' appreciation for "artisanal goods and farm-to-table connections."[52] Moonshine is also what distillers can sell quickly while waiting on their bourbon to age appropriately—it's a more immediate return on investment that shows some financial savvy. Because of this product popularity, most tourist locations (especially in East Tennessee) include references to moonshine and sell products made with it, including jellies, maple syrup, and barbecue sauce. Many restaurants in Southern Appalachia, especially upscale restaurants, recently began featuring moonshine-based cocktails.

Traveling along, we also saw complicating narratives, as with most origins, in moonshine's history and place in Southern Appalachia. Public memory surrounding moonshine and whiskey in the region spotlights the story of crafty and determined mountaineers outsmarting and outrunning authorities. The scene includes ramshackle structures buried deep in the woods and fast-moving cars carrying illegal liquor, featuring white men living fully (despite economic challenges) in the thick of this scene. Although these images might not be accurate, they contribute to overall ideas about the region.

The individual character that is central to public memory surrounding moonshine is the hillbilly. He (and the pronoun is specific here) is portrayed as the overall-wearing, corn pipe-smoking, banjo player who speaks broken English with a heavy Southern drawl. As one Tennessee distillery owner stated, "There are too many people from this area playing into the hillbilly stuff, everyone around here portrays us as hillbillies and make it into their product."[53] Helen Rosko claims that this image of Appalachians is "capitalizing on and a perpetuation of an inauthentic narrative of the region."[54] The allure of this portrayal of Appalachians is that it sells; tourists happily consume the image. As Kristen Baldwin Deathridge writes, "The marketing in all of Pigeon Forge is over the top and an assault on the senses, often catering to customers who seek a caricature of mountain people. 'Hillbilly' tourism has grown in Pigeon Forge since the opening of Great Smoky Mountains National Park in the 1930s, and many people love the area for its kitsch, not in spite of it."[55] In fact, Mark Roberts argues that this embrace of the hillbilly image on the part of Appalachians, what he calls "hillbillification," acts as a "kind of guerilla warfare, where regional people utilize the enemy's weapons—in this case, hillbilly stereotypes—to combat, or reverse, identity attacks."[56] Motivation aside, the inaccurate depiction of Appalachians is widespread.

The stereotypical moonshiner is almost always a man, even though, as Elizabeth Engelhardt points out, women also engaged in moonshine production to increase their economic opportunities when options were often limited. Women rarely appeared in stories told about the underground industry, though, and were even less likely to appear in the lampooned image of the whiskey maker.[57] Bourbon, whiskey, and moonshine are all associated with men, from the creation to the selling, and even to the drinking of the distilled beverages. "Bourbon," Seán McKeithan says, "has been written indelibly into the history of the white masculine South, by Percy, Faulkner, and our fathers, through advertising and through our consumption, for centuries."[58] Moreover, the men in these narratives are criminals, but their actions are dismissed with a wink and a nod, knowing that many in the community questioned the laws that placed them in that role. Historically, violence that accompanied moonshining was often ignored, with community members often overlooking "other forms of illegal and abusive behavior which took their toll on family and community life."[59]

One of the most venerated moonshiners, Marvin "Popcorn" Sutton, exemplifies this very image. In tourist heavy Pigeon Forge and Sevierville, we talked to local shop owners and distillers, asking them about their views on moonshine. Sutton's name came up frequently, with some lamenting his untimely death by suicide said to have been in reaction to federal charges related to illegal distilling and future prison time. His story is almost always recounted in discussions about moonshine in Appalachia, acknowledging the central role that he has in circulating memories. His 1999 self-published book (*Me and My Likker*), videos providing instructions on moonshining, and numerous souvenirs centering on his persona all drove interest in his life.[60] In 2008, a documentary (*The Last One*) brought national attention to Sutton and led to even more attention.[61] As Daniel Pierce writes, "Popcorn gave his fans what they wanted: the quintessential, bearded salty, overall and flannel-shirt wearing, 'meddlin' guvmint'-hating, good-old-boy moonshiner topped off with a pork-pie hat with a racoon's penis bone stuck through the crown."[62] Sutton "resembled a daguerreotype from an indeterminate Appalachian past."[63] Clearly, moonshiner stereotypes are connected to some accurate portrayals (as we will explore in the next section), but become exaggerated to embellish stories and to sell more liquor.

At the same time, another part of the dramatic moonshine narrative is the authority figure—the revenuers who collected taxes, the police who chased down the cars, the federal agents who took axes to the stills and burned down structures to prevent future distilling. While moonshine was and is a part of Appalachian tradition, it also symbolically acts as a "a generations-old middle finger to the establishment"[64] and "the contrarian uncle who lurked in the back of the national liquor cabinet, the rude, young, law-flouting spirit that never grew up."[65] Illegal moonshining provided mountaineers with a sense of identity, placing them in the role of the law-breaker. That illegality also created an alluring story to outsiders; it became common to "romanticize the life of the moonshiner as a modern-day Robin Hood, an outlaw who defies the oppressive forces of 'guvmint' and simply exercises his God-given right to make a little liquor."[66] At Call Family Distillers in Wilkesboro, North Carolina, for example, we were invited to try Uncatchable Moonshines named after Willie Clay Call, who is said to have outrun the law delivering to Winston-Salem and Charlotte, and sample their Forbidden Fire Whisky, said to have been first distilled by Lutheran Minister Reverend Daniel Call behind his general store.

Aside from the authorities, moonshine brings with it a great distrust of outsiders of any sort, creating a climate of suspicion, with Appalachians always on the lookout for informants.[67] As secret production happened, strangers might be met with a wary eye or even a shotgun. During our interviews, moonshine jars were brought out for a taste once we gained trust; sometimes they came from a back room, sometimes from underneath a counter, but always with a twinkle in the eye of the one offering a sip, taking pride in the role that moonshine has in the region's history, but also acknowledging its sense of taboo. Secrecy continues to be a part of the public moonshine memories. Our travels allowed us to experience being somewhat accepted as part of this tight-knit community when offered a sip on the sly, but this allure continues to draw in tourists, too, who feel slightly rebellious drinking liquor that is now legal and taxable.

Yet another part of the moonshine narrative centers on poverty. Not only is the distiller himself shown as struggling to survive, but he is also surrounded by a community facing the same issues. The common image of the moonshiner is not intended to sympathize with this economic issue, but to mock the ways of the hillbilly, perpetually poor because of a lack of intelligence and drive. The souvenirs on display at Tennessee Shine, for example, laughingly portray crude instruments meant to mimic modern technology or to highlight a lack of education. The "hillbilly flip phone" is a piece of wood, a "lucky lottery scratcher" is a piece of wood with a penny attached, the "hillbilly scratcher" is a piece of wood with a corncob attached. Tourist outsiders lampoon Appalachian poverty. While class issues are a part of public memory in this case, the focus on this memory quality hurts more than helps those facing deficiencies.

Similarly, the location of moonshining in public memory speaks of class and, specifically, classlessness. Most of the distilleries in the region connect their products to the history of the region, often using old, existing buildings, and outfitting them to accommodate their needs or bringing in pieces of authentic Appalachia into distilleries and tasting rooms.[68] This historical connection is effective because "visitors crave authenticity. People have choices for where they visit, and they want 'real' historical experiences."[69] Although it is hard to connect the new and polished distilleries with the barns, shacks, and lean-tos that housed much of the moonshine production of the past, the designers do their best to signal authenticity through distressed wooden shelves, hardwood floors, rocking chairs lining the entry porch, and crudely written signs denouncing "revenuers" and other "outsiders." Ironically, some of these distilleries spend a great deal of money trying to replicate a crude, classless scene.

The public memory narrative that we encountered at many of the tourist-heavy distilleries is a familiar image of Appalachians, unfortunately. If this memory acts in a constitutive fashion, though, its community building potential is not clear. Although the moonshine industry in Southern Appalachia has grown beyond the 'shine of the past, mainstream industries still build from images of that history.[70] The stereotype emphasizes limited resilience—outwitting authorities and outsiders, successfully distilling corn despite the difficulty of the process, providing a means of income for families and communities that might have had no other options—but this narrative does not communicate the strong resilience message that is possible through the story of moonshine, creating a limited and unproductive role for Appalachians.

ALTERNATIVE APPALACHIAN NARRATIVES

Despite the prevalence of many of these essentialist stories, alternative narratives surrounding moonshine and whiskey in the region create more productive sites of resilience and push against damaging images. These alternative public memories have always existed but rarely make their way to more popular imagining of moonshining. Instead of stories from "craft" or community distillers more likely to focus on regional traditions or family histories, mass-produced distillery marketing reaches much larger audiences. Many of today's craft distilleries, in fact, work to "combat what they perceive as negative stereotypes of the region, choosing instead to promote a narrative of moonshine that embodies tradition, craft, and resourcefulness."[71] These sites create the ultimate "neolocalism" feel, centering on usage of local resources and connections to the people and the land of the region.[72]

The moonshiners portrayed in these settings may not be dramatically different than the cartoonish images in many touristy mountain towns, but visitors get a more complex introduction to the characters. We visited Copper Barrel Distillery in North Wilkesboro, North Carolina, for example, and learned a great deal about the distiller—Buck Nance. Before taking a behind-the-scenes tour of the distillery, our "Spirit Guide," Anna, had us sit down to watch a documentary about the history of the business. The story as described in their introductory video, began when Vermont native George Smith decided he wanted to continue his family's rural traditions and eventually settled on opening a bourbon distillery in the small North Carolina town. As an outsider, he sought input from locals and was soon directed to talk to Buck, who ultimately became his business partner. Buck, however, convinced George that good moonshine could have as much taste complexity as bourbon and would yield a faster product. Almost ten years later, George and Buck have a successful business, with a second site scheduled to open in nearby Blowing Rock, North Carolina. The savvy business decision that the two made was guided by advice from Buck, who in some ways mirrors the stereotype of a moonshiner—white, male, clad in denim overalls, with a Southern drawl. And yet, we learned that Buck was far more than the cartoon hillbilly. Previously working for NASCAR as an engineer (a noteworthy connection, given the historical linkage between moonshining and NASCAR), Buck had been charged with designing the fastest cars possible.[73] As Anna walked us through the distillery, she explained that Buck had handcrafted all the steel-based equipment, working from drawings that his father brought back from World War II. Buck outfitted the former furniture manufacturing warehouse to accompany the distillery equipment, using his engineering background and handcrafting skills to work around preexisting parts of the space. While he was initially resistant to change and expanding with a "business guy coming up from Charlotte," recounting, "Oh Lord, I ain't getting in on that end of it," he quickly changed his tune when he realized that it was a sound financial option.[74] At first glance,

Buck was everything that you might imagine in a moonshiner based on the kitschy public memory narrative, but the distillery clearly wanted to tell more of his story. Whether the portrayal was completely reflective of his lived experience is not clear, but the rhetorical choices of the distillery in portraying him disrupted the story of the backwards, uneducated hillbilly. Indeed, there is now a vibrant "moonshine economy," where savvy businesspeople tap into this old hillbilly mystique to sell a lucrative product.[75] Positive portrayals of Appalachians who look and sound like the stereotypical moonshiner but who break that stereotype otherwise disrupt typical signifiers of poverty and may circulate alternative versions of public memory regarding class.

There is also a burgeoning market in celebrating the diversity of moonshine and whiskey history, for example, recognizing African and African American connections to the distilling process. Most notably, as previously discussed, Jack Daniel's distillery, one of the biggest names in the whiskey-making business, began in 2016 to embrace the origin of their product more publicly as connected to Nathan "Nearest" Green. As the company tells the story, Jack Daniel learned to make whiskey from a local minister and Nearest Green (then enslaved) prior to the Civil War; later, Green was hired to work at the distillery, with the company proudly proclaiming that "Jack Daniel not only never owned slaves but he worked side-by-side with them." A member of the Green family has been employed at the distillery since its inception.[76] Although the details continue to emerge, acknowledging the significant role that Green played is an important signal.

Since the story about Green broke, Uncle Nearest Distillery, has started selling whiskey using Green's recipe.[77] As we previously described, Green's story is on full display in the new Uncle Nearest Distillery, breaking away from the typical touristy stories of recipes handed down between (white) relatives. The entire space seems to disrupt the old narrative about whiskey, with visual markers (images of the Green family) changing the face of distillers and a history that is told both orally on the tour as well as in signs that insert different origin stories. One sign explains, "Whiskey came to America with the Scotch and Irish, but the technique of producing it here, was dependent on enslaved people who brought cultural knowledge of distilling & purifying water & alcohol through charcoal." Souvenir T-shirts were scattered around the room exclaiming, "I Am Making Black History"

Figure 12. "Making Black History" T-shirt at Uncle Nearest Premium Whiskey Distillery, Shelbyville, Tennessee. Author photograph.

(as opposed to the "Powered by Moonshine, High Octane Redneck Fuel" T-shirts on offer at Tennessee Shine). That day, visitors were delighted to hear that the company CEO and founder, Fawn Weaver, was making a visit and would sign purchased bottles. Tourists lined up to get pictures taken with Weaver, who started what the company claims is the "best-selling African American founded spirit brand of all time," her vision of privileging Green's story energizing the experience throughout the entire tour.[78]

Outside of the Nearest Green experience, more recent narratives also include women in the story, recognizing the role that they always played in the history. As Elizabeth Engelhardt points out in her analysis of women in moonshine literature, this taboo setting for women opened up more possibilities to "explore gender roles during a period of shifting definitions. Moonshine characters wrestled with new gender roles and the implications of strong women who were not confined to domestic spaces or domestic foodways."[79] Although Engelhardt's work centers on literary depictions of women, her argument also applies to the lived world of moonshine and whiskey creation. Historically, Mahalia Mullins, East Tennessee moonshiner, fit this description. Her story began as folklore in the late 1800s and is still celebrated through the Tennessee Vacation tourism web site and through her preserved cabin in Sneedville, Tennessee. Mullins was said to be "catchable, but not fetchable" because of the mountainous terrain leading up to her cabin as well as her weight.[80] Stories that go beyond the surface, however, explain that she was a single mother of many children, and that moonshine allowed her to provide for the family. Recent stories also point out that Mullins was considered "Melungeon, a [derogatory] name given to families of Black, white, and indigenous descent who settled in parts of Central Appalachia beginning in the late 1700s," and most likely fell subject to discrimination.[81] Despite the discrimination that she likely faced, Mullins was recognized as one of the most revered moonshine distillers in the area, with buyers coming from near and far to bring back some of her creation, said to be masterfully flavored with local apples.[82]

Uncle Nearest also highlights women's roles in the distillery. One placard in the showroom includes a drawing of Victoria Eady Butler, explaining that she is "the first African American Woman Master Blender at a major brand & great, great granddaughter of Nearest Green." Her talent in making whiskey, they explain, "was undoubtedly inherited." The CEO, a woman, is also spotlighted. At Copper Barrel, we learned that our guide, the co-owner's niece, was not only deeply involved in the production of whiskey at the main location but would soon be taking over as master distiller of a new location set to open. Anna was excited to become a part of the distillery story but explained to us that she had to convince her Uncle Buck that a woman could distill, starting with turning the water on and off and eventually slinging a bag of sugar over her shoulders to show a willingness for manual labor. She would become a part of the modern moonshine story, although it took effort on her part.

Part of the bad boy image of moonshining has also changed with legalization and widespread production. Distilleries are now featured in travel brochures, central to many Appalachian towns, serving as an anchor to the tourist industry. As Erin Carson writes: "It's a far cry from the days when moonshiners hid their illegal stills in the woods. No one a hundred years ago would've dreamed of placing their operations a few yards from the sidewalk on the main drag of one of Tennessee's biggest tourism towns, where the Salt and Pepper Shaker Museum and a replica of the Space Needle vie for your attention. And no moonshiner would have a gift shop to flaunt the enterprise."[83] The villains in these narratives, like the illegal moonshiners, have been relegated to the past. Given the economic boom that the industry has experienced and the global emphasis on using local resources for food and drink, the creators and consumers of moonshine and whiskey have changed. Most of the moonshine producers at this point are "Urban, middle-class professionals, or 'hipsters' who brewed or distilled alcohol as a hobby and decided to leave their jobs to open distilleries."[84] These aren't "dumb hillbillies," but savvy businesspeople who work "the other side of Thunder Road," offering white spirits featuring "open-pollinated corn," "Appalachian Spring Water," and historically accurate peach flavored shine.[85] And because distilling has been featured as an important part of Southern Appalachian culture, there is an eager audience taking part in the tradition. The tourists for this kind of adventure continue to flock to the region, seeing moonshine as "'cool' and 'edgy.'"[86]

The reason for distilling also changed slightly in these alternative stories. Much of what makes the modern-day moonshine and whiskey trend appealing is the relationship to regional history, with some Southern Appalachian distillers placing an emphasis on the importance of their work to this history. As one distiller explained to a researcher, "My whole idea is the art of making whiskey is being lost, and if I'm able to pass that down and showcase the art of making whiskey, that's important."[87] Heritage tourism appeals to many travelers who may see moonshine as a "symbol of Americana, a product that is 'authentic.'"[88] Drinking moonshine (and all its related liquors) provides a visceral connection to the land, so touristic experiences at distilleries let the visitor feel that they are in tune with the regional heritage. As McKeithan explains it, "Bourbon drinking can serve as a bridge into the past, allowing a drinker to tap into centuries of culture with a simple consumptive act."[89] Beyond the connection to history, this quintessential drink also provides a way to perform a Southern role, offering up "a piece of masculine identity that southerners can 'put on,' much like overalls, a seersucker suit, or a North Carolina twang."[90] Although the role is limited in many ways by expectations of what it means to be a whiskey-drinking Southerner, it shows the role of moonshine/whiskey in creating identity.

The economic reasons for producing moonshine are not completely removed from the explanations in the old narrative, but there are differences in this part of the story that also offer alternative constitutive possibilities. The move to legalize the production of moonshine in 2009 not only shifted the story away from the messages of illegality and morality that have been connected to the drink, but it also energized the economy in Southern Appalachia, allowing moonshiners to become entrepreneurs and savvy businesspeople, massively increasing their scale of production. Making a quickly produced white whiskey (unaged or barely aged whiskey) allows distillers to make a profit while waiting for the barrel-aged whiskeys and bourbons to be ready for sale.[91] Distilleries in Southern Appalachia and nearby parts of North Carolina have "sold millions of cases of 'white lightening' since 2010" and, although there has been a slight decrease in popularity in recent years, tourism surrounding moonshine is still very strong.[92] John T. Edge writes of the interest in moonshine, "As craft distilling boomed, moonshine, its little brother, attempted a transition from lowest common denominator drunk fuel to aspirational artisan beverage."[93] Perhaps ironically, the moonshine industry has formed a strong connection to many local governments, working together to bring in tourist dollars and "earning their support for what can be a controversial business option in small towns."[94] Although there may be some initial community hesitation, small towns see distilleries as helping to develop tourism economies. Copper Barrel's President and CEO, George Smith, was named a Main Street Champion, for example, for his help in revitalizing North Wilkesboro.[95] As Rocky Mount, Virginia's, town manager Matt Hankins explains the role of distillery tourism in the historic moonshine capital Franklin County, although moonshine production may sometimes conflict with "small town" community values, it is more likely seen as a way to bring in tourist dollars: "Franklin County—whether people like it or not—has the reputation of producing really great distilled spirits . . . So now we have somebody that's going to capitalize on that heritage and that reputation."[96] Neighboring town Boone's Mill Mayor Ben Flora also supports the industry development, arguing that moonshine is a "distinctive Franklin County heritage product that is now wondrously legal," adding humorously that the distillery really just produces "a Virginia agricultural product."[97] Instead of hiding away regional creations, many distilleries focus on the pride connected to the craft of distilling, highlighting the people and places that allow whiskey and moonshine to be celebrated.

Today, alternative moonshine narratives also tell a different story of the place where these distilled products are made. While almost all distilleries focus on the history of moonshine recipes and traditions, many smaller distilleries often focus more intensely on the land itself, sometimes claiming connections to the very land that they sit upon. The emphasis on land being used for tourism purposes, "using their individual rootedness to represent" the region, "but they are also working to sell the region with each jar of moonshine sold from their distillery."[98] Distilling provides another way to connect to local products, making it attractive to food advocates seeking local-made products, but also providing Appalachians and Southerners a point of pride that is more productive for the people and the region.[99]

Taking a step back to what some consider the "original moonshine of the colonies," we visited the Holman Distillery outside of Moravian Falls, North Carolina, where they make what the owner calls the "only true applejack" in the United States. The liquor is created by freezing, rather than boiling, apple cider, gradually scraping off ice layers until what is left is a higher concentration of alcohol. Although Prohibition made this cultural staple a thing of the past, applejack was a popular choice in the Blue Ridge Mountains for many years.[100] We wanted to see how the distillery was bringing back this regional tradition. After driving on winding mountainous roads through numerous apple orchards, farmland, and sparse houses, we met with John Holman for a private tasting of his creation. He walked us through the history and mission behind his business, frequently centering on the location and resources of the land. He explained that because his distillery sits in a valley with no farms and few houses even above his land, the water that he uses from the land is pure and that purity makes his products even more land-influenced and flavorful. When he started his business, he initially made a drink based on muscadine grapes, common to the area. Soon after starting to sell his creation, though, he had an eye-opening conversation with someone who asked, "What are muscadines?" He knew then that the message of the product would be lost if people couldn't recognize the ingredients. "Who doesn't know what apples are, though?" he asked. Determined to make a pure and historically based drink, he settled on applejack, developing a process to create an apple concentrate, not a separation (setting it apart from other similar products). Holman emphasized that each batch of applejack is different, completely dependent on the taste of the apples each year. We sipped on his various applejack versions, noting the differences in the experiences depending on the order of the drinks and the flavors that still lingered on our tongues. Sampling the green apple applejack, we agreed with John's description: "It tastes like green!" Many distilleries emphasize the land and climate affecting the product, but when you stand on site and view what is being described, it makes the explanation even more powerful and adds to the feeling of authenticity.

Similarly, Uncle Nearest Distillery frequently referenced the importance of land to the taste of the whiskey. Signs in the distillery explain that Lincoln County, where the whiskey was historically made and is now produced again, "became known for the good quality corn grown here," has a unique set up with "creek water flowing through miles of limestone," and holds the ground water at a perfect temperature. The land is featured even more prominently in a video on the web site and played as part of the tour that tells the story of the originator. The film opens with the narrator staring across a grassy field, slowly walking up to a house owned by the Green family. The narrator steps into the house, noting that it sits on "a special piece of American land," and continues to tell the distillery story as he looks out the window. The camera moves to a slow shot of a creek flowing over limestone and a sugar maple tree (used for charcoal filtration) while the narrator tells us that he (Green) "gave birth to Tennessee whiskey" on this land. The implied message is that although Green brought the techniques, it was both a combination of his skills and the land itself that led to the creation. This land is far removed from the stereotypical image of the mysterious mountainous woods hiding illegal undertakings; instead, distilled goods from the area are lauded as a reflection of a strong cultural tradition and the best qualities of the land.

Comparing these differing narratives, then—the damaging public memories and the stories being told by many of today's smaller distilleries —provides a clear image of the differences in the types of Appalachian citizen that can be constructed through rhetorical renderings of the role of distilling in Southern Appalachia. We conclude by discussing the implications of these different identities on offer.

PUBLIC MEMORY IN SOUTHERN
APPALACHIA CONSIDERED

Exploring the role of moonshine memories in shaping popular images of Southern Appalachia underscores the importance of accounting for public memory because these stories continue to represent the region to a broad audience. Even as outsiders recognize this portrayal as a caricature, many Appalachians exploit this imagery knowing that it meets tourist expectations. Preserving the traditions of distilling while melding together various components yields a very different outcome. The celebration of diversity brings more Appalachians into the story of the region and connects histories together in meaningful ways. In essence, bringing in a more robust understanding of the history and production of the product—folding that into public-facing narratives—elevates the status of distilling in the regional story. In other words, preserving and melding together create a more resilient role for Appalachians. Subtle shifts in the stories make an important intervention into the white, male narrative that is generally privileged in Appalachian public memory. As moonshine documentary film maker David Weintraub argues, the first moonshiners were African American and American Indian, and more work needs to be done to uncover and share their histories.[101]

Beyond this understanding of the specifics of moonshine memories, there are also broader conclusions to make about public memory research. This case study shows the importance of accounting for everyday images and memories, knowing that commonplace rhetorical messages can often be more powerful than overt constructions of narratives. These are "public discourses that continue to shape the way that we live," as Maldonado explains, but they are often overlooked.[102] Moonshine memories highlight the impact of popular culture on regional identity. The moonshine story also demonstrates how powerful public memory can be in shaping regions and identities connected to those regions, influencing how outsiders view a region, but also the roles that insiders enact based on those narratives. Public memory provides "a symbolic connection with the group and a sense of belonging."[103] Whether examining the mainstream moonshine narratives or alternative stories, there is an opportunity to connect with the region and to each other through this history. Creating a productive sense of belonging through public memory is vital and because public memory is selective, it is worth asking what narrative is being put forth and what kind of role it is creating for the region and its people.

Studying moonshine in Appalachia also isolates an example of an intervention into a problematic public memory, showing individuals who are intentionally (in some cases) fighting against inaccuracies. There is no simple way to replace damaging narratives with alternatives that tell a fuller story of the history; instead, competing narratives become a part of the circulation of ideas and may slowly alter public memory. As Blair, Dickinson, and Ott point out, "Groups tell their pasts to themselves and others as a way of understanding, valorizing, justifying, excusing, or subverting conditions or beliefs of their current moment."[104] More intentional public memory narratives are productive for a region, noteworthy in their overall contribution to public thought.

Finally, narratives surrounding moonshine and whiskey provide an example of public memory that accounts for race and class in a way that many do not. In this case, those memories are both destructive *and* constructive. The mainstream moonshine stories ignore race (defaulting to white) but place a heavy emphasis on class as an explanation for why Appalachians historically chose to participate in the illegal creation and sale of moonshine. Although there is attention to class, it is primarily used as a punching bag, offering up hillbillies as sacrificial lambs, too dumb to join the middle class. The alternative narratives are more intentional about examining race—pointing out distilling's complex and diverse history. Class is also often a part of these narratives, but there is more nuance in pointing out how moonshine provided for important regional economic stability. Not only is it important to explore how powerful these kinds of alternative narratives can be in region formation, but it is also important for scholars to continue searching for race and class representation in public memory. More significantly, our public memory research should continue to explore how and why certain negative constructions of identities can continue to be more appealing as well as the impact of those identities.

Although it is easy to brush off stereotypical images of Appalachians in public memory, this chapter shows the significance of these narratives in shaping regional identity. Even before the National Prohibition Act increased attention to their efforts and demand for their products, distillers weren't just lazy men lolling around on porches, but innovative men and women from a variety of cultures and histories finding ways to provide for family and community and celebrating an important part of the regional history and land. A more inclusive narrative of the regional point of pride offers much more to the region in telling the story of resilience—preserving tradition, fortifying community, and melding cultures—in Southern Appalachia.

Chapter 4

Creating Resilient Tourism in Appalachia

Almost exactly a year after the brutal death of George Floyd by Minne-apolis police officer Derek Chauvin and the nation's outpouring of outrage through protests and intensified pressure to enact racial justice, we arrived in Asheville, North Carolina. Vaccination had begun in earnest, mask mandates had been lifted, and people were everywhere, clearly in celebra-tory moods. In what is often recognized as the zenith of the possibilities provided by contemporary Southern Appalachian food tourism, it was still somewhat of a shock to see patrons enjoying meals indoors, stop-ping in various breweries located downtown and beyond, and sampling cocktails on the city's improved outdoor dining patio network, oblivious to or temporarily ignoring the world changes. A large food hall was set to open the following week, featuring the return of the original Asheville brewery—Highland Brewing Company—to downtown, as well as several locally owned restaurants. Many hotels were completely booked. We were in Asheville to watch it all unfold and we were curious. Would the nation's tumultuous year be reflected in the city's tourism scene? Would calls for post-pandemic hospitality industry reform, racial justice, and better cul-tural representation for minorities be evident in our experiences as tourists and researchers? In other words, could tourism better reflect the current moment, responding to the needs of residents while also continuing to appeal to travelers? We thought we would begin to investigate these ques-tions through a particularly coveted dining experience—dinner at Benne on Eagle.

Benne on Eagle is described as a modern soul food restaurant focused on African American cuisine of the Appalachians. With an Instagram profile highlighting its location in 'The Block,' Asheville's historically

African American neighborhood, and its spotlight on telling the stories of Affrilachia's[1] finest, in concert with glowing food media coverage and awards, we had high expectations. And the meal did not disappoint—an incredible tomato salad consisting of three different preparations and dotted with buttermilk cheese and basil, a crawfish rice dish with contrasting textures from its Carolina Gold rice, local bacon, and Old Bay puffed rice, and an inventive vegetarian jerk summer squash dish that echoed Caribbean influences with its spices, coconut rice and peas, and plantains. All were visually pleasing and deliciously complex. As we ate, we admired photos on the wall of Black women who had inspired the restaurant's chefs and owners and who had influenced Asheville's cuisine, shelves filled with influential African American cookbooks, and nods to Africa through carefully chosen wallpaper and decorations. Even the candle glowing in the restroom was made locally by the Hazelwood Soap Company. We finished eating, marveling about the whole dining experience, and yet, in the end, we realized we had just eaten at another impressive high-end restaurant. And we wondered—this restaurant, and others like it in the area, excelled at symbolizing the resilience of overlooked cultures and the importance of highlighting their contributions, but did it matter, ultimately?

In chapter 2, we discussed the role that tourism can play in both reinforcing problematic images of a region, as well as contesting those images, with culinary tourism serving a particular function in that experience. Here, we extend that discussion of tourism, taking the analysis beyond pathways and considering the larger scene of culinary tourism. There is an obvious economic benefit to a healthy tourism industry, but that success comes with other significant cultural advantages if it is thoughtfully constructed. Resilient tourism, that is, tourism that consciously works to strengthen a given region and its residents, happens by creating connections and a sense of consubstantiality through transcendent rhetoric. By focusing tourism on meaningful similarities among groups it is possible for individuals to not only connect on a deeper level, but to alter relationships with the region for residents and travelers. This type of tourism has the potential to undermine the otherizing of Appalachia and Appalachians, providing a clearer understanding of people and place that represents the area differently, offering residents more positive identities and material benefits. Culinary-based tourism is particularly well suited to create a transcendent experience because of all the ways the food speaks to travelers, as "the sights, smells, touches, sounds, and memories that accompany that food create a compelling message."[2] In this chapter, we explore the regional tourism context before turning to relevant literature on culinary tourism and resilience. We then analyze examples to theorize what resilient tourism might look like, suggesting how it helps preserve, fortify, and meld Appalachia's culinary traditions within a visitor's experience.

TOURISM AND TRANSCENDENCE

Tourism in Southern Appalachia effectively attracts more people to the region to learn about the culture, making a significant contribution to the economy. In fact, travel in the area has substantially grown in recent years, with 14 million visitors to the Smokies in 2021 contributing over 1.3 billion dollars to the economy.[3] But culinary tourism is also a powerful way to learn more about regions, with significant numbers of travelers choosing destinations based on food offerings.[4] These kinds of experiences provide an opportunity for travelers to merge the "exotic and familiar," partaking in a daily dining ritual, but doing so with different sensations, inviting travelers to remain open to new experiences and viewpoints. As we have previously argued, "Consuming food—through all of the senses—creates a strong shared experience that has the potential to help shape the identity of the individual."[5] Food-based travel means more than filling an empty stomach—it can create a deeper connection and improves understanding of others, given the right setting.

What is necessary for more meaningful travel—for long-term resilience—is thoughtfully understanding the regional intricacies for residents and the visitors. Images of the region compete with a continual stream of stereotypes like those previously detailed, so travel to a region alone does not necessarily shatter longstanding stereotypes that have grown out of otherizing. It might, in fact, strengthen misperceptions knowing that businesses and the tourism industry often cater to expectations hoping to draw in more visitors. One significant experience in travel, however, is an "encounter with difference," and what the traveler chooses to do with the difference—real or perceived—may be the key component to understanding the possible effects of travel.[6] Previous writings on tourism and transcendence help to develop an idea of what resilient tourism might look like.

Tourism more broadly carries a bad reputation. Mountain hillbilly tourist traps are targeted at a type of traveler because those consumers exist and there is a continued demand for that kind of experience. But beyond the worst kind of tourism, the role of tourist is inherently problematic, often "invasive and ignorant of their surroundings. Tourists make waste, take resources, destroy—or, at minimum, transform—places, and encourage local communities to literally sell themselves and to commodify their culture for money."[7] It is possible to create a more evocative tourist experience, however. Phaedra Pezzullo advocates for "toxic tours" (or environmental- and social justice–based tourism), but many tourist experiences focused on significant interactions between travelers and residents create an opportunity for "outsiders to travel in order to *be present* and, perhaps more importantly, *to feel present*."[8] Sustainable tourism that is "centered on needs and values profoundly different from those of consumption and fun that had characterized the language of tourism up to a few decades ago" provides a model for making these experiences more meaningful.[9] Rather than solely emphasizing *pathos* (or the emotional aspect), sustainable tourism highlights the *ethos* of tourism, connecting to "the emotions stemming from the human interaction of the traveller with the native populations" and potentially affecting the way travelers see themselves afterwards.[10] Heritage tourism in the form of food travel may be a strong pathway to this kind of experience.

Although travelers often seek experiences that are different than their own worlds, there is also an inherent search for connection while exploring. As discussed in chapter 2, heritage tourism seeks to provide travelers with an experience that connects them to regional histories, potentially altering the way individuals view the sites themselves. These place-making instruments are constitutive of memory practices and cultural/historical representation, providing resources and rationales "for public judgments about the present that are grounded in strategic animations of the past."[11] Tourists may reshape the past, present, and the places they visit, forming "alternative orientations to history."[12]

Food and drink's roles in constructing a place's authenticity, offering visitors particular identities and imagery and inviting cultural change, makes cuisine an essential part of heritage tourism.[13] Culinary tourism provides opportunities to interact with difference in non-challenging ways, or, perhaps more hopefully, to see the world in a different way that is empowering to tourists and residents alike.[14] Similar to other forms of heritage tourism, Appalachian culinary experiences risk becoming spectacles that de-emphasize critical reflection, reshaping the practice/production of traditional foods, where producers sacrifice quality or meaning in order to meet consumer demands to see the "show."[15] Concerns involving authenticity in rhetorically constructing regional identities can hamper culinary tourism's more empowering potential. Featured foods may provide a sense of uniqueness and foster connections between tourists and places, but they may also exacerbate difference or trivialize residents' experiences.[16]

Still, the possibilities of transgression challenge class-based stereotypes and encourage cultural openness. Eating "bizarre" fried Mars bars in Scotland or red-eye gravy in the Blue Ridge may be read as affirmations of class-based rules, such that eating something "disgusting" makes the eater the same; or, by playfully trying the creation, tourists might question cultural norms and practices and be "in" on the joke.[17] Culinary tourism thus reproduces food norms, simultaneously offering community membership or affinity, while sometimes channeling curiosity to "lead the consumer into a deeper understanding of the culture behind the food, into the logic of the Other."[18] Moreover, a wider variety of travelers may be drawn to food experiences rather than other tourist options such as museums, historical reenactments, or historical displays. Seeing food experiences as a meaningful way to share historical and cultural stories could shift the tourist industry to becoming a part of creating a resilient region.

That heritage and culinary tourism is compelling for individuals can partially be explained by moments of transcendence they experience. More broadly, transcendence as a rhetorical device is focused on lifting interested parties to move above and beyond differences. It has been described as "symbolic bridging and merging," allowing entities to reach a different point of view, as perspective shifting, and as providing a sense of movement, thus making space for a shift in perspectives.[19] Often studied as a persuasive tool in political rhetoric, transcendence accounts for ways that individuals and movements appeal to a larger cause in order to bring audiences together.[20] But the strategy is also at play outside of the political realm in sites of public memory and mediated narratives, for example, because transcendence messages are sometimes more subtle, working in non-discursive ways to highlight similarities that may function to unite individuals and allow specific differences to fade away.[21] Transcending division, however, does not necessarily mean abandoning individual and cultural characteristics. James Zappen explains that transcendent exchanges "can also seek to encompass a diversity of individual voices in larger unities that preserve, but transcend, any one of them."[22] Experiences that bridge gaps, open lines of understanding, and invite individuals to view people, ideas, and regions in a different way can also have a significant influence on our own identities and how we connect with others. Particular types of travel open up the possibility for transcendence through a more meaningful interaction with places and people, providing "opportunities to cultivate connections;" culinary tourism may create even more moving experiences for travelers.[23]

At the same time, rhetorical scholars have pointed out problems that can emerge with transcendence appeals. "Selective amnesia," Kristin Hoerl argues, is a risk when transcendent rhetoric obscures sociopolitical problems to smooth over differences and create connections, constructing "a myth of transcendence in which the traumas of racial injustice have been overcome."[24] Tourist experiences based on limited narratives might cause similar problems. Roger Gatchet and Stephen King, for example, analyze public memory narratives created in the BB King Museum, arguing that when transcendence is used "as a hegemonic means for forgetting or rewriting histories of marginalization and oppression" it becomes deeply problematic.[25] Resilient tourism avoids this problematic depiction of a region by offering more honest representations of histories, therefore inviting dialogue. As Constance Gordon, Phaedra Pezzullo, and Michelle Gabrieloff-Parish point out, meaningful travel experiences "that are shaped by local knowledge and grounded in historical roots of oppression" lead to individuals intervening in problematic systems.[26]

Resilient tourism may effectively bring people together to momentarily focus on similarities, leading to invitations to connect with the perceived other, and potentially affecting points of view. Identification already invokes transcendence, Kenneth Burke argues, "since the individual is to some extent distinct from his group, an identifying of him with the group is by the same token a transcending of his distinctiveness."[27] If food tourism reflects regional diversity, undermining the dominant narrative, it invites tourists to find commonalties with a wider community. This kind of perspective-changing tourism, though, takes effort from both those crafting the experience as well as the tourists; authentic experiences present more complex stories and require open minds.[28] In other words, merely eating at a restaurant that serves historically accurate foods even with descriptions to explain the cultural significance is only as good as the interaction between those making the offer and those taking the offering. Burke explains that transcendence is "best got by processes of dialectic" and emotionally moving travel experiences can work as a kind of back and forth—"the give and take of questioning and answering" between insider and outsider, learning more about each other through the experiences.[29] Meaningful tourism adapts to the needs of residents and travelers, changing with traditions and practices, and deeper understanding of regions, creating an in-the-moment, connection-focused experience. Resilient tourism creates a stronger region by building from area strengths, highlighting connections, adapting, and creatively engaging travelers.

This kind of experience, although powerful, is also fleeting, since "the transcendence of conflicts is here contrived by purely symbolic mergers, the actual conflicts may remain."[30] Consequently, resilient tourism does not erase divisions fully or make significant cultural change on its own, but decreases the otherizing and alienation that plagues Appalachia, in particular. Given the conditions required of this kind of tourism, it might seem an impossible pursuit, but our field work experiences provided examples of both messages/experiences that fail and those that come closer to creating moments that invite change. This is an aspirational rhetorical experience, then. By highlighting positive tourist experiences we hope to encourage discussion of tourism more broadly and to motivate and incentivize development of resilient Appalachian tourism experiences.

LOST OPPORTUNITIES IN MOUNTAIN TOURISM

Many mountain tourist traps share messages that reinforce the backwards region narratives that haunt the area, including depictions of poverty as laughable and an area that is defined by its whiteness. Although this image is often driven by entrepreneurs who are trying to design a business that profits from tourists, the ramifications of this kind of message are long lasting because of the cultural meanings that they circulate. Damaging tourism appeals to these stereotypes serve as a "double-edged sword" by providing economic influences, but also negatively affecting cultural identity by exploiting stereotypes.[31] The growth of the tourism industry in the area in the early twentieth century presented travelers who expected a hillbilly encounter because of the flood of literature and other depictions that drew this image of the region.[32] As Joshua Newman notes, tourism in Appalachia often features locations "where young men and women dress in overalls, sing bluegrass, and speak with the drawls of their ancestors—but often do so at the service of very different impetuses than those who came before them."[33] "The worker," as he concludes, "is at once the producer of commodities and the commodity itself in this touristic phantasmagoria."[34] In these kinds of travel experiences, Appalachia and Appalachians remain foreign—the other, leaving no room for identification or connection since the region and people that these messages create rarely exist.

The family-owned Hillbilly Hideaway in Walnut Cove, North Carolina, for example, has offered homemade food that tastes of authentic mountain dishes since 1977. The experience may invite some guests to connect to mountain culture through its highly rated food, but the broken-down pickup truck serving as a welcome sign, rough log cabin setting, and jumbled baskets hanging from the ceiling keep some tourists culturally distanced from their hosts by confirming stereotypes about the way "hillbillies" continue to live. It has become popular, too, for outsiders to make fun of the tourist traps serving pancakes and watered-down cotton candy moonshine in Gatlinburg and Pigeon Forge, Tennessee, but residents are more likely to use the hiking trails rather than eat at the Lumberjack Feud or Hatfield and McCoy Dinner Shows.

Even tourist areas that highlight the history and culture of the region may fail to meaningfully connect travelers to the region to the degree required for more transcendent experiences when the intent to connect is not the primary motive. For example, many mountain towns offer quaint downtown areas filled with locally owned shops and restaurants. Restaurant spaces bring together residents and tourists, offering local specialties made with regional products. Given the interest in locavore (eating local foods whenever possible) culture, the menus frequently spotlight those regional products, bringing attention to regional traditions, crops, foodways, and such. We saw examples of this type of downtown scene in places such as Hendersonville, Brevard, and Asheville, North Carolina; as well as in

Abingdon, Virginia; and Johnson City, Tennessee. We drank a Fightin' Parsons Pale Ale at Wolf Hills Brewing in Abingdon, named after a preacher who was said to have kept a rifle by his side to protect early Abingdonians from village raids. We sampled a smoked trout spread with fried saltines at Timber! in Johnson City, a casual cafe sourcing ingredients from the area's surrounding rivers, lakes, and mountains. These experiences are more locally connected and create an opening for resilient tourism, but they do not necessarily provide unique connections to the people and the land that have the potential to change travelers. In fact, we found that many of these towns offered similar dishes with similar products (albeit using regional producers), making it almost possible to forget which town you were in while enjoying the restaurants, gift shops, and activities on offer.

Restaurants that attempt to create a more meaningful experience, inviting diners to learn more about the food that they are ordering, also contribute to a better travel experience. As previously discussed, Benne on Eagle in Asheville brings in different elements—food, menu descriptions, images on the walls, cookbooks displayed to highlight influences, and even its location —to engage visitors in a more meaningful way. Previous chef Ashleigh Shanti looked to the past for inspiration and sought to bring those practices into the present, even partnering with local African American women who had been active in the Asheville food community for years. Shanti drew from the underrecognized narrative of Black women in Appalachian food, inspired by Malinda Russell's recipes, for example, to highlight the history that is often erased.[35] Self-published in 1886, Russell's *A Domestic Cookbook* was the first-known cookbook written by an African American author and is remarkable not only for its early publication date but also for its recognition of other cooks who helped teach her techniques and recipes.[36] What one restaurant has accomplished for recovering African and African American contributions to Appalachian food history is noteworthy. The experience, though, is only available to certain people since it is an expensive restaurant, and it is also a fleeting moment for those who dine there. There are signs of engagement with community and heritage at Benne on Eagle, but a meal alone can only go so far in creating experiences that might invite transformation. Culinary tourism alone does not necessarily create a moving experience, although it can be an important part of inviting understanding; resilient tourism moves beyond a single experience. Placing the business more in the community's hands—depending on local workers who live nearby, including more local businesses in every aspect of the production, and bringing in more voices—makes it more meaningful than just a dining experience. Yet, even when it is a strong example of respecting culture, experiences do not directly address the root of continued community problems, such as histories of racism and erasure, discriminatory policy, and a lack of safety nets for employees.

Some high-end resorts in the region also aim to provide a localized tourist experience but fail to truly connect travelers with the area and its people. Primland resort in Meadows of Dan, Virginia, for example, promises a "luxurious back-to-nature escape."[37] The resort's main dining page offers to satisfy "the finest of palates with sustainable authenticity," emphasizing the use of seasonal and natural ingredients, although the highlighted dishes of potato and truffle gnocchi and ocean-fresh scallops don't necessarily tie the food to the region.[38] The more casual dining option on site makes one nod to local traditions, enticing travelers to "get a taste of the region's rich bootlegging history with home-brewed moonshine inspiring a range of happy hour cocktails."[39] Digging deeper into the menus, it is also possible to find region-inspired dishes such as mountain asparagus soup, Carolina rabbit, and North Carolina rainbow trout, although they are listed without any context. Again, however, only a certain type of traveler can stay at the resort, with most rooms costing over one thousand dollars per night. Primland's director of Food and Beverage, Karl Kazaks, told us that some of its clients arrive in private helicopters or airplanes, even eliminating the possibility for exploring the area on the drive to the location. Although these travelers might experience something new and even reflective of the region, this setting does not yield a transcendent experience.

Similarly, Blackberry Farm in Walland, Tennessee, emphasizes its placement in the Great Smoky Mountains, allowing visitors to experience "breathtaking scenery, decadent cuisine and pleasurable pastimes."[40] The resort offers dishes that are "rooted in what comes from our farm as well as the region," with the fine dining option housed in a "turn of the century bank-style barn" on the property and described as "Foothills Cuisine [trademarked] which is rooted in our Appalachian ingredients from around the region as well as farm products harvested just a few feet from the front door."[41] The menu reflects these claims, with ingredients such as ramps, forest mushrooms, and local meats included, although there is no context given for the dishes. The resort advertises a "Smoky Mountain Table" event that invites travelers to "connect with the Great Smoky Mountains" through food and drink, but with a $900 per person room fee, it is unlikely to draw a diverse crowd.[42] Area resorts clearly have found a market for Appalachian tourism and offer it up through housing, dining, and hosted events, but despite efforts to highlight the region while offering luxurious experiences, they fail to bring travelers and residents together in meaningful ways.

These kinds of travel experiences do provide some connections to the region but have limitations and can even be detrimental to the region. For example, development of these properties in the heart of mountain land has a potential for negative environmental impacts. The tourism industry that began to grow exponentially at the turn of the twentieth century valued environmental protection because tourists came to the region to experience the wilderness and the (thought to be) curative natural springs; this desire "directly and indirectly spawned efforts to preserve and conserve environmental resources."[43] But the demands on the region once tourism expanded also "induced a wave of development that substantially modified the landscape."[44] Given clientele expectations, the properties provide the finest accommodations and experiences, depending not only on the creation of the properties, but also the day-to-day upkeep, "rapidly transforming rural villages into bustling tourist meccas."[45] There is also a process of taming nature in order to accommodate nonnative visitors. The region is venerated for its wilderness, but many tourists still want to start their day with a latte at a hipster coffee house, enjoy foodie experiences in the woods, and sleep in a climatized hotel with all the latest amenities, including constant connection to the modern world through the internet.

The social and cultural impact of this kind of tourism can also be problematic. Many area workers mentioned to us that they were unable to live near the resorts since property values increased with area development. Although some of the workers are from the region, the Primland general manager admitted that they also recruited workers from the Philippines and Old Edwards Inn in Highlands, North Carolina (another high-end location), fully staffs their restaurant with seasonal international workers. Moreover, the overall region tends to change with this kind of development since "local residents adapted their way of life to accommodate the modern tastes and desires of their urban guests."[46] Appalachian food itself may also change as it becomes more popular through tourism, with the region's "rituals and symbols rapidly mined for export."[47] If, for example, only fresh produce and upscale takes on traditional Appalachian dishes are featured, those who cannot afford or cannot access these forms of the cuisine continue to be denigrated for their consumption of packaged and convenience foods, perpetuating the dichotomy in which Appalachia's foods are typically discussed.[48]

In the end, this kind of high-end tourist experience works *within* the region but does not always work fully *with* the region. Expensive mountain shops, restaurants, and resorts bring travelers to the area, but primarily offer a parachute tourism experience, in which travelers land in a particular area and only end up experiencing a segment of the region. This tourism elevates mountain culture, perhaps highlighting the sophistication of its culinary history and available local foods but leaves little room for understanding the region more broadly. It markets the parts of Southern Appalachia that sell, ignoring regional struggles such as socioeconomic disparity and the whitewashing of Appalachian history. Generating profit is the main goal of most of the tourism examples thus far, so it is understandable why they are less concerned with cultural enrichment and creating understanding. Despite the economic gain for the region, however, what is left behind in this version of tourism is potentially damaging in some cases, disconnected from the larger region, and far from supporting resiliency in the region. Creating experiences that are economically lucrative and ethical is critical for building a sustainable Southern Appalachian tourism industry and changing tourism more broadly. Rhetorically, these experiences should preserve important parts of cultures, fortify the community, and meld traditions that better reflect the entire region.

RESILIENT TOURISM EXPERIENCED

Given the failures of many kinds of tourism, seeing and experiencing resilient tourism in practice helped develop a clearer image for us. Examples are sometimes difficult to find, where food builds on and reflects regional resilience to provide possibilities for experiences that invite transcendence, offering a tourism model that we suggest should be the desired *telos* of Appalachian experiences. But they are there. We made our first trip to Southwest Virginia in the summer of 2019. This was an exploratory re-search trip, but we were overwhelmed with texts over the next few days as we traveled the region. We wanted to cover multiple locations and experi-ences and soon decided on an annual (before COVID-19, anyway) summer event—The Mountains of Music event called "Homecoming" that takes place over a week in multiple locations throughout Southern Appalachia. As the organizers explain the location—traveling the Crooked Road—travelers are able "to experience authentic musical traditions that have been shaped by some of the greatest names in American music."[49] Along the route, organizers highlight restaurants and places to stay that provide local-ized experiences. The route is available year-round, but the "Homecoming" event is a series of community events that happen over one week. Each day, travelers and residents can attend concerts (some are free, and others have a nominal fee), take part in community meals or eat at local restaurants high-lighted on the itinerary, learn about the arts and crafts of the region, and participate in educational events. On the first night, we participated in one of the community-based, farm-to-table events held within a small historic hotel that had been renovated and served as a jewel of the town. The meal provided an opportunity to appreciate locally grown and prepared foods, while also hearing a bit of regional history.

We learned how Marion, Virginia, was being revitalized. World re-nowned guitarist and Southwest Virginia cultural ambassador, Wayne Henderson, helped to create a folk school offering traditional music classes and wait-listed workshops for participants to build their own guitars. Local advocate Joe Ellis continues to restore the town's historic buildings as part of "Joe's Magnetic Theory of Tourism," where "Tourism creates a magnetic attraction to draw people to an area. These magnets are powered by history, unique architecture, and natural beauty. The more unique something is, the more powerful its attraction."[50] Afterward, we made our way to the "Kickin' It" Dance Review held in the Lincoln Theater, erected in 1929 and renovated after many years of being in disrepair. There, full of local foods and knowl-edge of the region from the dinner, we watched residents play traditional Appalachian instruments like the fiddle and banjo, with people clogging and buck dancing, and generally celebrating the region's cultural traditions. In this one night, we had been introduced to multiple area characteristics and learned about them through interactions with locals.

The next day, we attended a gospel concert at the Slate Mountain Evangelical Presbyterian Church, where we watched the Doyle Lawson and Quicksilver band entertain a mix of locals and tourists. Driving through the rural Southwest Virginia countryside, we came upon the small church and knew we were in the right place based on the rows of cars lined up in the parking lot and beyond. Before the musical event in the sanctuary, the church community hosted a potluck in the fellowship hall, spotlighting many traditional Appalachian dishes, crockpots filled with green beans alongside Jello salads, the dessert table filled with pound cake, molasses cookies, and chocolate delight, a pudding, pecan crust, cool whip concoction, perfect in the summer heat. By the end of the trip, we also made our way to Floyd, Virginia, where locals were happy to talk to us about the town's music tradition at the Floyd Country Store, "a great little country store in the Blue Ridge Mountains of Virginia," where musicians and locals participate in a Friday Night Jamboree featuring bluegrass and traditional music.[51] At its cafe, visitors could eat a country bowl, pinto beans served with collard greens, chow chow, and cornbread, before the show. They could also try other local foods and drinks that were spotlighted in main street stores and restaurants, such as famous chocolate and cream cheese pie at Tuggle's Gap, a roadside diner open since 1938, or ramps and kombucha from Gnomestead Hollow Farm and Forage.

This experience was a mix of planned and unplanned activities, free and ticketed events, fine dining and home cooking, young and old in attendance, with a mix of locals and tourists. In three days, we interacted with locals who were excited to share their traditions and we listened and ate with open minds. There was a heavy focus on what they viewed as traditional food and activities, and we learned more about the communities through those experiences. We also heard stories of communities coming together to save and restore buildings and traditions, sending a message of resiliency. Ashli was familiar with much of this effort from childhood and return visits home, but it was an introduction for Wendy, who experienced more of a connection to and understanding of the area after the trip. In other words, the tourist experiences met many of the expectations for more meaningful travel—a transcendent experience. Of course, we were fortunate to be able to travel in the region for that amount of time and, as white women, we found a place in the dominant stories offered—a luxury that some would not have. There is no doubt that our particular backgrounds yielded a different travel moment than some might have and it is worth noting this difference in order to reflect on what other transcendent travel experiences might need to include. For example, this particular "Homecoming" year did not highlight a very ethnically diverse Appalachian history, although other years were different. In 2018, the "Homecoming" event featured African American influences on the Blue Ridge and bluegrass music, its "Songs in the Key of Blue" theme including a poem from awarding-winning Virginia Tech professor Nikki Giovanni, and musical performances from bluesman Jimmy Duck Holmes along with National Heritage Fellow and blues harmonica master Phil Wiggins.[52] Our own experience was far from perfect, but we never expected to find a perfect example of this type of meaningful tourism.

Cherokee, North Carolina, provides another opportunity for more connected tourist experiences, although first impressions seem otherwise. For a period, Cherokee history was erased from the story of Southern Appalachia or, if it was included, Cherokee Indians appeared as enemies in the stories of frontier men battling to tame the land. Once the travel industry realized that the Cherokee Indian story could be exploited to make the region more exotic, their story held a more central role in the narrative of the region as it emphasized the importance of ancient customs in an old land.[53] As Brenden Martin explains, "Much like the mountain whites who embraced the hillbilly stereotype to draw tourists, Cherokees proved to be just as apt at adopting cultural stereotypes of American Indians to meet the expectations of visitors raised on the images of Indians in popular culture."[54] Officially started in 1912, though some records indicate events from the late 1700s, the Cherokee people of the Qualla Boundary took more control over their story, creating the Cherokee Fall Fair (previously discussed) as a way for tourists to experience their world. Admittedly, the main thoroughfare leading into Cherokee is still filled with the stereotypical imagery of head-dress-wearing, tomahawk carrying Indians, but there is a more thoughtful narrative elsewhere and especially when experiencing the Fair.

Aaron Copeland's iconic "Appalachian Spring" came on the radio as we were driving into town for the 110th Annual Fair late on an early October night. The next morning while waiting for the Fair to open, we visited the beautiful amphitheater for the seventy-year-old outdoor drama, "Unto

These Hills," which tells the story of the Cherokee people. Ashli had seen the play as a child and wanted to look at its setting with fresh eyes, apart from the fond family memories and rousing sounds of Copeland floating in her mind. We spoke briefly with two caretakers checking on the Eternal Flame that stood at the entrance, meant to memorialize Cherokee people who had lost their lives during Removal and to symbolize friendship between Cherokee Indians and non-Indigenous people. The show had changed, they told us, and we should check it out; we learned later that it now included many more opportunities for Cherokee Indian performers, stronger roles that de-emphasized Euro-American ideals of American Indians, and the removal of the crowd favorite character, Tsali, portrayed as a martyr, for an emphasis on Selu, the corn mother. According to James Bradley, executive director of the Cherokee Historical Association who oversees the new production, "this show is pretty Cherokee-centric," making some nostalgic viewers complain that "they don't get it."[55] People were still adjusting to the new version and to the news that the Fair would be held in a new place for the first time in 109 years, but many opportunities to experience more resilient tourism remained—from conversations, to new taste experiences, to observing Cherokee Indian ways of life that are not always easy to access for outsiders. If people driving through Cherokee's stereotypical main drag with its fake Indian trinket stores and over the top Cherokee Indian Shows would visit the Fair, it could do even more rhetorical work in sharing a resilient story that melds the Cherokee people's unique food culture into what it means to experience Southern Appalachia.

It was Veterans Day when we visited the Fair, and the opening ceremony, now held at Harrah's Cherokee Casino Conference Center, offered veterans a buffet of pinto beans, macaroni and tomatoes, ham steak, and cornbread, catered by Cherokee Indian owned Granny's Kitchen. Angela Toomey sang beautifully in Cherokee, the word *tōhi* (peace and wellbeing) echoing throughout the Hall. Principal Chief Richard Sneed and Walker Gaskin of North Carolina Veteran Affairs delivered speeches and gave attendees challenge coin mementos, pointing out that Cherokee Indian service members served at five times the rate of any other American military. The exhibit hall featured Cherokee Indian foodways awarded ribbons akin to a state fair, but highlighted items we hadn't known enough about—Cherokee Indian butternut pods, Turkey corn beads, and Yellowhill Community honey. The

Figure 13. Cherokee Indian crafts and canned goods at the Cherokee Indian Fair, Cherokee, North Carolina. Author photograph.

Fair's theme was "Say it in Cherokee" and we took away a deeper appreciation for the culture's uniqueness as well its commonalities with other parts of Appalachia.

Beside an array of carnival rides sat three Indian taco/Cherokee frybread vendors, one offering Indian dinners, and another selling tacos and tamales. Asking the ticket takers which one we should try first, they directed us to Nikki's Frybread, a third generation frybread maker. Many people know that frybread was once shunned by Indigenous people because it was made by Western government-supplied food products of low nutritional value—lard, flour, and oil.[56] Today, though, some have reclaimed frybread, and we chatted with one of Nikki's cooks, who proudly told us, "I heard this is your first Indian taco," and explained why she was sure we would love hers, featuring frybread covered with bean chili, cheese, tomato, and more. We then bought chestnut bread from the next vendor, who described it to us, even though she was exhausted: "I'm too busy to talk—I keep telling myself

'Just one more day.'" In a tent using home kitchen equipment and assisted by children and other family members and friends, she and others along the vendor lineup prepared for the evening's rush. Another vendor told us how components of her traditional Indian dinners quickly sold out, her customers still coming for chicken, cabbage, and beans. Sitting down to enjoy our purchases, we noticed two women with Cherokee High School Class of 1975 T-shirts, and asked if they would be willing to talk about their meals. They were sisters who now lived in Tennessee and Georgia, coming back yearly to the Fair. Offering us a bite of bean bread studded with pinto beans, they warned us that we might not like it. We did, though, noting different textures, but similar flavors to the cornbread and beans we grew up eating. The sisters told us that they were disappointed that the Fair had moved from its traditional grounds to the casino, which now stood on the ground where they had once ridden thrill rides at Frontierland as children, their grandmother buried at the amphitheater where we had started our day. We needed to come back, they said, to experience it the *right* way. One of their grandsons added that we needed to see the crowds at night and watch the men's stickball games: "We go for Wolftown!" he said proudly, speaking of his relatives' community within Cherokee. He told us to try sweet frybread topped with powdered sugar and strawberries, his aunt adding that although frybread used to be plain, there were constant changes and innovations.

After lunch, the contrast between old and new, local and commercial, insider and outsider, and kitschy and genuine intensified. Tourists could stay at the gleaming Casino hotel, buy frozen lemonade and cotton candy, and later attend the Fair's Boyz to Men concert, or choose between many varieties of frybread and watch the baby crawling and traditional Cherokee Indian fashion contests, each item handmade. On the way out of town, we stopped in the Museum of the Cherokee Indian, smiling at T-shirts that changed the iconic "Entering the Blue Ridge Parkway" sign to read "Entering Indigenous Land," while another shirt was emblazoned with the words "Merciless Indian Savages" quoted from the Declaration of Independence. A new exhibit called "Disruption" had opened, an art intervention designed for EBCI members to respond to the museum's removal of non-Indigenous donated funerary and culturally sensitive objects; as its executive director Shana Bushyhead Condill described to a reporter, "Hey, what if we were at the table as we're talking about telling our own story? Now there are so many of us that there's no doubt we're going to be the ones telling our own story."[57] Our last stop was at a youth stickball game between the Hummingbird and Big Cove communities, tiny shirtless boys chasing a small ball to their respective goals, guided in this ancient game by elders who decide when a child is old enough to play. Hours later, Ashli arrived in Southwest Virginia where her parents had just sat down to beans and cornbread—Did she want some? Both communities extended their foods to us, but the Fair provided a rich opportunity to experience familiar tastes and experiences expressed differently, transcending differences to meld the traditions together. Along with new exhibits, new restaurants, and new experiences, tourists to the Fair are guided in how to value and appreciate this foundational part of Southern Appalachian culture—a strong example of resilient tourism.

Residents from areas surrounding Southern Appalachia have additional opportunities to experience resilient tourism. At Old North Farm, for example, a working farm about an hour outside Charlotte headed into the mountains, attendees having dinner at farmer Jamie Swofford and baker Keia Mastrianni's "Supper and Storytelling" event enjoy regional history and traditions as they eat, seated under a tent on the edge of the fields on a chilly spring evening. Following a brief tour of the farm's varied crops and farming methods, guests are guided to appreciate particular qualities of the dishes placed in front of them, a food tourism experience that has become increasingly popular nationwide. Partnering with Mike Costello and Amy Dawson of West Virginia's Lost Creek Farm who offer a James Beard Award nominated "Farm and Forage" dinner series, Jamie and Keia's North Carolina version combined supper and stories to connect guests to mountain food culture in ways that honored its past, combatted stereotypes, and also showcased their potential. For instance, chicken and dumplings is an Appalachian dish often presented as stick to your ribs, humble, carbohydrate-heavy, and penny-stretching. Here, however, guests are presented with a vintage, inexpensive, flower printed plate, three small cubes of cream-colored pastry atop a green sauce flecked with herbs and asparagus, alongside a small sausage patty. As Mike explains, he wanted to offer a dish that represented his Aunt Floda's chicken and dumplings, who was beloved in his community, her dish earning pride of place among all the other dishes

Figure 14. Chicken and dumplings at the Supper and Storytelling Event, Shelby, North Carolina. Author photograph.

at its annual spring picnic. Telling the audience a little bit about his aunt's skill, Mike stops to play a snippet of his mother talking about the dish, recalling that, "What I remember about her dumplings is that they were just as light, almost like a cloud, nothing was heavy about it at all. It was just, it was light as air. And then her chicken down in the gravy part of it was always so good too, but the dumplings were what everybody really loved. No one even tried to bring anything else, any other kinds of dumplings." Looking down at their plates again, seeing the modern presentation of his family's dish, guests taste a similar lightness in their own dumplings, but now coupled with regional morel mushrooms, wild onion, and chicken to form the sausage. North Carolina is represented in the (green) gravy, made from wild herbs like nettle and two fork, an herb that is sometimes known as the arugula of the forest. This dish contradicts what diners expect from chicken and dumplings, nodding to an honored tradition, but adding a contemporary feel—pretty, light, and special, not basic.

Similarly, guests try the infamous Appalachian ramp, a wild onion. They learn about the community ramp fundraisers they support each spring as they try a delicate soup that is a play on the beans, ham, potatoes, and cornbread with which they are often traditionally served. The white bean soup is topped with a bright green ramp oil and crumbled, dried, and ground ramps, served in a simple white bowl that contrasts with the green of the wild onion. A pickle plate arrives between courses featuring sweet and sour green strawberries and pickles made from foraged bamboo shoots and the couple's turmeric; the traditional bread and butter pickles that some might expect are there but are made from sunchokes from another local farm. Later, Jamie tells the group he wants to "debunk, right now" the stereotype of Appalachian cuisine being meat heavy. He points out the variety of grown, preserved, and foraged vegetables on the plate that dominate the small piece of pork belly from a farmer recently moved to the area, the meat braised in North Carolina Cheerwine soda that is then reduced to provide the sauce.

Diners are provided with many other stories during the evening that challenge expectations about what mountain food is and might be. Those narratives range from the difference between traditional uses of lard in baking that is often now replaced with butter, to how mountain people fermented vegetables for hundreds of years before kombucha became popular, and how the host's grandfather was an original version of the now trendy foragers, harvesting ditch lilies (orange day lilies found on NC roadsides) and using every part of the flower. Keia tells the guests at the end of dinner that it has been a "beautiful pleasure to be with y'all tonight," but guests may indeed take away a new perspective about the enduring beauty that is found in sharing these types of traditional foods. As special as this evening was, it is an experience that may remain out of reach for many regional tourists; the ticket cost and distance from the city might deter some, and of course, this type of experience is geared toward visitors who have an intense interest in food and who already want to learn more. This type of transcendent experience, however, is not limited to people choosing to attend a dinner series.

Transcendent experiences are more spontaneous and sometimes fleeting. Chatting with someone about their products, either at a farm stand, community store, local restaurant, or other tourist stop sometimes offers brief moments of connection. We talked about why apples were used to create moonshine and applejack in the NC mountains, and how important clean water is in that process. We learned which peaches are able to grow in Cana, Virginia, off the Blue Ridge parkway, its owners working hard to keep their small orchard alive. In Tennessee, we ate at small cafes that were trying out new dishes and methods to stay open during the pandemic, chatting with owners about their efforts. The experience can be casual, but most importantly there needs to be a desire to learn and connect.

MAKING TRAVEL MATTER

The idea that tourism can both make much-needed contributions to Southern Appalachian economies while also creating an environment that fosters resiliency might be difficult to envision for travelers, business owners, and community leaders. Examples we have highlighted, however, show the potential for change in these different communities. Fostering a resilient environment through culinary experiences is particularly important, given the ability for food and food rhetoric to open individuals up to new discussions. Here, we highlight the characteristics of resilient tourism more broadly. If resilient tourism hinges on making connections between travelers and insiders, these experiences must reflect the region and its people as honestly as possible. Messages should include a full story of regional history and reflect how the culture/region has changed. Consequently, as those regions, cultures, and people shift, the accompanying tourism experiences should also, bringing past and present together.

Another critical element of resilient tourism is being invested in the region and the people. It takes effort on the part of residents, travel industry representatives, as well as visitors to the region, to intentionally come together to create an experience that allows for connecting with each other on a different level. Travelers often have personal reasons for participating in heritage tourism. Although they may care about the region because of a personal connection, however, they are not always invested in the region, nor does the travel experience change that perspective. The heritage traveler might leave with a different understanding of their background and take those memories with them, while residents are left solely with the economic benefits.

Resilient tourism experiences should transform what we know and think of one another, using transcendent rhetoric to invite individuals to rise above differences and highlight shared experiences. It is this type of tourism that provides a more meaningful connection between travelers and residents. At the same time, it is hard to craft this kind of experience and travelers must be open to options. Tourism can only begin to change a region and its visitors, but it is one more element in the push toward creating a resilient community.

What might it look like for towns and regions to combine the resiliency elements that we have discussed and work from there to craft a travel experience? It takes community leaders, business owners, and government representatives coming together and being more intentional about creating a particular experience. Others might follow once they see that there is interest in telling a more diverse story of the region, in shaping public memories around the resiliency of the people, and in showing how communities care for each other and extend that care to visitors.

Reflecting back on our Asheville adventures that took place after the changes that the pandemic and Black Lives Matter movement brought to the world, it was not surprising to see a tourist industry that continued to move along as if nothing had changed. It was soothing, however, to find at least one experience at Benne on Eagle that seemed to acknowledge this change not by directly addressing racial erasure and injustice, but celebrating a more honest history of Appalachian foodways built on a multitude of cultural traditions that have gone unrecognized and unacknowledged for far too long. In a more recent visit, we were thrilled to discover even more examples of this kind of experience. On a rainy Saturday morning, we took a walking tour with Hood Huggers International, an organization working to highlight the many African American contributions to life in Asheville, learning about its pioneering architects, civil rights leaders, and entrepreneurs, including restaurant owners and food vendors. As its director emphasized, the organization's name was selected because they wanted people, especially Black visitors and residents, to love their 'hood the way that tree huggers love and protect the environment. At an event later that evening, we ate dishes that used Malinda Russell's historical recipes to offer diners incredible tastes of regional produce and products, dinner organizers encouraging participants to understand Malinda as a professional chef, an expert, not a poor Black East Tennessee woman doing her best with what was left over from her employment for whites. Although this type of tourist experience is still difficult to locate and participate in, the ideas are percolating and circulating and there are sure to be more advancements that build off this work.

Chapter 5

Community and
Food Care Rhetoric

There are touches of Southern Appalachia to be found on plates and in your glasses as you wander through downtown Asheville, grab a post-hike beer in Brevard, or fuel up for a bike ride on the Virginia Creeper trail outside Damascus, Virginia. It is a delicious and exciting time to find traditional, local mountain ingredients being celebrated by tourists, from Eastern Tennessee's Benton's country ham in their mac and cheese or sorghum syrup in glasses of dark ale. Interest in these food experiences brings tourism dollars and fresh perspectives about regions, strengthening some forms of resilience discussed in the last chapter. It is sometimes easy for tourists to overlook communities in need as they enjoy these local finds, however, the stories of those planting the seeds, processing the animals, or placing their order at a drive-through to stretch their food dollar hidden out of sight. Food experiences offer ways for tourists to connect more firmly to places they visit but may also keep local perspectives tucked quietly away.

Amidst a post-pandemic summer of food and drink tourism recovering lost revenue, for example, Appalachian communities in Kentucky and Southwest Virginia were decimated by historic floods. Many residents were left with nothing and made the difficult choice to leave the area, their communities unrecognizable. What, then, do food rhetorics offer these and other similarly challenged Mountain towns? These aren't the places tourists typically go, reinforcing the *poor, sad* Appalachia (our emphasis) narrative, and featuring media interviews with despondent residents lamenting their losses in a familiar twang. After the reporters leave and residents use any remaining resources to pick up the pieces of their lives, however, these communities continue to fortify and care for one another. Residents argue that what really defines Appalachia is an interest in caring for their own; as culinary author and resident Ronni Lundy emphasizes, "working for and with one another is an important aspect of mountain culture."[1] Food is central to this ethos of resilience. This chapter examines whether Southern Appalachian food rhetorics support those frequently left out of the tourist tableau, offering places for them to see themselves in a regional food narrative that is often too celebratory and utopian.

When exploring the relationship between Southern Appalachian food and resilience, it is impossible to fully understand the connection without asking whether, and how, care is performed in communities through food. Although the importance of "self-care," the notion that people need to take time to improve their physical and mental health, has become more recognized, this rhetoric sometimes reinforces "the most self-reliant and individualistic inclinations in our culture."[2] Without a collective, community-based understanding of care that is rooted in place, particularly in under-resourced or marginalized Southern Appalachian communities, building resilience through food rhetoric is unattainable. Black food justice movement advocates argue for the need to recognize the importance of care work, particularly by Black women, as traditions that build resistance and resilience in urban Black ecologies that are often structured by violence and vulnerability.[3] We explore whether Southern Appalachian food rhetoric expresses care for mountain communities in these more resilient ways, one of the few options left in challenged communities. These expressions of care deserve to be valued and appreciated for what they manage to do in often difficult to imagine circumstances. Does this rhetoric help fortify communities, filling in the gaps where governments fail or refuse to care? Does its circulation help contribute to a broader, less individualistic story of Appalachian resilience? Black foodways scholars Ashanté Reese and Symone Johnson point out that care should be thought of as mutual aid, a more agentic alternative to charity, that interrogates why communities face systemic challenges and solves problems through collective action.[4] Similarly, we go off the tourist trail and into the gardens, farms, and myriad mountain community food initiative locations to contend activism in the mountains often features place *topoi* to present an active form of resilience that uses food to enact community care. This regionally specific *form* of place-based advocacy has been overlooked in our disciplinary scholarship but deserves more attention. Local advocates use place-based *topoi* to activate residents, preserving mountain traditions while fortifying the community and bringing more people to the table. Although more resources are needed to build resilient Appalachian communities, the importance of locating these regionally based *topoi* should be instructive in other regions.

Although the use of this strategy is not surprising because protecting and supporting their "place" has long been central in creating Appalachian community mobilization, this tendency is often overlooked in tales about how the Mountains could be saved by others.[5] Reformers came to the mountains to tame perceptions of agricultural savages and teach so called better farming and cooking practices, encouraging Appalachians to move away from what was perceived to be bad cooking (cornmeal, grease, fatback, few vegetables) and using poor equipment (iron skillets, a single source of heat). Examinations of community care through food continue to counteract these notions of a singular Appalachia of uniform histories, cultures, and economies. People used their place to care for each other, building coalitions across different groups, and challenging claims of interracial division and/or monolithic whiteness. By pushing back against insider/outsider and redeemer/redeemed character dichotomies, place rhetoric provides possibilities to connect Appalachian food traditions to the broader American experience. Emphasizing place finds innovation in what is already here; in the process, stories about Appalachia continue to become less about what is missing.[6] Place becomes an active heuristic in maintaining Appalachian resilience while offering broader forms of representation.[7] To be clear, putting an emphasis on the appeal of place in food care faces limitations, material and otherwise. Much more needs to happen to build resilient mountain communities than praising the bounty that a community garden provides.

Despite these challenges, to elucidate how the appeals of place in food care rhetoric are catalytic, helping to construct broader, more relatable narratives of community resilience, we first contextualize the need for food care activism in Appalachia. We then detail rhetorical obstacles these efforts encounter, especially the need to address regional socioeconomic problems. Drawing on notions of performance and affect in crafting appeals to place, we assess three broad examples of community care through food, emphasizing how place helps construct an alternative understanding of what it means for a community to be resilient over time. By exploring how communities use food to care for their people both in and out of tourist towns, how place features prominently in Cherokee community food care rhetoric, and how food care presents a different understanding of land for Black Appalachians, we show how place *topoi* help situate Southern Appalachia as part of a broader vision of a stronger, more resilient America, not a broken one. Our conclusion assesses how food care appeals might be structured in Southern Appalachia and beyond to further galvanize community membership and change.

APPALACHIAN FOOD ACTIVISM, THE "NEW" AGRARIANISM, AND COMMUNITY RESILIENCE

Dependency narratives may chastise lazy hillbillies for their fatalistic acceptance of their lot, but a look at the history of Appalachian activism tells a different story of communities working together to protect their place, including through food.[8] Radical activism was not brought to the Mountains by outsiders, but was homegrown, and activists continue to build unions and coalitions to support a number of causes, develop mutual aid programs, open and maintain health clinics and food banks, work to abolish the prison industrial complex, and protest in favor of LGBTQ+ rights.[9] Community care through food, too, has always been present. Cherokee people have long used ginseng root for medicinal purposes and to establish a non-extractive trade economy, *Foxfire* books recorded traditional community expertise and taught self-sufficient agricultural skills, and the countercultural back to the land food movement of the 60s and 70s offered residents manifestos such as *Living the Good Life.*[10] In the 90s, Asheville's Appalachian Sustainable Agriculture Project developed the region's first local food guide, markets, and a farm-to-school program; later, it transitioned more than 426 Western North Carolina farms from tobacco to food production, one of the few areas to gain net farmland.[11] Collaborations such as the Equal Plates Project in Asheville continue to address high rates of food insecurity.[12]

This renewed landscape of community care through food is often seen as a bright light in driving regional social change and positive social outcomes, although skepticism remains. Contemporary food activism risks echoing familiar problems, such as providing a "strongly aspirational" story that circulates a new aesthetic that risks merely mining the old one— "reconnection to a 'real,' yet carefully distanced, 'post-racial' South of old time hog killings, canning, preserving, and distilled whiskey."[13] Glamorized local food cultures remain out of reach for many, with food sovereignty advocates arguing, for instance, that moving past "white shoppers who support farmers' markets" requires "land ownership, investment, and both individual and family financial return."[14] Leaders also face high land prices and climate change, employees who cannot afford to live in their communities, the loss of affordable space for entrepreneurs, and pressure to develop already limited farmland. What's true in Southern Appalachia follows more general critiques of food activism movements, where a focus on education and gastronomy contributes gradually to economic and cultural change, but often remains an underdeveloped rhetoric of community organization.[15] Detractors argue food movements must extend beyond narratives of "education, experience, and exposure to artisanship, seasonality, and flavor" to creating real change based on "activism, protest, coalition building, and legislation that supports sustainable agriculture."[16] To build stronger relationships between individuals and their communities such that they are able to exercise collective power, advocates need to address the rhetorical barriers of time, money, and skills that some lower socioeconomic and middle class community members face.[17] Especially critical is the need to address how the sustainable food movement overlooks widespread racial food inequities, instead profiting from the "land and free labor of Indigenous and Black people."[18] It is worth asking whether more recent Appalachian food care rhetoric offers something new, able to "resist, rather than reify, the power dynamics that they seek to address."[19]

Situated within the new agrarian movement, food activism within Appalachia and in other places is imbued with both hope and anxiety.[20] Agrarianism refers to the "sets of attitudes and practices guiding a way of living" to "constitute a culture rooted in the values, practices, and structures of local food systems" long tied to American ideals about connectedness to community and land, democracy, and transformation.[21] The enduring adaptability of the agrarian myth has potential in shaping Appalachian community resilience through food, providing a renewed sense of stability and meaning and a sense of a shared destiny "emanating from the land and our relation to it." The myth encounters several obstacles in terms of execution, however, such as being used superficially as a "shield of public defense" for self-interested and unethical agendas.[22] Still, rhetorical scholars argue that the new agrarianism has the potential to connect to the food justice and food sovereignty movements, where the retelling of agrarian narratives has transformative potential in bridging deep rifts among Americans.[23] We *want* to believe in the ideal of the mythic farmer, despite our convenience food, lack of knowledge of the industrial food system, or distance from farm communities. Scholars argue that many Americans still "hold values that align with agrarianism" despite their differences, where the hardworking yeoman farmer, surrounded by green pastures and acting as "civilization's caretaker, preserver of local communities, and possessor of practical knowledge" is able to invite audiences to change our relationships to food.[24] The new agrarianism represents an "ethic of resistance" that faces challenges but seeks to generate more than nostalgia, "stir a collective soul," and summon a cultural identity that is yet to be realized.[25]

Several rhetorical obstacles hamper the ability for Appalachians to successfully tap into the new agrarianism myth. One is the ongoing romanticization of Southern/Appalachian food that ignores the realities of food's gendered and raced elements in praise of farmers, farming, and farmers' markets.[26] As Ashanté Reese observes, there is a dearth of scholarship about the role of Black women in the food justice movement, leaving a need to call attention to how these women "make sense of and navigate the food system, make ways out of no way, and live lives that do not start or stop at the door of the supermarket."[27] To wit, older forms of the myth deployed by Southern Agrarians were problematic for their racism and desire to preserve small farms despite urgent needs for change in agricultural labor systems. Still, Reese and others continue to see value in using agrarian values to re-imagine more equitable and sustainable foodscapes.[28] Kenneth Zagacki observes how a North Carolina localized farming resistance campaign transcended traditional ideological boundaries by using the agrarian myth to bridge divisions tapping into a "unique and often submerged form of patriotism to challenge the combined forces of the federal government and large corporations."[29] Today's iterations must similarly blend a more heterotopic "militant pastoralism and spiritual awakening" to connect more people over what it means to be American.[30]

Another structural factor that remains a barrier to successfully performing community care through food rhetoric in Appalachia, is, of course, a high rate of endemic poverty. Notoriously hard to define, with elements of income, wealth, education, social connections, and cultural consumption all affiliated with the idea, social class and socioeconomic discourses present a significant challenge for food care rhetorics.[31] If agrarianism and new food movements more broadly contend with charges that they are unrealistic, elitist, or utopian in their visions, these concerns are magnified in this historically under-resourced area. Indeed, although the South has been associated with "uniquely White, rural, and primitive" poverty, Appalachia's version is associated with white trash, redneck, and hillbilly monikers that elide race, denote inferiority, and signal the inability to achieve economic success or upper/middle-class norms.[32] To wit, in Appalachia, "among a people of immense pride, independence, fierce family loyalty, fatalism, and rich cultural heritage," poverty persists among those "trapped" "higher in the mountains and up the remote hollows."[33] Associating Appalachian poverty with whiteness overlooks how a variety of its people experience being poor, even as this tendency characterizes the entire population as overwhelmingly white and unredeemable.

Working class rhetorical strategies must also respond to often unspoken cultural norms that demarcate and stratify, moralizing class as matter of character, not economic means.[34] Stereotypes about the "rural bogeyman" remain, separating and stratifying Appalachia away from the American mainstream, allowing more "cosmopolitan people" to project their own bigotry and bias.[35] A continued "universalized sense of middle-classness" contributes to the broad tendency for Appalachian social problems to be coded as familial and individual, dislocating collective action and concealing economic inequality and structural racism.[36] To move past this characterization, food care rhetoric must make class more visible, illustrating how different people are connected at society's margins.[37] It must reduce the stigmatizing cultural distance between "low class, white trash" poverty and other lived poverty experiences, yet keeping in mind specific Appalachian financial "contextual realities," working class "providing and protecting" norms and differing senses of prudence.[38] Offering a "nexus of the textual and corporeal," helps fuse poverty with power imbalances, pointing out how Appalachian stereotypes are class-driven—its people visibly marked from eating so called bad or cheap convenience or fast food, suffering from obesity, poor dental hygiene from sugar consumption, and/or recognizable by their thinness and pallor.[39] To remove more of poverty's shaming visibility, activism must direct attention away from the shamed label of Dollar General Diner and toward the predatory Dollar General Corporation, where eating crops grown by the community or ministering to others through food becomes a resistant, viable alternative.[40] Overcoming these rhetorical obstacles helps create a more receptive audience and a rhetorical climate more conducive to policy changes.[41]

When Appalachian food care rhetoric draws on the new agrarian myth, it helps highlight interrelationships between race, gender, and land that undergird the region's class structure while also making these struggles more connected to people's lived experience outside the region. Agrarianism helps locate opportunities to create common ground and solidarity among oppressed groups. For example, if Americans still broadly adhere to the value of agrarianism, those on the receiving end of food care initiatives become part of the mainstream, the deserving working poor, not individual failures that garner little sympathy.[42] Tapping into a new agrarianism helps locate the emotional experience and connection to place that food rhetoric offers broadly, showing how people use food to successfully care for themselves and others. Sharing more rural "alt-country" success stories is critical in reshaping regional identities and national destinies.[43] These appeals help the movement become more polycultural, representing the varied concerns of a community, moving beyond a mere vision of living "tied to the land, the seasons, family, community, and agricultural practices" and creating political pressure that motivates change.[44]

In particular, appeals to a new agrarian myth in Appalachian food care must move beyond discourses of self-reliance that do not serve as active forms of long-term community resiliency. As rhetoricians Philippa Spoel and Colleen Derkatch explain, within some self-reliance frameworks "what looks like resilience or 'bouncing back' may represent not dignified independence and self-sufficiency but scrambling and improvisation as citizens are increasingly burdened with responsibilities that formerly belonged to the state."[45] Not everyone has the time, ability, and resources to be self-reliant, and successful performances of resiliency cannot only offer "entrepreneurial" ideologies; indeed "taking responsibility" is not always the issue in addressing food insecurity.[46] Asking people to be more food literate, too, merely "substitutes the material good of actual food with the immaterial good of knowledge about food."[47] Reese and Johnson synthesize the limitations of these appeals in the Black community by arguing that some charity-based forms of community care be understood as performative "policing based on 'prescriptive' ethics;" instead, she re-imagines care as a praxis of mutual aid, where "people's needs are met and their humanity is not weighed against arbitrary measures of deservedness."[48]

In light of these shortfalls, rhetorical scholars argue that we must "do resilience differently" to more "tangibly recognize and meaningfully address the socioeconomic, material inequities that produce food vulnerability."[49] To both move beyond thinking about resilience as a crisis response and build structural, sustainable community strength, attending to everyday forms of resistance helps build knowledge, skills, community, and economic independence.[50] To be more than an individually focused response to catastrophic events food care rhetoric must provide new ways to understand regions and people, pushing back against structural factors and offering intentional collective responses that critique structures of power.[51] Importantly, this work calls attention to the "everydayness" of caring through food; that is, community members may recognize structural racism and class inequalities while also manifesting "belief in community-driven change in those raised beds."[52]

PERFORMING COMMUNITY FOOD CARE, AFFECTIVE INVESTMENT, AND THE OPPORTUNITY OF PLACE

If agrarianism retains qualities that broad swathes of Americans support, appealing to Appalachia's place helps fortify communities by connecting them to others. Place *topoi* draw on local experiences and expertise so that traditional knowledge and skills are valued, but also appeal to more audiences, tapping into broader claims about "regionality, seasonality, environmental sustainability, and culture that are powerful, disruptive counter narratives."[53] Appeals to place may be tailored to address low-income community members who cannot see themselves as active participants in food care initiatives until concerns about access, labor, and lack of capital are addressed. These appeals extend beyond a region's "outputs," such as ingredients or techniques.[54] They give place an active voice and role, going beyond marketing appeals featuring utopian messages to offer more connections to perceived authentic places and people that encourage reflection about audiences' own places and food cultures.[55] When Chef Sean Brock emphasizes

American slavery's role in shaping Southern foodways, he encourages others to take a different, perhaps deeper, look at their own cuisines.[56] Qualities of land and place may also strategically connect agrarian visions in both rural and urban communities, as in Appalachia, where there is a mix of political conservatism and activism.[57] To provide a deeper examination of the possibilities of place in food care rhetoric, we connect it to notions of performance and affect in rhetorical studies. We then provide examples where place presents different narratives of representation, offering opportunities for connection that help build active forms of Appalachian resilience.

Simply invoking the name of place does not connect people to build collective agency and resilience; rather, catalyzing place associations makes these appeals more broadly relatable and persuasive. The ability to perform and enact a sense of place helps create performative food care rhetorical ecologies, where instances of performance or repeatable, "influential acts of naming and identification" create pathways that shape our understandings of place over time.[58] These pathways are always in conversation with each other, shifting and changeable. As Kathryn Trauth Taylor explains, when African Americans perform Appalachia differently through poetry readings, music, and more, these performances circulate and influence others, able to "transgress, establish, negotiate and redefine Appalachian identity."[59] Performances are pathways in an active, ecological system that form an "ongoing space of encounter" interrupting homogenous, collective understandings of Appalachian history, rejecting outsiders' views, and drawing connections between insiders' experiences."[60] Crucially, performances of being "Affrilachian" "were not circulated until they were named, not meaningful until they were performed, and not rhetorical until those performances inspired new conceptions of Appalachian identity."[61] Different food care performances connect and re-inscribe, people telling their stories while challenging understandings of the region.[62]

Beyond connecting residents to performances that resonate with their experiences, appeals to place must also create affective investment in Appalachia to connect with the broader experience of others. As rhetoricians Ashley Mack and Bryan McCann explain, these strategies are the "inarticulable affective commitments that are mobilized through discourse and social conditions" cultivating a shared sense of belonging and intimacy, delineating whose pain matters, and cultivating concern.[63] The inability to create affective investment in the lives of community members keeps the needs of Others, often Black and working class people, relegated to the bottom of priority lists.[64] To create affective investment in the lives of working-class Southern Appalachians, rhetoric must cultivate a sense of common cause and compassion, a "felt experience of closeness, empathy, or perhaps even responsibility to the Other."[65] People are not always invested in the plight of working class Appalachians, instead choosing to engage in self-preservation or avoidance, making it easier to justify policy and practice that protects the status quo.[66] "Violence" and "street culture" (i.e. Black urban culture) became tethered rhetorically in New Orleans following a Mother's Day shooting; similarly, in Southern Appalachia, *fatalism*, and *bad food habits* became linked.[67] As Sarah Ahmed asserts, then, emotions *do things,* shaping affect as they are exchanged, sometimes mobilized in the service of violence, othering, and disdain of raced and classed communities.[68] Conversely, our research demonstrates how affect is used in care rhetorics to build feelings of hope and mutuality that circulate new associations, encouraging public investment in Appalachian communities.

Shining a Spotlight on Food Care in the
Shadows of Mountain Tourism

Advocates use the foods of their places strategically to perform care, creating buy in and commitment by those with resources, and an increased sense of community membership and dignity for those in need. Whether attracting attention to towns overlooked on tourism itineraries or providing for those excluded from its economic impact, advocates provide a multi-sensory and participatory affective entry point in supporting communities. Tiny South Pittsburg, Tennessee, for example, sits about forty minutes outside of Chattanooga in a valley walled in by the South Cumberland Appalachian Mountain range and the Tennessee River. In a town of just 3,000, unemployment is 4.7 percent, higher than the US average, still struggling after Walmart opened and a highway bypass was built.[69] Once a year, though, the town hosts the National Cornbread Festival in association with Lodge Cast Iron, the town's primary employer, and the area comes alive, more than 30,000 visitors putting over one million dollars back into the community.[70] Festivals bring visitors to new places through their unique offerings, such as ramps in North Carolina, slaw dogs in West Virginia, or hot rods and moonshine in Wilkesboro, all boosting local economies. The National Cornbread Festival illustrates how people in this community also use food to create affective investment through multifaceted, engaging celebrations of people, local food, and traditions. Named one of the top twenty events in the Southeast, the festival brings people to the area that might not have otherwise visited to watch the National Cornbread Cook-Off. Ten finalists use Lodge cast iron skillets and Martha White Tennessee-made cornmeal to prepare dishes using ingredients not typically associated with cornbread—Asian vegetables, Cajun spices, and Mediterranean cheeses. On Cornbread Alley, different local groups, including the Boy Scouts, local churches, and women's organizations, compete for the honor of winning the best cornbread dish honor, and visitors shop stalls boasting handmade cornbread-themed merchandise.

Food becomes a place-based instrument of community care when South Pittsburg visitors and residents celebrate cornbread. Preparing for the festival creates a sense of excitement among the town's residents: "right after Christmas there's just a feeling that comes over the town and you know it is cornbread time in Tennessee."[71] As the date gets closer, residents anticipate which foods will be featured by the vendors and make plans; as one woman explains: "there's just a spirit that catches on a week or two before . . . it's in the air, and people will mow their yards, and clean their windows, and plant their flowers."[72] Booth volunteers share stories about South Pittsburg's residents and history, one booth honoring local cook Patsy by sharing her cornbread salad, recipe taped proudly on the window. At The Bean Pot booth, the women of the First Baptist Church weighed in about sweet and unsweet cornbread. We were also invited to the hospitality tent to try our first cornbread omelet, made for us by Lodge employees moonlighting as chefs, clearly proud of the delicious crispy dish made with corn meal, egg, and tomato. You could buy local honey, listen to local musicians, or see women's quilting skills at the town's heritage museum. These small-town festivals do rhetorical work in creating affective investment among residents and others by galvanizing volunteers, providing a place to build community, and enacting pride. As one organizer explains, "We saw pride leaving our community, people giving up on our downtown, and we hated to see it." 1,000 out of the town's 3,000 residents now volunteer, engaging in town beautification, trash removal, and event staging, helping visitors

*Figure 15. Doing fieldwork at the National Cornbread Festival,
South Pittsburg, Tennessee. Author photograph.*

experience the "sights, sounds, taste, and history of the people of South Pittsburg."[73]

The festival thus creates a sensory pathway for visitors to feel personally invested in the types of small towns South Pittsburg represents. That is, cornbread is sometimes associated with stereotypes about what's wrong with Southern regions. It isn't healthy, it isn't a prestige food, and it may conjure images of mountaineers in overalls, smoking a corncob pipe after a supper of cornbread and buttermilk. The festival combats this image by offering different ways for people to engage with this foodway. Visitors shop for handmade items (all juried to ensure authenticity), attend the opening night street dance, place their vote for the best dish, or talk with high school student volunteers relying on festival money to fund team sports. Cornbread bridges the community with its visitors; trying to "bring the American spirit out of all of us," illustrating one way the new agrarian myth might be rhetorically enacted.[74]

Across the mountain range, city advocates use food care rhetoric to build affective investment in their communities beyond tourism. Greenville and Spartanburg, South Carolina, and Asheville, North Carolina, are tourist destinations, with Greenville boasting more than 1.3 billion dollars in visitor expenditures, Spartanburg seeing close to 600,000 visitors to its Cultural District, and Asheville continuing to dominate the industry.[75] Behind these booming facades, tourists may not detect a significant problem —food insecurity. Spartanburg sits in the most food insecure county in South Carolina, Greenville has close to fifty percent of public-school students who qualify for free or reduced-price lunches, and in Asheville, one in four children face hunger.[76] Repeated visits encouraged us to look closely at what one of our interviewees called the "tale of two cities," with development largely serving the privileged. We learned how food care rhetoric helps build community resilience outside of the tourism spotlight.[77]

Appeals to a sense of place are paramount in efforts to create affective investment for underserved communities in several community food initiatives. Place appeals are used successfully to attract tourists, but some communities recognize the importance of using them to increase involvement from residents. As Jordan Wolfe, executive director of the Hub City Farmers Market in Spartanburg, Rob Cain of Mill Village Farm in Greenville, and Madi Holtzman, managing director of Asheville's Equal Plates Project told us, local food attracts tourists to experience the offerings of place, and, in doing so, encourages interest in more equal access to food for community residents. For instance, on a cloudy summer morning at the Hub City Farmers Market in Spartanburg, we saw an ambitious, visually integrated community project come to life in a historic African American neighborhood that had been designated as a food desert. All in one beautiful place, kale, rainbow Swiss chard, corn, potatoes, cabbage, and basil grew neatly in raised beds, active bee boxes flourished, the Monarch Cafe served healthy food seven days a week, and a pavilion provided space for culinary training and events. The area created broad community appeal, where 800 people per week visited and could shop more equitably with tokens instead of cash. In Greenville, Mill Village Farms similarly tackled the city's lack of racial and socioeconomic diversity in its food system, designing its urban farms to address its belief that "access to healthy food shouldn't be limited by where you live or how much you make."[78] Community gardens aren't new ideas, but Mill Village Farms relied on pastors to promote healthy living in Greenville's historically African American churches and to build trust, working with businesses to offer entrepreneurship classes and funding, and providing workers for a local restaurant. These initiatives turn places of disrepair into thriving landscapes that help build community-wide affective investment.

Similarly, two Asheville initiatives succeed in creating deeper ties to underserved communities through place-based food experiences. Walking into the Equal Plates Project, set in a community center surrounded by a vibrant community garden on Asheville's Southside, two of Asheville's fine dining chefs, Kikko Shaw and Kendrick Burton, make meals for 300 daily recipients. One chef carefully picked leaves from a cilantro plant to make a summer zucchini dip, another sliced freshly grilled chicken, assisted by two community volunteers helping to package the meals. As Madi Holtzman explained about what looked like the kitchen of a high-end restaurant, these chefs created restaurant quality meals featuring first-rate foods, not castoff seconds, sourcing ingredients from local farms, employing local people, and selling meals to charter schools to fund their efforts while creating better linkages among the community.[79]

On a Sunday morning at Haywood Congregation's Welcome Table, when we sat down for breakfast, the potential in involving various parts of the community through place-based food experiences was heightened. Served by community volunteers and featuring meals provided by local farms and restaurants, we ate homemade biscuits, jalapeno cheese grits, and brisket hash provided by 12 Bones, a barbecue restaurant situated in Asheville's trendy river district that we had visited two days before. Now, served alongside bright blue linen-wrapped cutlery and fresh mountain flowers, we felt the welcoming atmosphere of a resilient community working together. As our elderly unhoused dining companion remarked as she invited us to help identify one of the flowers in the vase, Welcome Table volunteers were angels, making good on what the Welcome Table described as creating "Holy Chaos on Holy Ground."[80] As the clouds were breaking this Sunday morning, the sun starting to shine, the dining room offered hope and dignity, served by volunteers feeding people who slept by its doors and in the parking lot. Similar to Equal Plates, diners were treated like everyone else.

After a weekend of seeing many homeless people filling the doorways of downtown Asheville, tourists literally stepping over them to shop and eat, these spaces tried to use food to create fortifying, connective experiences despite evident challenges. Reading the Welcome Table's covenants provided dissonance that much was still needed in order to construct a collectively resilient community—"Food speaks the language of love. There's always enough, and more. Grace is on the menu. The answer is yes. Families eat together."[81] Still, these initiatives were tackling food insecurity in more integrated ways that encouraged community involvement beyond voluntarism. These actions created a space where people matter—they plant, cook, eat, and serve neighbors together, sharing messages of commitment, belonging, and intimacy. More community resources were clearly needed, but the rhetorical importance of this care work should not be discounted.

"You Can't Be Cherokee without Cherokee Plants"

Exploring the food sovereignty movement in Cherokee Indian communities located related, but different, messages about how food crafts resilient community care.[82] Advocates similarly recognize how a community's food traditions serve as rhetorical opportunities to interest and connect residents. Place *topoi* predominate in American Indian community food care rhetoric but are also used to reclaim Native control over local food systems, reduce food insecurity, and recover food traditions and techniques.[83] As one Indigenous cultures professor explained to reporters the importance of maintaining a connection between place and Native cultures, "Our access to and use of the land is so tied up with identity. It's who we are as a people."[84]

Indigenous food activists seek to make present what has been absent by highlighting ingredients and techniques once unique to tribal lands.[85] Sioux Chef Sean Sherman, for example, jokes that Indigenous cooks "aren't trying to cook like it is 1491" by avoiding Western products such as sugar, flour, and butter; rather, they privilege land and place to secure access and recognition of foods adopted by other cooks and protect their endangered plants and foodways.[86] In Cherokee Indian food care rhetoric in particular, place appeals also facilitate performances of identity that bridge disconnects in contemporary tribal society, but these *topoi* also link nature and sustainability in ways that can strengthen affective investment in Cherokee Indian communities among non-tribal communities. Our fieldwork demonstrated how food sovereignty advocates strengthen the performance of Indigenous identity by making place-bound traditional plants and crops essential, primary elements.

Since Removal separated Indigenous people from their food heritage, Cherokee Indian food sovereignty activists contend that recentering and recreating links to traditional foods holds the key to strengthening their identity.[87] Constitutively, saving seeds, preparing foods, and eating together reinforces a sense of Cherokee-ness. Indeed, the origin story of the Cherokee people privileges food, where the selfless actions of Selu, the first woman and Corn Mother, sacrifices for her children so that they can survive, eat, and thrive; her descendants also use corn to provide for Cherokee people for generations.[88] Corn crops are Selu's ancestral linkages, not just in terms of ingredients or the plant, but connecting with this honored person. As Cherokee Nation chef and food sovereignty advocate Nico Albert Williams, who resides in her post-Removal home in Oklahoma, told us, "As long as we're planting our Cherokee corn, we will be Cherokee. If we stopped speaking our language or if we stopped growing our corn, or if we completely leave our lands, then there won't be any more Cherokee."[89] Selu's corn only grows in certain places and in certain ways, needing tending and nurturing, so that performing active farming of the crop and cooking of the traditional corn-based dishes continues her legacy of providing for other tribal members. Through her Burning Cedar Sovereign Wellness Initiative, Albert Williams performs Cherokee Indian identity through the food she plants and dishes she cooks, and, because "we've saved those seeds since the beginning of our existence," Albert Williams considers her work sacred, not just for sustenance.[90] This emphasis on tending to and eating corn-based dishes to perform and embrace a sense of Cherokee Indian identity is also seen in the work of Cherokee Indian farmers Harold and Nancy Long, 2019 North Carolina Small Farmers of the year, who plant and save heirloom seeds, working with the farm extension to provide garden kits to up to 800 Cherokee Indian families. Bordered on two sides by tribal land, their farm was sold to white settlers who held it for more than 100 years following Removal but has been returned to their ownership. Food activist Tyson

Sampson's Bigwitch Indian Wisdom Initiative also re-establishes links to Qualla land because he believes "our identity *is* the plants," where talking about connections helps preserve Cherokee Indian identities.[91]

Cherokee Indian food activists also rebuild bridges between the past and present to help relocate lost senses of tribal identity. Particularly important considering cultural disconnection post-removal, identifying, gathering, and preparing traditional greens and mushrooms, for example, are performances that recenter tribal ways of life for those who no longer practice them. Back from a recent visit to Cherokee, North Carolina, Albert Williams stressed how important it was to experience traditional foods in the town of Cherokee to reconnect to history and identify what was lost as tribal members resettled in Oklahoma: "Folks over here in the Western band are disconnected in a lot of ways . . . we're trying to use food as a bridge to reconnect and begin to learn their language and try and bring all of these ways back home."[92] When she teaches people how to process and cook with corn and October beans and to make traditional dumplings, her work re-kindles lost elements of tribal identity that cannot be replicated without a specific connection to the fruits of Cherokee Indian ancestral land: "All of our medicines and our ceremonies and all of that revolved around that climate and that region and the specific land that we tie ourselves to. I think a lot of people, non-native folks, have a disconnect or the misunderstanding that, 'well, yeah, you were removed, but then, you just continue your culture wherever you end up.'"[93] Place becomes more than a collection of physical characteristics, a site of sensory experiences that are beneficial to healing, wellness, and sustainability. This emphasis is in keeping with Cherokee Indian culture broadly, because a foundational principal is that "healing cannot occur without an intrinsic connection to something larger than the individual."[94] Indeed, the Cherokee Indian concept of well-being, or *tōhi*, extends beyond individual health to the relationships between people and the rest of the world, "smoothly flowing, evenly and moderately paced, fluid, and peaceful."[95] Teaching people to produce their own food and prepare it, Albert Williams and others return traditional ecological knowledge and balance to the Cherokee people, creating what they believe is "actual food sovereignty."[96]

We then experienced the connective potential of tapping into the new agrarian myth firsthand by helping harvest the first returned ancestral crop of Catawba Nation River Corn—*Kus Iswa*. Arriving early on a Friday morning, the sun glinting on the grass and fields, before us lay two corn fields, one planted with traditional beans, one without. The stalks in the fields were high and brown, drying in the September heat, and at first, we couldn't discern which was an ear of corn and which was simply part of the plant. Soon we found a rhythm, pulling down an ear and twisting it from the stalk, country music playing in the background from someone's phone. As we filled sacks with ears of corn, Catawba Nation Natural Resources director Aaron Baumgartner stressed that we were not just participating in cultural traditions, we were working on a process of revival and renewal. Encouraging us to call these plants by their original name, he told us about the importance of this moment for the Nation. In the 1910s, Catawbas proudly brought their corn to agricultural expos, but similar to other tragic stories of the treatment of Indigenous people, the growing of this corn, an undertaking that took a significant amount of time to plant and harvest successfully, died out as their culture was slowly erased. Also called Lial corn, named after the white family who still had some of its seeds many years later, the seeds had finally been brought back to the Nation with the help of culinary historian Dr. David Shields. Peeling back the husks, we picked vibrant red ears, strawberry colored ones with flecks of red nestled within yellow kernels, rainbow ears with orange, red, yellow, white, and even grayish–purple kernels, and yellow, white, and hybrid ones, all to be sorted into two types of corn—food and seed. This harvest flourished despite drought, too much rain, sun, bugs, and the like, but also had withstood cultural suppression. The Nation was working with a chef who would nixtamalize the corn (referring to a traditional process that increases its nutritional value and removes toxins) and then help to prepare a variety of dishes with it. Back at the mercifully cool senior center, we all processed the corn in the same rhythm—husk, sort, braid. Senior women chatted as they worked, the center's hallway display cases were filled with handmade pottery and baskets and historical pictures showing groups of family members working in agricultural roles. The Nation's new farm offered a connection to those pictured, though they were from an earlier generation. Handling the corn made this link immediate, where harvesting connected place and people. We left sweaty, corn meal dust and dirt sticking to our legs and hands, thirsty, offering to bring students to help with the harvest the following year. We wanted them to also experience this powerful performance of cultural renewal and reclamation.

Although relationships to particular crops may differ in other communities, our research with Indigenous food activists suggests that plants and crops offer one way to locate place-based food appeals that help community members share in a common identity. The holistic Cherokee Indian philosophy about plants bridges gaps between rural farmers who want to talk about agriculture and urban activists who are interested in climate change, highlighting one possibility of how the new agrarian myth links communities who have different perspectives.[97] Among Catawbas, we saw how agriculture also provided a discourse of collective resilience. Powerful experiences among African American food activists would suggest yet another possibility—resistance.

Farming, African American Resistance, and Resilience

When he removed his shoes on the tour and let the mud reach his feet, the memory of her (his dead grandmother) and the memory of the land literally traveled from the earth, through his soles, and to his heart. He arrived "home."

—*Leah Penniman, Farming While Black*

The use of place in Affrilachian food care rhetoric has parallels with its use in Cherokee Indian communities, privileging history, honoring ancestors' abilities, and stressing the need to serve as stewards of the land to avoid replicating harmful white farming and land ownership policies and practices. Although they locate similar *topoi* as starting points, these stories of Black farming resistance move away from narratives largely centering on the pain and oppression of enslavement to highlight Black horticultural knowledge and expertise.[98] Our fieldwork experiences presented subtle differences in how activists used food to craft community resilience, with place used to both preserve and assert the authority of the Black experience in Appalachia's culinary traditions and to serve as a resource for performing resistance and liberation. We observed how food centers place and the body's relationship to it for reclamation and justice, as essential acts of defiant community care. The visceral experiences of food and farming were used to connect with racism, where bodies bear the brunt force of labor and

Figure 16. Harvesting Kus Iswa with the Catawba Nation, Rock Hill, South Carolina. Author photograph.

exclusion but also experience its physical rewards.[99] If racism "dislodges brains, blocks airways, rips muscle or cracks bones," farming and cooking is also felt corporeally, sometimes offering pleasure and a step "closer to the taste of freedom.'"[100] Broadly invoking Malcolm X's belief that "revolution is based on land," advocates crafted food inequity as a weapon of white supremacy, seeking to restore and repair these physical connections.[101]

Some Black farming communities' care rhetoric invokes the guidance of sacred African deities, but what we observed falls into another common practice—locating knowledge in historical pioneers to firmly seek respect and acknowledgement from other communities.[102] Activists draw on the historical work of Black farmers to reclaim the place of African Americans within the food system, but in the Southern Appalachians, they also highlight the mastery of Black women in forming the region's culinary legacy.

For instance, the Asheville Chow Chow Festival Event, "The Mystery of Malinda Russell," could have been just another ticketed dinner, featuring beautiful food with carefully matched wine pairings. There were clues it would be different immediately—tickets came with instructions to read an online PDF copy of the formerly enslaved Black woman chef's 1866 cookbook, *A Domestic Cook Book: Containing a Careful Selection of Useful Receipts for the Kitchen.*[103] Sitting down at shared tables, a menu copied from the only known remaining volume of this fragile text listed ten of Malinda's recipes we would experience, the antique look of the document helping to create anticipation for 200 diners trying "Malinda's Dressed Okra served on Salt Rising Bread," "Malinda's Fricasseed Catfish with Carolina Gold Rice," and "Malinda's Allspice Cake with Orange Blossom Chevre." We received additional historical and culinary context from Chef Ashleigh Shanti and four expert panelists, Cynthia Greenlee, Leni Sorensen, Toni Tipton-Martin, and Ronni Lundy. Malinda's ability to create and publish her recipes in a volume meant for an audience of professional Black women chefs was an act of independence, a miracle, at a time when being a Black woman was incredibly difficult. This remarkable achievement is echoed in tastes of salt rising bread, where creative Appalachian bakers have to "catch" yeast out of the air; by discovering that her cookbook contains *ten* different complex recipes for gingerbread (wild ginger only grows at certain elevations like those in Appalachia); and noting her recipes' terse instructions, no instructions given for choosing a pan or temperature. It becomes clear that her intended readers were educated, professional women who did not need stepwise instructions. As Chef Shanti explained about the efficient style of the recipes, "She has an incredibly simplified way of conveying all this florid, overly technical language we use today."

Bite by bite, the presentations broaden the audiences' understanding of who Black women were in the 1860s and what they managed to do in their kitchens. Once dismissed as "incapable of originating their own thoughts about creating recipes," tasting Malinda's recipes dispels these myths. Their performance shifts the overall narrative that has defined the Black experience in terms of land and food labor; indeed, Malinda provides African Americans with a different relationship by helping other Black freed businesswomen and catering professionals to scale their work, moving their home cooking recipes into professional catering adaptations.[104] Malinda's story offers healing and identification, providing a sense of agency for people to change how their own narratives are shared.[105] As Toni Tipton-Martin put it, "Your life is hard, but not as hard as hers was." This dining experience is inspirational—if a free woman of color can operate a business at that time while raising a disabled child, they, too, can continue to change things.

The experience also helps challenge perceptions of who shaped the place of Appalachia. These performances more firmly meld the Black experience as an Appalachian one; as Ronni Lundy explains, performing Malinda's story "busts the myths that we were some sort of genetic strain of Scots-Irish people . . . they tell the many, many stories of Black Appalachians who were able to make their way because of food."[106] As a Black vintner, Black professor/culinary historian, Black former journalist and writer–editor, and Black chefs share her remarkable story, they collectively define a presence that marks Black culinary contributions as undeniable and professional, an important part of Appalachian, not just Black Appalachian, cuisine. They speak of and beyond Black communities to reduce the distance between one community's experience of food to another's. Malinda is East Tennessean, publishes recipes that are still recognizable by twenty first century diners, and makes Black women's culinary stories Appalachian ones.

Broadening the story of Appalachia is rhetorically significant, but so is the insistence on making Black Appalachian foodways a vehicle for continued liberation. Driving through historic African American West Asheville looking for the Burton Street Peace Garden, we first missed this powerful expression, passing hip black-painted cinder-block buildings sitting next to smaller older houses, newly built homes with broad decks and Black Lives Matter signs decorating neat yards. Walking up the quiet street on a Friday afternoon, we quickly realized this was not another community garden, but part of the 100-year-old African American Burton Street community fondly called Pearson Hill, honoring founder E. W. Pearson. Beside the gate sat a laminated sign describing Asheville's anti-racism proclamation, a large poster celebrating the contributions of African American "outdoor heroes," and a bright blue welcome sign advising visitors to "take deep breaths and only what you need, but take time to relax and enjoy." To our left sat an enormous metal statue of a man and a dog, in one of the man's hands a bouquet of metal flowers, in the other, a gun, beginning to indicate that this space was a verdant experiential Black Asheville history museum.

Planted on a hill, the lower areas of the garden were filled with late summer okra, squash, and edible flowers, and slowly walking up the incline, our steps were directed by paths that led to the rhetorical message becoming stronger with each step—food could help create social justice.[107] A metal exhibit filled with empty prescription pill bottles sat amidst plants and a laminated poem lamenting the drug overdose epidemic in the Black community. Just beyond it, empty industrial waste barrels sat at the intersection of two old College and MLK Jr. street signs, juxtaposed with a "water quality is poor" sign. Each part of the garden was devoted to a particular topic of concern within the Black Asheville community—a small shed encouraged Black children to embrace building and mechanical skills, documents in a library shed featured local activist DeWayne Barton calling for more inclusion in an "African Americans in Western North Carolina" conference, and a hand painted mural proclaimed that their "'hood is Black excellence." It became overwhelming—cast-off toys, dolls, metals, tools, wood, and vegetation juxtaposed together, the most devastating scene an outdoor room of metal folding chairs placed in front of an image of George Floyd and plastic guns strewn nearby on the ground. Each chair held the image and story of a Black man who lost his life to police violence and the collection stood beneath a mural of smiling Jaleaha, a young Black girl similarly killed. Spaces were devoted to religion, to redlining, and to community building strategies, laminated descriptive placards highlighting found objects. You move through time and space in an immersive manner, entering in the beauty of the crops, directed through difficult exhibits, ending with a community stage and kitchen space, farm stands offering brightly colored assorted peppers, okra, and free garden seeds on a sliding scale honor system. Inviting us to try out the new wooden stairs he had just built, a volunteer noted that most visitors were from out of town, but he was trying to attract more locals to the space. Tourist downtown with its restaurants and breweries sat about three miles away, but similar to what had also happened in the city's African American East End, the "local, face-to-face, sustainable food network" that had once existed and thrived had been erased by the "one-two punch of 'urban renewal' and the national shift of food retailing to the supermarket."[108] Activists were trying to bring this food network back to life by making the connection between food justice and racism experienced and

Figure 17. Mural in the Burton Street Peace Garden, Asheville, North Carolina. Author photograph.

felt in the Peace Garden, making these issues powerfully present for more audiences.[109]

The Peace Garden experience made it almost impossible for a visitor not to feel a visceral link between the past and present, making a clear tie between food, oppression, and liberation, whether you took the time to read all the signs or not. The garden helped repair individual relationships to the land by showing how spaces can be used to grow community, but also fortified this community, fueling a sense of collective response and resistance to food injustice.[110] Helping a Black Ashevillian to "care yourself into freedom," it connects a solo Black body with a collective one.[111] Food here is not about oppressive history, but creates "everyday pockets of respite," building food sovereignty and social justice to help the community practice resilience in their kitchens and beyond.[112] In this space, food creates new associations and meanings; here, land itself becomes vital to Black resistance, an active, resilient form of Black liberation.[113] Walking through the canopy of George Washington Carver Edible Park the next day, this connection was again made clear, food crossing lines in an attempt to bridge communities. Our Hood Huggers International tour guide, Daniel, chose to end our tour of Black Asheville here in this space managed by the city's historically African American East End–Valley Street volunteers. Encouraged to take what we wanted from its 40 varieties of fruit and nut trees, Daniel invited us to step over an imaginary line between the park's boundary and the historic East End African American community center. Daniel told us we were part of this community now, this 'hood, encouraging us to share the seeds of information about Black Asheville's legacy of resilience.

CONCLUDING, LOOKING FORWARD

Again and again, we found community members throughout the Southern Appalachians using place *topoi* to situate Southern Appalachia's food resources as *part* of a broader vision of a stronger, more resilient America—not a broken one. These are not uncomplicated messages of patriotism, urging residents to ignore real problems; rather, they use specific qualities of region to spark interest and action in supporting their own. Of course, advocates recognize that food is not the only thing needed to build stronger communities. Instead, they note that communities should use food to construct a regionally specific agrarian vision that attempts to bridge different people, varied causes, and possible solutions together. Challenges abound. We are in a very divisive historical period, the "dis-United States," with disagreements over election fraud, vaccines, gender politics, race, and more, but some scholars argue that Americans still largely agree on some basic issues, some of which are being held hostage by a political party representing a minority of voters.[114] It is also true that food movements are popular cyclically, and people lose interest. Still, the ability to position the foods of place as already-available innovative resources has a role in meeting a variety of community needs and bridging ideological boundaries. Southwest Virginia author and former political candidate Anthony Flaccavento reflects on using food to help successfully support and develop Abingdon, Virginia's mountain communities, for example, noting much of what people need is already here if they take time to see it, with some in that community becoming "food citizens" who not only value fresh food but the "farmers who grow it and the land from which it comes."[115] These are not nostalgic, sentimental reminders of food traditions experienced by a privileged few, or presented as utopian dreams of political investment, but provide food-based practical solutions to real problems. In Southern Appalachia's place-based rhetoric of new agrarianism, food is used to help creatively re-invent and support those communities when there is, at times, not much else available.[116]

In this chapter, we have detailed multiple performances of place and attempts to create spaces where people feel more connected and affected by their food choices, working to catalyze more resilient community responses. Although place provides a common ground among people, acting in support of others encourages community members to value those place-based connections. Performing care provides more encounters with others and the rhetorical action is, therefore, more meaningful. Building affect between groups—enhancing the emotional connections and feelings of closeness with other community members—also provides more incentive for longterm change.[117] More specifically, investing in food and foodways of a shared place gives back to the community, feeding those who are both physically and culturally hungry and looking for a way to connect back to their roots. Cherokee Indian activists work to heal their people through food. In Spartanburg, Asheville, and Greenville, and beyond, food care fills in resource gaps left by tourism economies. In Asheville, Black food activists teach lessons about their historical and contemporary part in the city's stories. As Black Asheville native and writer Cynthia Greenlee complains about being asked why she is visiting the city: "We are not latecomers, interlopers, the seekers casting about for New Age energy and vegan biscuits . . . some of us are moving back and staking our claims."[118] In each case, our fieldwork echoed what Ashanté Reese found in the predominantly Black areas of the Washington, DC, food activism community—"residents' understanding of self-reliance was grounded in historical and spatial contexts," where gardens and other initiatives fed the community, but in ways that supported youth, entrepreneurship, and relationships.[119]

Clearly, these rhetorics of Southern Appalachian new agrarianism will not succeed in building collective community resilience without more changes in policy and the creation and sharing of more resources. As Reese aptly summarizes in her work spotlighting Black food activism, "calling attention to the agency of residents dealing with food inequalities does not diminish the realities of structural constraint."[120] Black farmers only run 1,500 out of the 46,000 farms in North Carolina, for example, and despite almost overwhelming interest in farmers markets in some areas, their impact on local communities is still limited because the people who most need it cannot or do not always access it.[121] As Indigenous Chef movement leader Sean Sherman emphasizes, food is certainly not a cure all, but it is a piece of a solution: "The culinary approach has such a role to play, to get people excited about these foods, to show they can taste good, but there's this idea, like . . . they're gonna be healthier and really happy, but that's bullshit. The issues go a lot deeper. There's a lot of intergenerational trauma."[122] We saw work to address these issues by connecting individual responses to more collective ones, using local, traditional diets to emphasize accessible, inclusive systems that did not rely on the logics of self-reliance. These efforts interrupt the so-called bootstrap logics that plague Appalachia in particular and help identify strategies that make resilience through food care an issue for communities as a whole.[123] On an individual level, these efforts also do important work, showing community members how their efforts are part of the community and helping to provide some with senses of agency, opportunity, and confidence. As another African American Asheville community farmer explains, monetary gains are critical, but so are senses of representation and connection, or the "personal relationship with agriculture" that some of these initiatives we explored *in situ* provide.[124] Much of what we experienced linked issues of food access and quality (and their health correlates) to economic and demographic dynamics in a more performative, lived kind of way. The rhetors use the food of their particular places to embrace some of the macro (policy, sociocultural norms), local (community environments), and individual (personal choice) levels needed to create more resilient communities.[125] Our examples recognized that food care rhetoric must engage these questions of systemic connections, even if it does not have all the answers.

Some continue to argue that Appalachia is at a crossroads where the ability to use local natural resources to support sustainable development and livelihoods is possible, but difficult.[126] There are promising developments in Western North Carolina tourism where model experiences of "integrated tourism," blend elements of the land (soils, plants, food) and landscape (scenic quality) to link rural and urban resources together with regional identity for greater success.[127] Food care advocates similarly intertwine elements of place with a community's people to go beyond "do gooding," charity or volunteerism, to fortify and try to change communities from the inside out, prioritizing residents who rely on the elements of place and its affective power to rise beyond the "failures of the state and an economy that continues to depend on public-private partnerships to meet people's needs."[128] They are instead creating a vision that benefits from the state but recognizes their resilience exists with or without it. Southern Appalachian people might identify with their agricultural landscape and the sense of place it offers, but in the concluding chapter, we further argue how policy change and investment is still needed to build a stronger rhetoric of resilience.

Chapter 6

Digging Deeper into Appalachia's Stories of Resilience

The thoughts for this project began to form in the summer of 2016. On the way to where Ashli grew up in Southwest Virginia, the author passed over the New River Bridge near Sylvatus. Amidst the beautiful scenery sat a huge, white sign, penned in shaky handwriting, was the word "TRUMPF" in bold red letters. After canoeing with her family along the second oldest river in the world, encountering an American Indian pow wow by happenstance, and enjoying food from her family's garden, the author kept thinking about the sign. It symbolized more than a call to vote for a presidential candidate. Sitting alongside a tumble-down farmhouse in a largely white part of the state, the sign's angry letters appeared to connect one Sylvatus resident to the media's repeated claims that residents of greater Appalachia were looking for someone to speak out for *their* interests, a candidate who, in coded, racialized language, would "Make America Great Again." Coverage of Sylvatus followed this common pattern, part of a wave of stereotypical imagery that increased in volume in the lead up to the election.[1] For instance, Sylvatus was first called Shade of Death because of its heavily forested character; in the 1880s, ore deposits created a prosperous mountain community, complete with a depot, bank, Slim Jim soft drink manufacturing plant, town hall, and three saloons.[2] Predictably, locally made corn whiskey and peach and apple brandy led to shootings, and discoveries of higher grade ore elsewhere forced the mine to shut and discontinued the railroad.[3] The community appeared to decline slowly after the 1940s. From the outside, the Sylvatus community plays into typical media stereotypes surrounding Appalachia; however, if you take a closer look, there is more to the story of this and other Southern Appalachian towns. For all we know, there is more to the story of the sign, too.

In our research, we sought to find food stories that would offer different versions of the region's narrative, helping to fuel alternative conversations about its people. We found them, in Sylvatus and elsewhere, where we learned how communities used food to help bolster resilience but often confronted many challenges when searching for how to do so. Today, much of the region looks the same and confronts similar economic and social challenges, heightened by the pandemic, and perhaps more deeply divided than before, but our trip taught us how (and why) it is important to look deeper. Southern Appalachian communities rely on food in building resilience, preserving important traditions, fortifying communities, and melding cultural touchstones with new influences, despite these often-difficult circumstances. Sitting in her parents' home again following our last fieldwork weekend, Ashli was offered a plate of pinto beans and cornbread, and she thought about how this one simple dish had been reflected in so many of our different conversations and experiences. Its ingredients were symbolic of her family, but as we had learned, they also reflected many other families and communities. She thought about the bean bread she had eaten at the Cherokee Indian Fair, its cornmeal providing a different texture from her family's plain cornbread. She thought about the homemade corn tortillas we enjoyed in Blowing Rock, North Carolina, made by a Mexican newcomer/chef. She remembered the delicate taste of Malinda Russell's recreated Green Cornbread, three dozen ears of fresh corn grated and mixed with a bit of egg, milk, and salt. They were all simple corn-based recipes but symbolized significant and varied stories of community resilience.

Studying food rhetorically, immersing ourselves in the different food experiences on offer in the region, emphasized how food speaks about Southern Appalachia's resilience in varied ways. Traveling throughout the region, conducting interviews, having unplanned conversations, and enjoying sips and tastes allowed us to participate in parts of Southern Appalachia's story that even some of its residents may not yet have experienced. For example, when we left the Cherokee Indian mother town's, Kituwah, corn field, we felt like our world was splitting open. We learned that EBCI members had been arrested by the National Park Service for harvesting ramps sustainably on their own land and that tribal members had applied for numerous agricultural grants to help protect its sovereignty once again.

We learned about our own ancestors' culpability in minimizing these types of stories of marginalized peoples' land in favor of others. We saw how culinary tourism acts in the region but were also confronted by what it was unable to do, wondering whether the industry would be able to offer more transcendent, inclusive experiences on a broader scale. We were surprised, not by how much food initiatives cared for communities, but by how they are used to provide visions and dreams for the future. In this final chapter, we reflect on what our research taught us about Appalachian foodways, Appalachian resilience, and resilience rhetoric. Our findings shed light on how other regions might be studied through their foodways rhetoric and suggest how to use the food of our places to circulate more and different stories.

LEARNING TO PRESERVE, FORTIFY, AND MELD THROUGH APPALACHIAN FOODWAYS

As we began to make our way across the region, resilience quickly surfaced as a *topos* in so many locations. Although we initially expected it to be only one of many topics, we eventually saw connections between the different food messages about the region and all those themes circulated around the idea of strengthening community through food. There were various ways that this discussion about community emerged, but three main *topoi* surfaced, sometimes appearing separately, sometimes overlapping, and sometimes seemingly focused on different audiences. From harvesting corn, chatting with canners, or tasting modern interpretations of historic dishes, there was a clear interest in preserving regional food traditions—people embraced mainstay dishes, familiar flavors, and time-tested production practices. Focusing on resurrecting and promoting regional food traditions was a message that largely focused internally—leading Appalachians to value food traditions that might have been forgotten or devalued. In many ways, preservation is focused on developing pride of place. Businesses and communities survived and even thrived when they honored what has been valued over time, but also introduced new practices and flavors that found acceptance. We experienced what folklorists Henry Glassie and Emily Hilliard call the temporal nature of tradition, acting as "a moving target constantly churning."[4] Still, the desire to preserve traditions and the status quo may continue to keep communities from moving forward; interviewees told us they wished for economic opportunities, more restaurant options, and safer spaces, worried about their neighbors of color. We were constantly reminded that traditions are not inherently good and must be negotiated, communities making decisions about what will be carried forward or left behind, and some not included in this conversation.[5] Calls to preserve the old ways may keep struggling communities in *stasis,* but in the wake of the historic floods in the summer of 2022, a new urgency arose from some, with communities recognizing that "we can't build back the same way as we were living before."[6]

At the same time, we saw how this desire to preserve strengthened a variety of communities, connecting one generation to the next and providing for their members. Not everyone needs to know how to can, but knowing that your family has that generational knowledge and skill is valuable and reaffirms your culture. Indeed, what an emphasis on preservation highlights is that Appalachia would not *be* as resilient without the diversity of people and traditions that built it. No exploration of resiliencies in the region is complete without fully accounting for the combination of traditions that emerged over time. Preserving means sharing these histories. As rhetorician Patricia Davis and colleagues contend, part of the larger process of what some scholars would call *decolonizing* the South means that we do not ignore those voices and communities that were oppressed and unheard, but illuminate the central role that these groups played in making this a place of resilience, where different cultures brought and preserved the traditions that make the region what it is today.[7] This understanding of preservation's role in building Appalachian resilience emphasizes that the region will become more resilient if it continues to work its rich histories into the narratives that circulate, showing how they fortified a variety of its communities. That work is happening. In Brevard, the Transylvania Heritage Museum received a North Carolina Humanities Engagement Grant to create a program about Cherokee Indian culture and its influence on the area, while an exhibit on display during our visit shared large colorful maps of Appalachian migration patterns.[8] National publication *Travel and Leisure's* August 2022 issue then circulated some of these types of messages, including a feature about Appalachian cuisine in Tennessee that discusses preserving tomatoes and pork in the typical language of getting by, but also pointing out the start of the Trail of Tears at the Hiwassee River Heritage Center, noting "those homesteads where people were dragged from their

*Figure 18. Appalachian-inspired charcuterie board at
Taste Restaurant, Bristol, Virginia. Author photograph.*

homes."⁹ In the spring of 2023, the popular *New York Times* column "36 Hours In," told Asheville visitors to look for the portrait of James Baldwin by a local artist as they enjoyed Benne on Eagle's homage to local African American culinary traditions.¹⁰

In these and other ways, the stories of cultural preservation are shifting, with residents and observers alike finding a more complete picture. Meanwhile, food continues to fortify Southern Appalachian from within, helping communities recognize themselves and their neighbors as part of a broader story of resilience. Rhetorical messages that empower a community take that first message of preservation and pride of place and shift the focus to lifting the entire community using the strength of tradition. Whether using the products of place to materially support people in need or to symbolically reaffirm a community's identity, food is central in this work. Each fall, the Appalachian Sustainable Agriculture Project organizes a family tour of twenty Asheville area farms that teaches the community where their food comes from and how to support it; each spring, GRINDfest Asheville promotes the work of Black food entrepreneurs in the city such as Slutty Vegan, a Black, woman-owned vegan food truck. Food connects communities to their places and provides opportunities for individuals to see themselves represented in their communities. As with preservation, food rhetoric may also solidify types of community that are destructive or continue to mark Southern Appalachia as a place of white supremacy, racism, and violence; fieldwork experiences firmly demonstrated how those who do not have particular white ethnic backgrounds are sometimes excluded. We saw efforts that recognized and tried to correct this problem, as in Asheville nonprofit BeLoved's initiative to offer kid-friendly chef kits and classes to help preserve the culinary traditions of communities of color, but it is still difficult to find experiences that celebrate food's power to fortify non-white communities outside some of the region's larger cities.[11] When used to build community, however, this *topoi* sets the stage for shifting the message to an external audience through a spotlight on a wider message of Appalachia.

Thinking of resilience as gaining strength while Southern Appalachia's cultures continue to meld together is admittedly hopeful, a desire for a regional vision that is more than the sum of its parts. As folklorist Emily Hilliard contends, though, although food and other forms of expressive culture may be disrupted by extractive industries, climate change, and structural inequality, for example, that cultural knowledge helps communities respond to and sometimes resist these destructive forces.[12] Crucially, though, cultures have *always* melded together to create what we know as Southern Appalachia and buffer its people against some of these barriers, whether it is through migrating crops, adapting dishes, or resisting co-optation. The challenge is to circulate these rich examples more broadly to counterbalance what is still presented as a unified, deficient area of sameness, finding in food cultures tools to "resist structural equality and oppression."[13] Further, adding to the stories of how cultures have melded together and continue to inform one another also interrupts the type of regional romanticization that leads extractive industries and unsustainable business practices to *develop* the land and *improve* its people, stuck together in their supposedly *one collective* past.[14] Residents interested in collectively creating a more sustainable future recognize the limitations of this narrative. Telling a more complex story of the region presents a more compelling message not only for more Appalachians, but also for others who do not fully understand the region and make harmful assumptions and claims.

These *topoi* are not only already apparent in the foodways rhetoric of the region, but could be used more broadly in regional discussions. As we have pointed out, there are limitations to the resilience *topos,* but the messages help strengthen communities and present a powerful message of endurance. These findings are most significant for understanding the region and the rhetoric surrounding and building it. However, there are also conclusions to be made about rhetorical messaging more broadly through food.

FOOD AS RHETORIC

Fundamentally, the rhetorical possibilities of food are a central part of understanding regions and places. Although this is not a new claim, the rhetorical nature of food is a topic that needs additional exploration. Locating these various expressions of resilience throughout the region's food cultures expands our understanding of how food acts as rhetorical text and how it provides access to messages about regionalism, identity, culture, and history that are of increasing interest to the discipline. We have devoted our scholarship to examining alternative rhetorical texts—trying to examine culture and identity from many different perspectives. Accounting for everyday rhetoric is necessary to form a clear image of the kinds of messages that shape how we see ourselves and others.[15] This project is a response to those calls for expanding the symbols that we interpret. And, especially in a place like Southern Appalachia, where white food traditions have become privileged over time as the region's *true* and *pure* culture, food messages offer a critical re-establishment of cultures that have been erased.[16] As Emily Hilliard writes about the importance of exploring these types of vernacular discourses in cultures that have been marginalized, "vernacular culture can be the most vibrant in small, marginalized communities invested in sustaining their cultural heritage . . . populations often hold onto their community traditions in resistance to assimilation and homogenization by the dominant culture."[17] This does not mean that people simply hold on to the old food traditions—what we found offered adaptations of important traditions into contemporary life.[18] The Peace Garden in Asheville used food to help tell a story of Black history in the area, but it also gave visitors seeds to grow their own. This project found multiple expressions of these vernacular *grassroots* food cultures that engage and augment "more formal and institutionalized mass and popular culture" in important, regionally specific ways.[19] Many people know about Asheville's dominant tale of craft beer and hip food. People there are working hard to add their stories to the rotation, as we experienced sitting in the pews one morning at St. Matthias Episcopal church, the oldest African American congregation in the city, built in 1894 by James Vester Miller, a once enslaved man. A few years ago, no Asheville tour told his story or provided the chance to see his beautiful church's architecture, but now they do. We also learned about more important figures in Asheville's Black history by visiting a brightly colored mural in the midst of its historic Black neighborhood, our guide telling us about the lives of each of the people featured.

Many scholars view food as a lens into studying different communities, but in our case, food provided an entry point into Southern Appalachian cultures that other rhetorical texts simply did not. There is a difference between reading a food travel article rhapsodizing about eating in one of the areas' so called authentic, down home cafes and talking with a restauranteur about why they cook what they do (or don't). For instance, in tiny St. Paul, Virginia, we learned that residents won't pay for a *fancy* pinto beans and cornbread dish that a new hip hotel restaurant tried serving but would support the town's new brewery and its brisket tacos, even convincing anti-alcohol religious opponents to let the business open.[20] Later, from the Packalachian Food Truck, which melds Appalachian and Pakistani food cultures, enthusiastic diners ordered kilt salad chaat and pawpaw mango lassi, kilt salad and pawpaws traditional regional favorites, but served South Asian style, the greens blended with warm spices and the cool yogurt drink served from a mason jar. These culinary preferences suggest a gradual openness to new cultures and flavors, but their ingredients are still rooted in familiar, regional ones. Similarly, watching and conversing with the tourists who visit Uncle Nearest's distillery shared a message about who might feel included in a particular experience. It was striking to taste whiskey among predominantly African American tourists when, so often in Southern Appalachia, that experience is dominated by white visitors and hillbilly/outlaw iconography. These days, rhetorical messages about Southern Appalachian food are found everywhere, touting the provenance of local or regional

Figure 19. Visitor learning about distilling process at Uncle Nearest Premium Whiskey Distillery, Shelbyville, Tennessee. Author photograph.

ingredients, but the opportunity to see how people experience these foods and drinks in place communicated more about how and whether they find them meaningful.

Southern Appalachian food is powerfully rhetorical, deeply moving, frightening, embarrassing, and comforting, sometimes all at once. That is, it is as rhetorically complex as any other cuisine. As people ate and drank, they talked to us, expressing pride, frustration, or joy. On more than one occasion, people asked us why we were taking notes as we ate, watched, read, took pictures, and listened, but they also understood and wanted to participate, sharing their plates, reactions, and stories. We took pictures of powerfully symbolic environments firmly sending messages of poverty, bigotry, and defiance, but even in the next few minutes, someone would smile as they told us more about where we were or what we were eating, and looking around, we understood the pride of place that we often saw at play. We knew, too, that we were sometimes included because we were white women, speaking with a similar accent. Sometimes we wondered if what we were documenting echoed what everyone else was writing and talking about for years—Southern Appalachian food was paradoxical. But then we realized that taken together, these foods were communicating resilience. These messages become more powerful as they are experienced in place.

For example, food rhetoric develops a sense of space and place, making regional definitions clearer and creating a sense of belonging. Critical regionalism concerns telling new stories about the region and food and drink is a natural way to do so, but it must account for how foodways maintain dominant or nostalgic interpretations, challenge them, or fall somewhere in between.[21] Traveling the region and talking specifically with those who have lived here helped to expand (or constrict) its regional boundaries, exposing these constructions, including the rhetorical forces that are not always easily visible. As critical regionalist Douglas Powell observes, "place is always mediated by preconceived notions" (including our own, of course), and to experience or acquire a sense of place is not to only consume, witness, or appreciate it as a rhetorical *text,* but to *participate* in it, which further creates that place.[22] In this way, we, as researchers, tourists, and residents alike, exist in these spaces, creating the place of Southern Appalachia as we participate in its culinary landscape, "asking how texts and their makers create versions of places" but also how we might intervene in these constructions.[23] As scholars and culinary tourists, our role is not solely to critique the Appalachia that has been constructed, but to experience and highlight those who are offering alternative visions, playing our own role in its cultural production.[24] We are cognizant that identifying elements of resilience rhetoric in Southern Appalachia risks codifying some characteristics that inadvertently omit other qualities or interests, but have drawn from our experiences in that place, molded *from* them, rather than trying to force them into a preconceived mold.[25] Fieldwork identifies how regions are formed by accounting for rhetorical activity *in situ,* in the moment, creating what Powell calls "a better kind of place."[26] Understanding food's role in creating this sense of place is critical.

Culinary tourism, then, has the potential to contribute to an understanding of place and offers possibilities for building understanding. Building more resilient tourism deepens what a visitor experiences, becoming more than a "kodak moment," a place to buy a T-shirt, or checking the latest *it* restaurant off their itinerary; focusing on meaningful travel experiences makes tourism more beneficial for residents and travelers alike.[27]

When tourist experiences and travel writing alike offer deeper histories of how crops came to this region and changed over time, these more accurate accounts of migration patterns do work in challenging the pioneer, Scots-Irish veneer that largely *costumed* the region. Observers argue that forms of resilient tourism are more sustainable for communities, respect fragile mountain sites, encourage locally owned shops and restaurants to feature local products and employ residents at fair wages, and increase community land ownership, but these types of tourism also often embody the elusive, often contested, *authenticity* that tourists crave.[28] These initiatives are successful because they attend to what these places have to offer their residents, not just tourists; as one tourism development director cautions, "If your residents don't visit your downtown, then your visitors won't either."[29] We wrote of our glimpses of these models in chapter 5, but others see its potential too. Regional policy change advocate and author Anthony Flaccavento concedes, for example, that Virginia's Appalachian region struggles in the wake of the coal industry's decline and as farmers transition away from tobacco crops, but argues that citizens, small businesses, and local leaders are working to build more *homegrown economies* around food, culture, and tourism, such as what is developing in Abingdon, Virginia and Brevard, North Carolina.[30] The rhetorical work that happens through culinary tourism, with food at the center of the regional story, provides yet another entry point into understanding how a larger region is experienced.

Similarly, telling a story of the resilience of the different people who came to create Southern Appalachia interrogates the public memory that has sedimented over time, simultaneously correcting assumptions about who lives here now. Studying food in this case provided points of access into Appalachian memories that might not have been immediately apparent. Celebrating the influence of Malinda Russell on Appalachian cuisine revises how we understand women, and especially Black women, in the public memory of Appalachian culinary history, reminding people that they were *always* here. Locating these culinary histories is part of ongoing efforts across the African American diaspora to bind the *fragments* of recovered and excavated histories with the ancestral knowledge and skills that these bodies contain to recognize these contributions and to create Black food futures.[31] Similarly, more work is being done to center Indigenous voices in the region's public memory as well as to celebrate their contemporary contributions, although rhetorician Tiara Na'puti contends that centering Indigenous voices simultaneously requires an emphasis on indigeneity while attending to how settler colonialism has erased these perspectives.[32] Frybread is now a celebrated part of some American Indian events, but the food had to be reclaimed first and regenerated as a chosen symbol of Indigenous foodways; others continue to argue that there is no place for this food story because it is a signal of colonialism, noting that "controlling food is a means of controlling power."[33] In this case, food presents an opportunity to discuss this complicated history. *Fabulachians*, a joyful term for gay Appalachians, gleefully insert their stories of being gay and cooking in Appalachia into this public memory too.[34] Stories of how Black Americans shaped Southern Appalachia's culture more broadly are also continuing to emerge. The last decade has seen a changing story of the history of bluegrass music, increasingly acknowledging its African American roots in a style most often associated with white musicians; Dr. Richard Brown is working to restore the legacy of Bill Monroe's mentor and son of a formerly enslaved man, Arnold Shultz, to this story.[35] We did our fieldwork during the pandemic and we undoubtably missed some of this type of reclamation work, but what is emerging is finding new audiences. More particularly, telling the story of place through food brings a different perspective to the discussion of region.

If building more resilient tourism remains partially aspirational, community care initiatives craft more resilient food rhetoric as acts of defiance. What we saw were not examples of individual Appalachians compelled by bootstrap logics of self-reliance, but rather, communities working together in landscapes that often ignored or minimized their needs. During the height of the pandemic, school bus drivers made voluntary deliveries to provide food boxes to children once schools went virtual; in Virginia, Sister Bernie Kenney's Health Wagon has delivered nutrition advice and preventative care in Russell county's remote areas.[36] All of the food-based action that we observed throughout the region, using food to perform care and strengthen the community, highlighted how community strength can be displayed outside of traditional discursive means of communication.

Ultimately, what makes the messages about regionalism and resilient tourism, migration, public memory, and care stronger in this case is not only the use of food as a means of sharing information, but also the way

*Figure 20. Frybread stand at Cherokee Indian Fair, Cherokee,
North Carolina. Author photograph.*

that the messages are circulated. This project thus contributes to notions
of rhetorical circulation, specifically accounting for how it functions in a
fieldwork context. Discursive circulation of rhetoric, is, of course, critical in deepening the story of Southern Appalachia and is ongoing. As we
were writing this book, for example, the story of Linda Skeens, a Southwest
Virginia woman whose cooking, baking, and canning recipes won almost
every category at the 2022 Virginia-Kentucky District Fair went viral.
Celebrated in song, memes, on TikTok, and finally, by Skeens earning a
cookbook publishing contract, people's interest in her work seemed more
than superficial, with people trying to find out more about her identity and
skills. A radio personality made a TikTok video in an attempt to find her,
garnering more than 400,000 views. It's a feel-good story, but Skeens views
her online fame as inspirational: "I actually hope a lot of people will start

canning again, baking again, and doing crafts because that's dying . . . so I hope people will take from the book and want to do it more."[37] Similarly, food media are increasingly creating space for more Indigenous voices, including stories about Sioux Chef Sean Sherman's Minneapolis–area all Indigenous restaurant, Owamni, and publishing his recipes. When the monthly magazine *Food and Wine* offers Sherman's recipe for sweet potatoes with maple chile crisp and multiple food culture publications share news of Owamni winning the James Beard Award for Best New Restaurant, these perspectives also gain traction in public discussion.[38] It is important to note that these conversations are not just happening in legacy food media. For example, Cherokee/Blackfeet Indigenous youth food activist Mariah Gladstone reaches out to fellow millennials through social media, keeping her cooking videos short in case of poor Internet connectivity due to reduced economic circumstances or isolated geography. She notes that as younger users tag their parents and grandparents and send back recipes they have modified, "they're getting their family members and other people involved, creating not just delicious meals, but also restoring knowledge on an intergenerational level."[39]

These stories influence how we discuss the communities with which they are affiliated, but we saw how the experience of culinary tourism itself plays a significant role in circulation. It matters that socially marginalized visitors see people who look like themselves when participating in Southern Appalachian food experiences. Increased efforts to appeal to Black tourists in Asheville ground their contributions in creating that culinary history but also cast a wider net as more and more tourists participate in them and share their experiences. We see this book and the work of others who seek to better document and share the variety of culinary traditions and communities as part of the work of increasing circulation, and part of that work is just getting more people to be there, in the moment, reliving these contributions and talking about them with others. As Chef Sherman explains about the power of eating in his Indigenous restaurant for the first time: "Some people do get very emotional when they come into the restaurant and experience this for the first time. I've seen a lot of people who just get really struck by it, especially Indigenous people, because it's not typical to be able to go someplace and see our Indigenous foods on the menu . . . see Native people cooking the food and serving the food and listening to

Native music coming out of the speakers and just the whole vibe."[40] Tourists also experience how Chef Sean Brock's new Appalachian restaurant, Audrey, takes items sometimes considered to be of lesser value, whether it is a quilt on the wall or lima beans and cabbage, and transforms them into new, special experiences.[41] They find these experiences at restaurants, but they may also occur in a gift shop or fruit stand, as we did when we laughingly chatted about Dolly Parton being turned into chocolate form by a local maker in East Tennessee or learned the story of growers who are still producing 1890s local Magnum Bonum apple trees, tasting the softer flesh of this older apple style in Southwest Virginia and then reading more about them by chance through a Facebook post. We remain mindful that tourism costs a great deal, and some people cannot participate, making these types of informal offhand experiences all the more important. New college programs, such as Maryville's "hospitality and regional identity" major offer another avenue for residents and visitors alike to learn about and appreciate Appalachian food and culture.[42] Ultimately, through the rhetorical vehicle of food, the messages about resilience in discussions of public memory, migration, tourism, and community care will continue to circulate.

RESILIENCE RHETORICS, BROADLY

In the end, our food related rhetorical fieldwork in this particular part of Appalachia helps develop a deeper understanding of resilience rhetorics more broadly. For good reasons, many rhetorical scholars have been cautious about celebrating resilience, focusing on all the ways that it can be harmful to individuals and communities alike. While we share that caution and have discussed many of the problems that can be connected to resilience appeals, it is also clear, based on this research, that there is a strength to resilience rhetoric in foodways narratives that should be accounted for in larger discussions of resilience.

Food offers a different perspective than other entry points into resilience because it is connected to communities in ways that are visible, tangible, and sometimes more accessible in terms of familiarity and approachability. In fact, food-based rhetorics offer a unique entry point into considering resilience because sometimes they represent the only commonality through which people who have nothing else in common are able to interact. Politicians talk about the need to become more resilient following the pandemic, pundits discuss potential impacts from climate change in an effort to prepare for them, and we are familiar with the charge to build mental health resilience. But as we found time and again, the community element is central to an understanding of effective types of resilience in Appalachia, and food was the frequent catalyst. Community-focused resilience is not just about coming together and helping others, it involves being more proactive and focusing not just on the immediate concerns (such as access to food), but also keeping the traditions of the region in circulation. Akin to growing cycles, the process is long and takes persistence and patience; similarly, community-based resilience focuses on long term and permanent solutions, not just quick fixes. Appalachians are used to relying on what they have to provide for one another when there are not enough available external resources or when policies or institutions fail to help construct long-term approaches. Despite this ongoing need for more resources, though, food and food traditions act as an internal community resource that has broad interest and appeal, perhaps helping a community to be more inclusive of a variety of its voices.

Tying resilience messages to land and to place also helps craft more powerful rhetoric. Because the foodways that we feature here are all based in products grown in the area, each rhetorical symbol—each type of food—has a deep connection to the region and the people through the shared land. There is a spirituality that lingers in discussions about the mountains, rivers, and fields that shapes what we know as Appalachia. Connection to land is explicit in most American Indian discussions about identity, as we have previously mentioned. This affinity for connecting to nature transcends any particular religion or spiritual beliefs and makes its way into popular culture. Naturally, then, appeals grounded in the land create strong connections among people who share that land. For example, new brewing initiatives in Native American cultures highlight the ingredients of a place but also uncover skill and artistry in a product often assumed to be a European import, simultaneously correcting "drunken Indian" stereotypes; as one brewer explains, "Our culture has always been mysterious to a lot of non-Natives, because it was illegal to practice our culture for a long time.

Now we put the stories on the cans and start a conversation. It demystifies it."[43] When tourists sample 7 Clans Bended Tree Chestnut Brown ale from Asheville, then, they try a brew modeled after traditional sweet Cherokee Indian chestnut bread, grounded in place and region, that also highlights the skill of the majority female members of the EBCI who own it. The signage, owner, and people working at Uncle Nearest Whiskey wax poetically about the magic of the land not only affecting the flavor of the whiskey, but it also tethers drinkers to the sacred land as they sip. Rhetorical appeals grounded in place are effective because of the natural connection to the environment, using material components to emphasize connections between people and land.

This rhetorical thread that ties resilience to community and place then naturally creates a connection to region that then makes powerful appeals to a sense of belonging. The idea of *place* is complicated and cannot be viewed as a set of physical characteristics, by its inhabitants, or its location; food helps to uncover the "betweenness of place."[44] For this reason, it is even more important to be inclusive and more accurate in discussing the ways that Southern Appalachian food traditions emerged and evolved. The tendency to use food to paint Southern Appalachia in broad strokes as a region is not unique, nor unique to the South in general, but better accounting for its food traditions helps illustrate what is, in fact, there. As a cultural commentator complained in the wake of Appalachian musician Loretta Lynn's death, for instance, her Appalachian identity obscured her legacy of resistance and feminism regarding women's healthcare and domestic violence, "because we hear the accent and automatically assume an unenlightened or backwards region, left behind in the wake of American progress."[45] Regionalism in food rhetoric puts the accent on different things, sometimes things that allow people to look closer. In particular, critical regionalism builds a sense of belonging because it helps people appreciate their regions in new or different ways. When we were kids, the sound of Dolly Parton's "Coat of Many Colors" made us cringe and we wanted access to more fast-food options in our hometowns, not only mom and pop shops and restaurants. Over time, though, Parton gained broad and deep appeal worldwide and the ability to grow your own food became considered as an impressive, sustainable skill. Critical regionalism helps people find new perspectives.

In sum, effectual resilience rhetoric preserves; it is aware of history and traditions of the region and respectful of what role that plays in developing community. To preserve correctly, though, as in the careful process of a water bath forming the seal to protect the produce inside, preservation must not be incomplete, intervening in inaccurate or partial histories to connect to community more fully. Resilience rhetoric better fortifies a community when it is closely tied to people and place, using what is familiar to perform care. Although food is a strong component of this argument, there are other possibilities for resilient rhetoric. For example, industries, arts, and crafts that are closely connected to the area, not just touted as lingering pioneer/mountain holdovers—such as forestry and logging, camping and white-water rafting, local music, handcrafted pottery, or body care products—all draw from the materials and skills of a community to shape solutions to problems and opportunities. In doing so, resilience rhetoric heightens regionalism, helping to create connections to place. The rhetoric is also community-based, in tune with the specific needs and characteristics of the area, but also able to recognize and meld these different components together to strengthen resilience. Resilience community rhetoric reacts to and includes the individuals who compose the community and has an interest in seeing those communities flourish. Because of this community focus, these messages and actions must be dynamic—reflecting the whole and changing with the needs of the community. Resilience cannot merely mean bouncing back but should also keep the bigger picture in mind— *bouncing in different directions* when change is needed.

When we began this project, we had no idea that the pandemic would present many discussions of resilience and that the concept would often be bandied about, sometimes flippantly. Conducting fieldwork, particularly in light of the challenges that the pandemic presented, provided a counterbalance to these more superficial uses. Researching resilience during a pandemic in a world that is increasingly divided, unequal, and often under-resourced in terms of supporting communities in need nevertheless provided multiple examples of this theme. We saw Cherokee Indian communities come together to stop high rates of infection, found small towns figuring out how to get food to hungry children when schools closed, and tourism destinations find ways to keep people coming. Of course, we also saw community efforts to remain resilient that failed, or at least changed course, but resilience takes a long view.

WANDERING ON

In search of some breakfast carbs and fall foliage views one October weekend, we set out on a drive through the High Country area of the Blue Ridge—northwestern North Carolina—ending up in Linville. Sitting at a stoplight at one intersection, we noticed a large collection of pro-Trump, Confederate, and *Don't Tread on Me* flags flying at a building across the highway. We approached the building—what we soon discovered was temporarily acting as a Trump campaign headquarters—and spotted Trump T-shirts for sale ("Jesus is my savior, Trump is my president"), Trump teddy bears on display, and handwritten words on its windows: "Southern Appalachian Lives Matter." We were struck by the dichotomy. On one side of the highway, we saw charming restaurants and produce markets and the vintage Pixie Inn, seemingly welcoming tourists with broad appeal. On the other side, there were messages that seemed to reject that welcoming environment in a barefaced message, conforming to the common pattern we had seen reflected in messages surrounding Southern Appalachia and its foodways. The next day, we wandered farther down the highway and discovered more examples that did not fit into the tired tales of Appalachia—the Vietnamese immigrant serving up food to locals in Banner Elk, a new brewery in downtown Johnson City, Tennessee, the Mexican immigrant serving comfort food in Blowing Rock, North Carolina, and locally sourced neo-Appalachian vegetarian cuisine served up in tiny Meadowview, Virginia, where we ate sitting outside under grapevines and shining stars, serenaded by cows and trains. Food helps this beautiful but endangered region survive and sometimes thrive, forming a significant part of its enduring resilience, but the ability for it to more fully support and reflect its many types of people and communities remains to be seen. Some were hungry for change, using food in their search to build stronger communities; others were not, their roots in communities justifying the status quo, food traditions symbolizing another reason just to stay the same. But food remained at the heart of it all, sending more messages about the complicated nature of regional resilience than we ever expected.

NOTES

INTRODUCTION: WHY APPALACHIAN FOOD (STILL) MATTERS

1. This was the term used by our interviewees and is widely used in the region.
2. Engelhardt, "Introduction: Redrawing the Grocery," 1.
3. Rich, "No Sympathy for the Hillbilly," https://nymag.com/intelligencer/2017/03/.
4. Catte, *What You are Getting Wrong*, 35.
5. Billings, Pudup, and Waller, "Introduction: Taking Exception," 9.
6. Massey, "Rhetoric of the Real."
7. Massey, "Rhetoric of the Real."
8. Kyle Smith, "Why 'White Trash' Americans," *New York Post*, July 30, 2016, https://nypost.com/2016/07/30/.
9. Batteau, *Invention of Appalachia*, 1.
10. Billings, Pudup, and Waller, "Introduction: Taking Exception," 2.
11. Shapiro, *Appalachia on Our Mind*, 1; Pudup et al., *Appalachia in the Making*; Batteau, *Invention of Appalachia*, 1.
12. Satterwhite, *Dear Appalachia*.
13. Harkins, *Hillbilly*.
14. Massey, "Rhetoric of the Real."
15. Roanoke Times Editorial Board, "Is Southwest Virginia in a Death Spiral?" *Roanoke Times*, September 7, 2017, https://roanoke.com/opinion/editorials/.
16. Shapiro, *Appalachia on Our Mind*; Pudup et al., *Appalachia in the Making*.
17. Satterwhite, *Dear Appalachia*, 225, 217.
18. Locklear, "Setting Tobacco," 38.
19. Ray, "Europeans."
20. Himes and Moore, "Hillbilly," 260.
21. Obermiller and Maloney, "Uses and Misuses," 103.
22. Catte, *What You are Getting Wrong*.
23. Cunningham, "Writing on the Cusp," 42; Locklear, "A Matter of Taste," 140.
24. Daniels, "Stay Here Anyway."
25. Maggie Hoffman, "Ronni Lundy Would Like to Show You What Appalachian Food Really Means," *Saveur*, September 7, 2016, https://www.saveur.com/.
26. Sarah Jones, "Can Local Food Help Appalachia Build a Post-Coal Future?" *Nation*, October 11, 2017, https://www.thenation.com/article/archive/.

27. See, for example, Harkins and McCarroll, *Appalachian Reckoning*; Smith et al., "Appalachian Identity."

28. Jones, "Can Local Food Help Appalachia?"

29. Eliza Barclay, "'Mountain Dew Mouth' is Destroying Appalachia's Teeth, Critics Say," NPR.org, September 19, 2013, https://www.npr.org/sections/thesalt/2013 /09/12/221845853/; Caity Coyne, "In McDowell County 'Food Desert,' Concerns about the Future," *Charleston Gazette-Mail*, April 7, 2018, www.wvgazettemail.com; Susan James, "MD Recruits Face Culture Shock in Appalachia," *ABC News*, September 30, 2008, https://abcnews.go.com/Health/.

30. Jane Black, "Next Big Thing," *Washington Post*, March 29, 2016, https://www .washingtonpost.com/lifestyle/food/.

31. Mike Costello, "Food Editor Mike Costello Shares His Vision for Appalachian Food. (It's complicated.)," *100 Days in Appalachia*, May 1, 2018, https://www .100daysinappalachia.com/2018/10/.

32. Cooley, "Southern Food Studies"; Edge, *Potlikker Papers*; Egerton, *Southern Food*; Engelhardt, *Mess of Greens*; Ferris, *Edible South*; Harris, *High on the Hog*; Miller, *Soul Food*; Shields, *Southern Provisions*; Twitty, *Cooking Gene*.

33. Courtney Balestier, "Best American Fruit You've Never Eaten," *Bon Appetit Online*, February 22, 2016, https://bonappetit.com/entertaining-style/trends-news /article/best-american-fruit-you've-never-eaten; Sheri Castle, "When a Southerner Tells You How to Cook Green Beans, Shut Up and Listen," *TheKitchn.com*, July 15, 2015; Cynthia Greenlee, "On Eating Watermelon in Front of White People," *Vox.com*, August 29, 2019, https://www.vox.com/first-person/2019/8/29/20836933/; Hilliard, "Foreword;" Lundy, *Victuals*; Sauceman, *Buttermilk and Bible Burgers*.

34. Ferris, *Edible South*, 231.

35. Engelhardt, "Beyond Grits and Gravy," 80.

36. Lundy, in Hoffman, "Ronni Lundy Would Like to Show You."

37. Lundy, in Hoffman, "Ronni Lundy Would Like to Show You."

38. Ferris, *Edible South*, 137.

39. Martin, *Tourism in the Mountain South*.

40. Martin, *Tourism in the Mountain South*; see Lucy M. Long's edited collection for folkloric analyses of culinary tourism, scholarship about Appalachian food tourism, "ethnic" culinary tourism, e.g., Long, *Culinary Tourism*; Long, "Introduction," *Culinary Tourism*; Long, "Cultural Politics."

41. Martin, *Tourism in the Mountain South*; Thompson, "Searching for Silenced Voices."

42. Engelhardt, "Gathering Wild Greens."

43. Brown and Brown, "Discourse of Food," 318.

44. Engelhardt, "Gathering Wild Greens."

45. Some residents prefer the "Mountain" instead of the "Appalachian" moniker. See Staley, "Identity in a Mountain Family."

46. Eric C. Wallace, "Chef Restoring Appalachia's World-Class Food Culture,"

Atlas Obscura, January 10, 2020, https://www.atlasobscura.com/articles/; Jones, "Can Local Food Help Appalachia?"

47. We use the term "American Indian" when referring more broadly to Indigenous populations. We use "Cherokee Indian" or "Cherokee People" when referring specifically to the Eastern Band of Cherokee Indians (EBCI), based on preferences that were shared with us by interviewees, precedent set by EBCI communication in the region and online, as well as suggestions from the Bureau of Indian Affairs and the National Museum of the American Indian. We recognize that there are many other preferred terms for Indigenous populations and Cherokee Indians in particular (e.g., "Kituwah," "First People," and "Tsalagi"). "Impact of Words and Tips for Using Appropriate Terminology: Am I Using the Right Words?" National Museum of the American Indian, https://americanindian.si.edu/nk360/informational/. "Editorial Guide," Bureau of Indian Affairs, https://www.bia.gov/guide/.

48. Fred Sauceman, "What Exactly is Appalachian Cuisine," March 13, 2015, https://www.whatitmeanstobeamerican.org/places/.

49. Long, "Culinary Tourism," 8.

50. Sauceman, "What Exactly is Appalachian Cuisine?"

51. Lucas Peterson, "Everything You've Always Wanted to Know about Ramps," Eater.com, April 10, 2015, https://www.eater.com/2015/4/10/8384255/.

52. Sauceman, "What Exactly is Appalachian Cuisine?"

53. Wallace, "Chef Restoring Appalachia's World-Class Food Culture."

54. Long, "Emergence of an Appalachian Cuisine," 8.

55. Coomes, *Country Ham*.

56. Wallace, "Chef Restoring Appalachia's World-Class Food Culture."

57. Long, "Emergence of an Appalachian Cuisine."

58. Sohn, *Appalachian Home Cooking*.

59. Mary Casey-Sturk, "Appalachian Foods: Defining Generations," *Smoky Mountain Living*, https://www.smliv.com/food/; Wallace, "Chef Restoring Appalachia's World-Class Food Culture."

60. Alan Muskat, "Mushroom Man," alanmuskat.com.

61. Casey-Sturk, "Appalachian Foods."

62. See the menus from *The Girl and the Raven* and the *Harvest Table Restaurant* (since closed) for contemporary examples: https://thegirlandtheravencafe.com/menu; https://www.harvesttablerestaurant.com/dinner-menu.

63. Sauceman, "What Exactly is Appalachian Cuisine?"

64. Wallace, "Chef Restoring Appalachia's World-Class Food Culture."

65. Long, "Emergence of an Appalachian Cuisine."

66. Hoffman, "Ronni Lundy Would Like to Show You."

67. Wallace, "Chef Restoring Appalachia's World-Class Food Culture."

68. Black, "Next Big Thing," https://www.washingtonpost.com/lifestyle/food/; Stokes and Atkins-Sayre, *Consuming Identity*.

69. Jones, "Can Local Food Help Appalachia?"

70. Hoffman, "Ronni Lundy Would Like to Show You."

71. Engelhardt, "Beyond Grits and Gravy"; Stokes and Atkins-Sayre, *Consuming Identity*.

72. Stokes and Atkins-Sayre, *Consuming Identity*.

73. Specialty Food Association, "Majority of Americans Showing Deeper Interest in Food," October 29, 2018, https://www.specialtyfood.com/news/article/.

74. Kant-Byers, "Revisiting Appalachian Icons"; Rosko, "Drinking and (Re) Making Place."

75. Poirot and Watson, "Memories of Freedom," 97.

76. Ray, *Highland Heritage*, 7.

77. Huber, "Riddle of the Horny Hillbilly," 74.

78. Robertson, *Poverty Politics*, 12.

79. Cunningham, *Apples on the Flood*, 122.

80. Robertson, *Poverty Politics*, 4; Denson, *Monuments to Absence*, 54.

81. Martin, *Tourism in the Mountain South*, xvi.

82. Black, "Next Big Thing"; Jess Daddio, "Appalachian Food Revolution," May 17, 2017, https://www.blueridgeoutdoors.com/go-outside/; Jones, "Can Local Food Help Appalachia?"

83. Kathleen Purvis, "Mining the Southern Mountains for Food Stories," *Charlotte Observer*, September 19, 2016, https://www.charlotteobserver.com/living/food-drink /kathleen-purvis/article102743072.html.

84. Lundy, *Victuals*; Engelhardt et al., *Food We Eat*.

85. David Glasgow, "Mapping Appalachia's Local Food System: 900 Entrepreneurs at a Time," USDA.gov, February 21, 2017, https://www.usda.gov/media/blog /2016/06/27/.

86. Jones, "Can Local Food Help Appalachia?"

87. Black, "Next Big Thing"; Jones, "Can Local Food Help Appalachia?"

88. Wallace, "Chef Restoring Appalachia's World-Class Food Culture."

89. Jones, "Can Local Food Help Appalachia?"

90. Farley, "Political Rhetoric of Property," 138.

91. Costello, in Jess Daddio, "Appalachian Food Revolution," May 17, 2017, https:// www.blueridgeoutdoors.com/go-outside/.

92. Jones, "Can Local Food Help Appalachia?"

93. Martin, *Tourism in the Mountain South*.

94. Engelhardt, "Beyond Grits and Gravy," 75.

95. Long, "Emergence of an Appalachian Cuisine," 13.

96. Long, "Emergence of an Appalachian Cuisine," 13.

97. Long, "Emergence of an Appalachian Cuisine," 16.

98. Jones, "Can Local Food Help Appalachia?"; Wallace, "Chef Restoring Appalachia's World-Class Food Culture."

99. Costello, "Vision for Appalachian Food."

100. Fabris, "Virginia County Bets on Moonshine Tourism in Rural Region," November 7, 2015, *Skift*, https://skift.com/2015/11/07/.

101. Hoffman, "Ronni Lundy Would Like to Show You."

102. Long, "Emergence of an Appalachian Cuisine," 18.

103. Long, "Emergence of an Appalachian Cuisine," 18.

104. Shapiro, *Appalachia on Our Mind*, 63.

105. For example, Locklear, "Fragrant Memories"; Locklear, "'A Comfort'"; Engelhardt et al., *Food We Eat*; Edge et al., *Larder*; Wallach, *Dethroning*.

106. Eller, "Foreword."

107. Wood and Lowery, "As We Cooked," 85.

108. Engelhardt, "Trying to Get," 4.

109. Cunningham, *Apples on the Flood*.

110. Amy Rogers, "'Raise Your Glass'–and Sandwich–to Pink," *WFAE.org*, March 14, 2013, https://www.wfae.org/wfaeats/2013-03-14/.

111. Blethen and Wood, *From Ulster to Carolina*.

112. Williams-Forson, *Building Houses*; Witt, *Black Hunger*; Wallach, *Every Nation Has its Dish*; Zafar, *Recipes for Respect*. See also Cooley, *To Live and Die*; LeBesco and Naccarato, *Edible Ideologies*; Ferris, *Edible South*.

113. Grey, "A Growing Appetite," 319.

114. See, for example, Catte, *What You are Getting Wrong*; Engelhardt, *Tangled Roots*; Harkins, *Hillbilly*; Hsiung, *Two Worlds*; Ledford et al., *Back Talk*; Locklear, "A Matter of Taste"; Long, "Culinary Tourism"; Engelhardt and Smith, *Food We Eat*; Obermiller and Maloney, "Uses and Misuses"; Shapiro, *Appalachia on Our Mind*; Williamson, *Hillbillyland*; Whisnant, *Modernizing the Mountaineer*.

115. Grey, "American Food Rhetoric;" Singer, Grey, and Motter, *Rooted Resistance*; Conley and Eckstein, *Cookery*.

116. Goldthwaite, *Food*; Frye and Bruner, *Rhetoric of Food*; Cramer, Greene, and Walter, *Food as Communication*; Boerboom, *Political Language of Food*; Schneider, "Good, Clean, Fair"; Stokes, "You Are What You Eat."

117. Presswood, *Digital Domestics*; Kelly, *Food Television*; Tippen, *Inventing Authenticity*; Walden, *Tasteful Domesticity*.

118. Jones, "Producing Heritage;" Prody, "Call for Polycultural Arguments," 110.

119. Davis, *Laying Claim*; Kelting, "Entanglement of Nostalgia."

120. Stokes and Atkins-Sayre, "Southern Skillet."

121. Engelhardt, "Beyond Grits and Gravy."

122. Brown and Brown, "Discourse of Food."

123. Dubisar and Hunt, "Teaching Ethos," 76.

124. Several articles discuss the need to legitimize Appalachians as their own storytellers, e.g., Costello, "Vision for Appalachian Food."

125. Cooley, "Southern Food Studies;" Romine, "God and the Moonpie;" Scott Romine and Jon Smith, "Against Cornbread Nationalism: How Foodways Partisans Misrepresent the South" (Call for Papers, 2016).

126. Romine and Smith, "God and the Moonpie."

127. Cooley, "Southern Food Studies," 5; Romine and Smith, "Against Cornbread Nationalism."

128. Green, "Mother Corn;" Wood and Lowery, "As We Cooked."

129. Balestier, "Eating to Go."

130. Allen Batteau, *Invention of Appalachia*, 10.

131. Hauser, "Attending the Vernacular," 17; Middleton et al., "Articulating Rhetorical Field Methods in *Readings*," 38; Hess, "Critical-Rhetorical Ethnography," 56; Senda-Cook et al., *Readings in Rhetorical Fieldwork*; McKinnon et al., *Text + Field*.

132. Senda-Cook et al., *Readings in Rhetorical Fieldwork*, 5. Pezzullo, *Toxic Tourism*, 11.

133. Middleton et al., "Articulating Rhetorical Field Methods;" Gordon et al., "Food Justice;" Pezzullo, "Resisting 'National Breast Cancer Awareness Month;'" Spurlock, "Performing and Sustaining;" Rai and Gottschalk Druschke, *Field Rhetoric*; Dickinson, "Space, Place."

134. Ferris, "'Stuff' of Southern Food," 300; Rai and Druschke, *Field Rhetoric*, 4.

135. Middleton et al., "Articulating Rhetorical Field Methods," 40. Moving forward, rhetorical scholars employed fieldwork to examine gender, politics, advocacy and activism, coalition-building, and more.

136. Stokes and Atkins-Sayre, *Consuming Identity*, 11.

137. Eller, "Foreword," xi.

138. Penman, "Field-based Rhetorical Critique;" Rai and Druschke, *Field Rhetoric*. Other disciplines employing ethnographic fieldwork also struggle with this issue. See Long, "Introduction." All disciplines employing fieldwork must guard against romanticizing or generalizing from data.

139. Folklorists and food studies scholars use ethnographic methodologies to look at individual expressions of identity through food rather than critiquing media representation common in rhetorical scholarship. See Long, "Introduction."

140. Billings and Kingsolver, *Appalachia in Regional Context*.

141. Wanzer-Serrano, "Rhetoric's Race(ist) Problems."

142. Appalachian Regional Commission, "Subregions in Appalachia," https://www.arc.gov/map/.

143. Lundy, *Victuals*.

144. Geographically, Appalachia is said to include all of West Virginia and parts of 13 other states—Alabama, Georgia, Kentucky, Maryland, Mississippi, New York, North Carolina, Ohio, Pennsylvania, South Carolina, Tennessee, Virginia, and West Virginia. In terms of physical landscapes, topography, and other geographical signifiers, these states blend urban and rural areas. Appalachian Regional Commission, "About the Appalachian Region," https://www.arc.gov/about-the-appalachian-region/.

145. Long, "Emergence of an Appalachian Cuisine."

146. Engelhardt, "Beyond Grits and Gravy," 78.

147. Engelhardt, "Beyond Grits and Gravy," 79.

148. Long, "Culinary Tourism," 8.

149. For a related perspective, see Wilkerson, *To Live Here*.

150. Billings and Kingsolver, *Appalachia in Regional Context*.

151. See Billings, "Introduction."

CHAPTER 1: REGIONAL RESILIENCE IN APPALACHIAN FOODWAYS

1. Chris Kenning, Connor Giffen, and James Bruggers, "'I Can't Do it Again': Can Appalachia Blunt the Devastating Impacts of More Flooding, Climate Change?" *USA Today*, August 7, 2022, https://www.usatoday.com/story/news/nation/2022/08/07/.

2. Molly Born, "In Appalachia, a Decades-Long Wait for Running Water," *Washington Post,* July 4, 2021, https://www.washingtonpost.com/national/. "Flooded with Opioids, Appalachia is Still Trying to Recover," *Washington Post,* July 24, 2012, https://www.washingtonpost.com/health/.

3. Kenning et al., "I Can't."

4. Jane Black, "Long Misunderstood: Appalachian Food Finds the Spotlight, *New York Times*, September 11, 2019, https://www.nytimes.com/2019/09/09/dining/.

5. Diane Flynt, unpublished interview with Ashli Quesinberry Stokes, November 8, 2019.

6. Catte, *What You are Getting Wrong*.

7. Davis et al., "Decolonizing Regions"; Moss and Inabinet, "Introduction."

8. Davis et al., "Decolonizing Regions," 352; see also Moss and Inabinet, "Introduction," 8.

9. Bean et al., "'This is London,'" 431; McMurry, "Rhetoric of Resilience."

10. Depew, "Introduction."

11. Buzzanell, "Organizing Resilience;" Scharp et al., "Communicative Resilience;" Walker and Cagle, "Resilience Rhetorics in Science," 3.

12. Buzzanell, "Organizing Resilience," 14–18; Buzzanell and Turner, "Crafting Narratives;" Scharp et al., "Understanding the Triggers."

13. Association for the Rhetoric of Science, Technology, and Medicine, "RSA 2018 Preconference CFP," http://www.arstmonline.org/meetings/prior-cfps-schedules/; Bean et al., "'This is London,'" 431; Johnson, "Resilience;" McGreavy, "Resilience as Discourse."

14. Walker and Cagle, "Resilience," 3.

15. James, *Resilience and Melancholy*.

16. Spoel and Derkatch, "Resilience and Self-Reliance," 1, 3. https://10.13008/2151 -2957.1298.

17. Okamoto, "'Resilient as an Ironweed;'" Wilson, "Community Resilience."

18. Walker and Cagle, "Resilience." By "intervention" we do not suggest that the region is lacking, deficient, or otherwise needs remediation. https://pubs.lib.uiowa.edu /poroi/article/id/3343/.

19. McGreavy, "Resilience as Discourse."

20. Charland, "Constitutive Rhetoric."

21. Smith et al., "Appalachian Identity."

22. LeBesco and Naccarato, *Edible Ideologies.*

23. Warner, "Publics and Counterpublics."

24. Hariman and Lucaites, "Performing Civic Identity," 90; Warner, "Publics and Counterpublics," 62; Stokes and Atkins-Sayre, *Consuming Identity*; Bostdorff, "Public Address Scholarship; Myres, "Five Formations."

25. Jasinski and Mercieca, "Analyzing Constitutive Rhetorics."

26. Charland, "Constitutive Rhetoric"; Jenkins, "Modes of Visual Rhetoric"; Lee and LiPuma, "Cultures of Circulation," Black, "Rhetorical Circulation," 638, 636.

27. Stuckey, "On Rhetorical Circulation;" Warner, "Publics and Counterpublics."

28. Bates, "Circulation," 45.

29. Billings and Kingsolver, *Appalachia in Regional Context*, 6.

30. Satterwhite, *Dear Appalachia*; Satterwhite, "That's What They're Singing About."

31. Farley, "Political Rhetoric," 138.

32. Wood and Lowery, "As We Cooked," 84.

33. Bruce, "Challenging National Borders; Jasinski, *Sourcebook on Rhetoric.*

34. Jasinski, *Sourcebook on Rhetoric*, 581.

35. Tippen, *Inventing Authenticity*, 75–76.

36. Tippen, *Inventing Authenticity*, 108.

37. McGreavy, "Resilience as Discourse."

38. Emily Adams, "Wrigley, Appalachian Food Summit Host 'Corbin Cornbread Convention," *Times Tribune*, August 17, 2017, https://www.thetimestribune.com/community/.

39. Costello, "Vision for Appalachian Food."

40. Definitions above from "Preserve," Dictionary.com, https://www.dictionary.com/browse/preserve; and "Preserve," *Cambridge Dictionary*, https://dictionary.cambridge.org/us/dictionary/english/preserve.

41. Caroline Stewart, "Road Trip Through Appalachia," *Humanities* 43, no. 2 (2022), https://www.neh.gov/article/.

42. Christina Gardner, unpublished interview with Ashli Quesinberry Stokes, November 3, 2020.

43. Travis Milton, unpublished interview with Ashli Quesinberry Stokes and Wendy Atkins-Sayre, October 16, 2020.

44. Ronni Lundy, "Salt of the Earth," *Garden & Gun*, August/September 2016, https://gardenandgun.com/feature/; Abigail Tierney, "A Guide to the Blue Ridge Parkway," *Garden & Gun*, June/July 2019, https://gardenandgun.com/feature/.

45. Egerton, *Southern Food*, 179; Ferris, *Edible South.*

46. Katlin Kazmi and Mohsin Kazmi, "Okra is Bhindi, Bhindi is Okra," Thepacka-lachian.com, https://www.thepakalachian.com/.

47. Jewel Spencer, unpublished interview with Ashli Quesinberry Stokes and Wendy Atkins-Sayre, June 9, 2019.

48. Tyson Sampson, unpublished interview with Ashli Quesinberry Stokes and Wendy Atkins-Sayre, April 30, 2021.

49. Elysia Slake et al., "Agriculture & the Environment: Sorghum & Millet Sys-tems," EPAR Research Brief, 213; *Evans School Policy Analysis & Research Group*, August 31, 2013, https://epar.evans.uw.edu/research/.

50. Ronni Lundy, *Sorghum's Savor*, Elizabeth Flock, "This Sorghum-Brined Chicken Recipe is a Lesson in African American History," PBS News Hour, August 1, 2017, https://www.pbs.org/newshour/; Emine Saner, "From Porridge to Popcorn: How to Cook with the Ancient Grain Sorghum," *Guardian*, May 24, 2021, https://www.theguardian.com/food/2021/may/24/.

51. Glenn Roberts, unpublished interview with Ashli Quesinberry Stokes, March 5, 2022.

52. Elizabeth Flock, "Sorghum."

53. Lundy, *Sorghum's Savor*.

54. Glenn Roberts, unpublished interview with Ashli Quesinberry Stokes, March 5, 2022.

55. Sharpless, *Grain and Fire*.

56. Lundy, *Sorghum's Savor*.

57. Karen Chavez, "National Park Wants to Tell the Stories of Black, Enslaved People," *Asheville Citizen Times*, March 2, 2021, https://www.citizen-times.com/story/news/nation/2021/02/28/.

58. Emine Saner, "From Porridge to Popcorn: How to Cook with the Ancient Grain Sorghum"; Margaret Roach, "Where Adventurous Gardeners Buy Their Seeds," *New York Times*, January 13, 2022, https://www.nytimes.com/2022/01/13/.

59. Splendid Table, "Women Brewers," *Splendid Table*, September 9, 2022, https://www.splendidtable.org/episode/2022/09/09/.

60. Emine Saner, "From Porridge to Popcorn."

61. Margaret Roach, "Where Adventurous Gardeners."

62. Jim Beckerman and Shaylah Brown, "More Americans are Craving the Vi-brant Tastes of Pan-African Cuisine," *NorthJersey.com*, December 3, 2020, https://www.northjersey.com/in-depth/food/2020/12/02/5585506002/.

63. Paliewicz, "Bent but Not Broken," 5.

64. Joe Reagan, unpublished interview with Ashli Quesinberry Stokes and Wendy Atkins-Sayre, December 5, 2020.

65. Definitions above from "Fortify," Dictionary.com, https://www.dictionary.com/browse/fortify; and "Food Fortification," World Health Organization, https://www.who.int/health-topics/.

66. Zack Harold, "A Taste of Home–How Pinto Beans and Cornbread Became an Appalachian Tradition," *West Virginia Public Broadcasting*, March 11, 2022, https://www.wvpublic.org/section/arts-culture/2022-03-11/.

67. Zack Harold, "A Taste of Home," *West Virginia Public Broadcasting*, March 11, 2022, https://www.wvpublic.org/section/arts-culture/2022-03-11/.

68. Zack Harold, "A Taste of Home," *West Virginia Public Broadcasting*, March 11, 2022, https://www.wvpublic.org/section/arts-culture/2022-03-11/.

69. Tonya Carroll, "Cherokee Indian Fair," *Western Carolina University Digital Heritage.org*, 2009, https://digitalheritage.org/2010/08/.

70. Some Eastern Band of Cherokee Indians refer to the land as Qualla Boundary, using the Cherokee word. National Congress of American Indians, "Eastern Band of Cherokee Indians in North Carolina," https://www.ncai.org/tribal-vawa/sdvcj-today/.

71. Definitions above from "Meld," Dictionary.com, https://www.dictionary.com/browse/meld, and Robert L. Wolke, "Melted? Melded? Mixed Up?" *Washington Post*, March 19, 2003, https://www.washingtonpost.com/archive/lifestyle/food/2003/03/19.

72. Travis Milton, unpublished interview with Ashli Quesinberry Stokes and Wendy Atkins-Sayre, October 16, 2020.

73. Ray, "Migration," 209.

74. Carstarphen et al., "Rhetoric, Race, and Resentment," 257.

75. Keia Mastrianni, "Chef Ashleigh Shanti Brings History, Memory, and the Art of Gathering to the Table," *Southern Living*, October 13, 2022, https://www.southernliving.com/food/. As noted, Shanti has since left this restaurant and is now working to promote African American–owned restaurants.

76. Mackensy Lunsford, "Ashleigh Shanti Steps Down from Benne on Eagle with Plans to Create Restaurant Group," *Citizen Times*, November 20, 2020, https://www.citizen-times.com/story/news/local/2020/11/20//3778838001/.

77. Uncle Nearest, Inc., "Uncle Nearest Premium Whiskey," https://unclenearest.com/.

78. Fawn Weaver, "Uncle Nearest Premium Whiskey: Fawn Weaver," *How I Built This,* an NPR podcast hosted by Guy Raz, October 4, 2021. See URL for more information—https://www.npr.org/2021/10/01/1042481944/.

79. Weaver, "Uncle Nearest."

80. Leticia Ruiz, unpublished interview with Ashli Quesinberry Stokes, September 18, 2020.

81. Mohsin and Kaitlin Kazmi, unpublished interview with Ashli Quesinberry Stokes, December 5, 2020.

82. Karmen George, unpublished interview with Ashli Quesinberry Stokes, November 3, 2020.

83. Christina Gardner, unpublished interview with Ashli Quesinberry Stokes, November 3, 2020.

84. Tennessee Department of Tourist Development, "Soundtrack of America Made in Tennessee," https://www.tn.gov/tourism/news/2018/2/8/.

85. Spoel and Derkatch, "Resilience."

86. James, *Resilience and Melancholy.*

87. Herrman et al., "What is Resilience?"; Walker and Cagle, "Resilience," https://pubs.lib.uiowa.edu/poroi/article/id/3343/.

88. McGreavy, "Resilience as Discourse;" Bean et al., "This is London;" Pezzullo, "Contaminated Children," http://muse.jhu.edu/article/565698.

89. Stormer and McGreavy, "Thinking Ecologically."

90. Rodriguez and Opel, "Addressing the Social Determinants of Health," https://pubs.lib.uiowa.edu/poroi/article/id/3341/.

91. Paliewicz, "Bent but Not Broken."

92. Spoel and Derkatch, "Resilience as Discourse," 3.

93. McGreavy, "Resilience as Discourse;" Stormer and McGreavy, "Thinking Ecologically;" McGreavy, "It's just a cycle," https://pubs.lib.uiowa.edu/poroi/article/id/3344/.

94. Bruce, "Challenging National Borders," 222.

CHAPTER 2: *DUALCHAS,* CONNECTION, AND FOOD MIGRATION IN APPALACHIA'S CULINARY TRADITION

1. Samantha West, "Who Was Jenny Wiley?" Prestonburg, Kentucky Tourism, https://prestonsburgky.org/.

2. Denise Smith, "Will the Real Jenny Wiley Please Tell Her Story?" Appalachian Heart Wood, February 7, 2014, https://appalachianheartwood.blogspot.com/2014/02/.

3. Ray and McCain, "Personal Identity."

4. Ray, "'Y'all Come!"

5. Austin, "Narratives of Power."

6. Blair Bowman, "Trouble with Terroir," *Scottishfield*, March 26, 2021, https://www.pressreader.com/uk/scottish-field/20210505/.

7. Moss and Inabinet, *Reconstructing Southern Rhetoric.*

8. Atkins-Sayre and Stokes, *City Places*; Powell, *Critical Regionalism*; Rice, "From Architectonic to Tectonics."

9. Randolph, "Making of Appalachian Mississippi."

10. Juliet Shields, "Did Sir Walter Scott Invent Scotland?" Lecture at the Museum of London, January 17, 2017, https://www.gresham.ac.uk/watch-now/.

11. Shields, "Walter Scott."

12. Ray, "Y'all Come," https://www.gresham.ac.uk/watch-now/; "About Ulster Scots Research," Ulster University, https://www.ulster.ac.uk/research/topic/english/.

13. Wilson, "Material Culture," 194.

14. Vats, "Racechange;" Bowman, "Tracing Mary Queen of Scots"; Lindenfeld, "Visiting the Mexican American Family"; Urry, *Tourist Gaze.*

15. Ray and McCain, "Personal Identity," 984.

16. Bowman, "Tracing Mary Queen of Scots."

17. A holiday in Scotland celebrating national poet Robert Burns that is now celebrated in a variety of Scottish diaspora communities. Ray, *Highland Heritage*.

18. Clukey, "White Troubles;" Ray, *Highland Heritage*.

19. Anderson, *Imagined Communities*.

20. Ray, *Highland Heritage*, 151–52.

21. Bowman, "Tracing Mary Queen of Scots."

22. Long, *Culinary Tourism*, 20.

23. Vats, "Racechange," 125.

24. Timothy and Amos, "Understanding Heritage Cuisine and Tourism."

25. Farmelo, "Another History of Bluegrass," 198.

26. Chavez, *Queer Migration Politics*; Lechuga and de la Garza, "Forum," 38; De-Chaine, *Border Rhetorics*.

27. Flores, "Constructing Rhetorical Borders;" Ono and Sloop, *Shifting Borders*; Chavez, "Queer Migration Politics."

28. Gupta, "A Different History," 41.

29. Knight and Shipman, "Food in Contemporary Migration Experiences."

30. Ryan et al., "'Must Have Been the Chinese I Ate,'" 316; Buettner, "'Going for an Indian.'"

31. Drymon, *Scotch Irish Foodways*.

32. Webb-Sunderhaus, "Keep the Appalachian."

33. Olson, "Agricultural Themes," 64.

34. Van Wagenen, *Golden Age of Homespun*.

35. Anson Mills, "Anson Mills," http://ansonmills.com.

36. We use the Scottish spelling (whisky) in this chapter to discuss the historical tracings to Scotland. In other parts of the book, we use the American spelling (whiskey).

37. David Shields and Zoe Nicholson, "Old Ones: Landrace Oats of America," Carolina Gold Rice Foundation. Carolina Gold Rice Foundation, April 10, 2018, http://www.thecarolinagoldricefoundation.org/news/2018/4/10/; Nelson, *Art of Scottish-American Cooking*.

38. Shields and Nicholson, "Old Ones," http://www.thecarolinagoldricefoundation.org/news/2018/4/10/.

39. Shields and Nicholson, "Old Ones," http://www.thecarolinagoldricefoundation.org/news/2018/4/10/.

40. Drymon, *Scotch-Irish Foodways*.

41. David Shields, "Landrace Oats, The Important Historical Varieties," *Foodlore & More,* January 15, 2021, https://davidsanfordshields.substack.com/p/issue-5-grain-part-1-oats.

42. Nelson, *Art of Scottish-American Cooking*.

43. Brown, *Scottish Cookery*; Christine Knight, "Negative Stereotypes of the Scottish Diet," *Appetite*, 103, 369–76.

44. Fiona McCade, "Porridge is Key to a Long Healthy Life," *Scotsman*, January 7, 2015, https://www.scotsman.com/1516136.

45. McCade, "Porridge is the Key."

46. Kathryn Burnett, "Taste of Tradition: A Critical Examination of the Relationship between Heritage, Food, and Tourism Promotion in Scotland," *Local Food and Tourism*, World Tourism Organization, 2003, https://research-portal.uws.ac.uk/en/publications/.

47. Burns Birthplace Blog, "Land O' Cakes," March 4, 2014, https://burnsmuseum.wordpress.com/2014/03/04/.

48. Lockhart, *Scots and Their Oats*, 5.

49. Gavin Love, unpublished interview with Ashli Quesinberry Stokes, October 25, 2021.

50. Claire Finney, "Oat Revolution: Coming Soon to a Fine-Dining Table Near You," *Independent*, January 29, 2020, https://www.independent.co.uk/a9308156.html.

51. Finney, "Oat Revolution." https://www.independent.co.uk/life-style/food-and-drink/features/.

52. Drymon, *Scots-Irish Foodways in America*.

53. Drymon, *Scots-Irish Foodways in America*.

54. Pete Wells, "A Thanksgiving Lesson in a Handful of Corn," *New York Times*, November 22, 2021. https://www.nytimes.com/2021/11/22/dining/native-americans-thanksgiving-corn.html

55. Long, "Culinary Tourism," 181; Nadeem Akhtar et al., "Post-COVID Tourism: Will Digital Tourism Replace Mass Tourism?," 5352.

56. Magnolia Network, "From the Source: Corn," Season 1, Episode 6, *Magnolia Network*, https://magnolia.com/watch/show/579650dd-0a78-5fd8-9d06-1a26fa3b193c/.

57. Magnolia Network, "From the Source."

58. Magnolia Network, "From the Source."

59. Diamond, "Beyond the Festival Afterglow."

60. Drymon, *Scotch Irish Foodways in America*.

61. Richard Crossdale, "Secret Still," *Unfiltered: The Scotch Malt Whisky Society*, https://smwsa.com/pages/unfiltered-magazine; German and Adamson, "Illicit Origins."

62. Bowman, "Trouble with Terroir."

63. Valerie Schrader, "Public Memory, Affect, and the Battle of Culloden: A Rhetorical Analysis of Two Exhibits at the Culloden Visitor Centre," presented at the National Communication Association Conference, 2021.

64. Crossdale, "Secret Still."

65. Opening film at The Scotch Whisky Experience, https://www.scotchwhiskyexperience.co.uk/.

66. "The Foundation Documentary," Copper Barrel Distillery, https://copperbarrel.com/.

67. Bowman, "Trouble with Terroir."

68. Ray, *Highland Heritage.*

69. Interview with Grandfather Games attendee, July 9, 2021.

70. Anonymous interviewee, unpublished interview by Ashli Quesinberry Stokes and Wendy Atkins-Sayre, July 9, 2021.

71. Timothy and Amos, "Heritage Cuisines and Tourism."

72. Ashton Lattimore, "How a Wave of Honest History Museums is Changing Black Tourism," May 8, 2018, https://slate.com/human-interest/2018/05/.

73. Omnia Saed, "At Colonial Williamsburg, a 'Landscape of Resistance' is Thriving Once Again," *Atlas Obscura*, November 9, 2021, https://www.atlasobscura.com/articles/.

74. Omnia Saed, "Landscape of Resistance," https://www.atlasobscura.com/articles/enslaved-peoples-gardens.

75. Lattimore, "Honest History Museums."

76. De Jong and Varley, "Food Tourism Policy;" Everett, "Beyond the Visual Gaze?"

77. Pezzullo, *Toxic Tourism,* 9.

78. Murdy et al., "Role Conflict." paraphrase

79. Rappas and Baschiera, "Fabricating 'Cool' Heritage," 649; Breathnach, "Looking for the Real Me."

80. Lattimore, "Honest History Museums."

81. Moss and Inabinet, *Reconstructing Southern Rhetoric.*

CHAPTER 3: MOONSHINE MYTHOLOGIES IN
APPALACHIAN PUBLIC MEMORY

1. Rosko, "Distilling a Commercial Moonshine;" Martin, *Tourism in the Mountain South.*

2. Edward Martin, "Controversy Stirs N.C. Liquor System," *Business North Carolina*, January 1, 2022, https://businessnc.com/; Virginia Distillers Association, "Virginia Spirits," https://www.virginiaspirits.org/.

3. Erin Carson, "How Ole Smoky Distillery Made Moonshine's Illicit Past into a Tourist Draw," *CNET*, September 13, 2021, https://www.cnet.com/features/.

4. Although most of the chapter will discuss moonshine, we will also include examples of whiskey and occasionally use the words interchangeably. The two products are linked not only through the same distillation processes, but also common histories and traditions in the region; whiskey is aged moonshine, at its most basic. Moonshine is also occasionally used to refer to any illegally distilled products.

5. Hall, "Toward a Culture History."

6. Peine and Schafft, "Moonshine, Mountaineers," 108.

7. Stewart, *Moonshiners and Prohibitionists*, xii.

8. Bill Kopp, "New Documentary Dispels Myths about Moonshining," *Mountain Express*, June 25, 2021, https://mountainx.com/movies/.

9. Edge, *Potlikker Papers*, 222, 224.

10. Edge, *Potlikker Papers*, 221–22.

11. Thompson, *Spirits of Just Men*, 160.

12. Carson, "Ole Smoky Distillery."

13. Dabney, *Mountain Spirits*, xiii.

14. Thompson, *Spirits of Just Men*.

15. Thompson, *Spirits of Just Men*, 79.

16. Pierce, *Corn from a Jar*, 6–7.

17. Peine and Schafft, "Moonshine."

18. Peine and Schafft, "Moonshine," 99–100.

19. Thompson, *Spirits of Just Men*, xxix.

20. Pierce, "Jim Tom Hedrick."

21. Wiggington, *Foxfire Book*, 301, 344.

22. Thompson, *Spirits of Just Men*, xxv.

23. Mickie Meinhardt, "Stories in the Shine," *Bitter Southerner*, June 30, 2020, https://bittersoutherner.com/2020/.

24. Kosar, *Moonshine*, 22.

25. Thompson, *Spirits of Just Men*, 79.

26. Ishii, "Alcohol and Politics," 672.

27. Clay Risen, "When Jack Daniel's Failed to Honor a Slave, an Author Rewrote History," *New York Times*, August 15, 2017, https://www.nytimes.com/2017/08/15/dining/.

28. Risen, "Jack Daniel's."

29. Engelhardt, *Mess of Greens*.

30. Pierce, "Jim Tom Hedrick," 51.

31. Stewart, *Moonshiners and Prohibitionists*.

32. Thompson, *Spirits of Just Men*, 158.

33. Licensed Beverage Industries, *Incredible Moonshine*.

34. Licensed Beverage Industries, *Incredible Moonshine*, 1.

35. Licensed Beverage Industries, *Incredible Moonshine*, 5.

36. Powell, *Critical Regionalism*; Rice, *Regional Rhetorics*.

37. Phillips, "Introduction," 2.

38. Bodnar, *Remaking America*; Casey, "Public Memory."

39. Sheldon, "Public Memory."

40. Maldonado, "Commemorative (Dis)Placement," 240.

41. Maldonado, "Commemorative (Dis)Placement," 246.

42. Bodnar, *Remaking America*, 13–14.

43. Maldonado, "Commemorative (Dis)Placement," 249.

44. Blair et al., "Introduction," 7.

45. Blair et al., "Introduction," 14.

46. Lynch and Stuckey, "'This Was His Georgia,'" 392.

47. Reyes, "Introduction," 2.

48. Davis, *Laying Claim*, 9.

49. Locklear, *Appalachia on the Table*.

50. Poirot and Watson, "Memories of Freedom," 97.

51. Heuman and Langford, "Tradition and Southern Confederate Culture."

52. Edge, *Potlikker Papers*, 225.

53. Rosko, "Distilling," 352.

54. Rosko, "Distilling," 352.

55. Deathridge, "Heritage Spirits," 256.

56. Roberts, "Performing Hillbilly," 81.

57. Engelhardt, *Mess of Greens*.

58. McKeithan, "Every Ounce a Man's Whiskey?" 17.

59. Stewart, *Moonshiners and Prohibitionists*, 7.

60. Popcorn Sutton, *Me and My Likker* (Popcorn Sutton, 1999).

61. Pierce, *Corn from a Jar*, 94; Hutcheson, Neal, dir. *The Last One* (Raleigh, NC: Sucker Punch Pictures, 2008), DVD.

62. Pierce, *Corn from a Jar*, 94.

63. Edge, *Potlikker Papers*, 221.

64. Carson, "Ole Smoky Distillery."

65. Edge, *Potlikker Papers*, 221.

66. Pierce, *Corn from a Jar*, 6.

67. Pierce, "Jim Tom Hedrick;" Stewart, *Moonshiners and Prohibitionists*.

68. Deathridge, "Heritage Spirits."

69. Deathridge, "Heritage Spirits," 247.

70. Rosko, "Drinking and (Re)Making Place."

71. Rosko, "Distilling," 231.

72. Rosko, "Drinking and (Re)Making Place," 353.

73. Thompson, *Driving with the Devil*. Neal Thompson, *Driving with the Devil: Southern Moonshine, Detroit Wheels, and the Birth of NASCAR* (New York: Crown Publishing, 2007).

74. Nance, "The Foundation," https://copperbarrel.com/about-us/.

75. Edge, *Potlikker Papers*, 224.

76. "How Jack Daniel Came to Make Whiskey," Jack Daniel Distillery, https://www.jackdaniels.com/en-us/vault/.

77. Risen, "Jack Daniel's."

78. Dominique Fluker, "How Fawn Weaver Created Uncle Nearest Premium Whiskey from Hidden History," *Forbes*, March 9, 2022, https://www.forbes.com/sites/dominiquefluker/2022/03/09/.

79. Engelhardt, *Mess of Greens*, 49.

80. "Mahala Mullins' Moonshine Cabin, "Welcome to Tennessee," https://www.tnvacation.com/local/.

81. Katie Myers, "The True(ish) Story of Tennessee Moonshiner Mahalia Mullins," *West Virginia Public Broadcasting*, April 19, 2021, https://wvpublic.org/.

82. Myers, "True(ish) Story."

83. Carson, "Ole Smoky Distillery."

84. Stewart and Lippard, "Revival of Moonshine," 13.

85. Edge, *Potlikker Papers*, 223–24.

86. Stewart and Lippard, "Revival," 12.

87. Rosko, "Distilling," 233.

88. Stewart and Lippard, "Revival," 12.

89. McKeithan, "Every Ounce," 7.

90. McKeithan, "Every Ounce," 8.

91. Stewart and Lippard, "Revival of Moonshine."

92. Stewart and Lippard, "Revival of Moonshine," 1–2.

93. Edge, *Potlikker Papers*, 222.

94. Deathridge, "Heritage Spirits," 256.

95. NC Main Street & Rural Planning Center, "North Wilkesboro–George Smith," March 19, 2019, North Carolina Department of Commerce, https://www.ncmainstreetandplanning.com/post/.

96. Casey Fabris, "Virginia County Bets on Moonshine Tourism in Rural Region," November 7, 2015, *Skift,* https://skift.com/2015/11/07/.

97. Fabris, "Virginia County Bets on Moonshine Tourism," https://skift.co/2015/11/07/.

98. Rosko, "Distilling," 361.

99. Thompson, *Spirits of Just Men*, xxvii.

100. Julia Moskin, "America's First Moonshine, Applejack, Returns in Sleeker Style," *New York Times*, February 2, 2021, https://www.nytimes.com/2021/02/02/dining/drinks/applejack.html.

101. David Weintraub, "The Spirits Still Move Them," Documentary film, *Center for Culture Preservation*, 2021.

102. Maldonado, "Commemorative," 249.

103. Blair, Dickinson, and Ott, "Introduction," 7.

104. Blair, Dickinson, and Ott, "Introduction," 6.

CHAPTER 4: CREATING RESILIENT TOURISM IN APPALACHIA

1. A term coined by poet Frank X Walker to denote African American contributions to Appalachian culture. See Taylor, "Naming Affrilachia," https://enculturation.net/naming-affrilachia.

2. Stokes and Atkins-Sayre, *Consuming Identity,* 49.

3. Ryley Ober, "Tourism to the Blue Ridge Parkway Creates $1.3 Billion in Economic Benefits for 2021," *Asheville Citizen Times*, July 11, 2022. https://www.citizen-times.com/story/news/2022/07/11/.

4. Long, "Cultural Politics," 318.

5. Stokes and Atkins-Sayre, *Consuming Identity*, 33.

6. Denson, *Monuments*, 54.

7. Pezzullo, *Toxic Tourism*, 2.

8. Pezzullo, *Toxic Tourism*, 9.

9. Antelmi, "Sustainable Tourism," 96.

10. Antelmi, "Sustainable Tourism," 96.

11. Poirot and Watson, "Memories of Freedom," 112.

12. Gordon et al., "Food Justice," 311.

13. Timothy and Amos, "Understanding Heritage Cuisines."

14. Vats, "Racechange;" Bowman, "Tracing Mary;" Lindenfeld, "Visiting."

15. Everett, "Vernacular Health."

16. Ray, "Y'all Come;" Vats, "Racechange."

17. De Jong and Varley, "Food Tourism Policy," 212.

18. Long, "Cultural Politics"; Ray, *Highland Heritage*, 4.

19. Burke, *Attitudes Toward History*, 179; Jasinski, *Sourcebook on Rhetoric*; Gatchet and King, "'I Call Him Father of us All.'"

20. Goldzwig, "LBJ;" Stewart et al., *Persuasion and Social Movements*.

21. Gatchet and King, "I Call Him Father of us All';" Hoerl, "Selective Amnesia."

22. Zappen, "Kenneth Burke," 281.

23. Gordon et al., "Food Justice," 311.

24. Hoerl, "Selective Amnesia," 179.

25. Gatchet and King, "I Call Him Father of us All," 55.

26. Gordon et al., "Food Justice," 311. In their research, the travel experiences that they are describing are food justice advocacy tours.

27. Burke, *Rhetoric of Motives*, 326.

28. We note here that the idea of authenticity is obviously problematic, but we envision travel experiences that reflect the lived experience in Appalachia, historically and today.

29. Burke, *Language as Symbolic Action*, 188; Burke, *Rhetoric of Motives*, 53.

30. Burke, *Attitudes Toward*, 180.

31. Martin, *Tourism*, xiv.

32. Martin, *Tourism*, 56.

33. Newman, "Appalachian Appellations," 360.

34. Newman, "Appalachian Appellations," 364.

35. Shaan Merchant, "This Revolutionary Chef Wants to Topple the Table," *Ozy*, January 29, 2021, https://www.ozy.com/the-new-and-the-next/416566/.

36. Monica Burton, Osayi Endolyn, and Toni Tipton-Martin, "The Legacy of Malinda Russell, the First African-American Cookbook Author," *Eater*, February 23, 2021, https://www.eater.com/22262716/.

37. Primland Resort, https://aubergeresorts.com/primland.

38. Primland Resort, https://aubergeresorts.com/primland.

39. Primland Resort, https://aubergeresorts.com/primland.

40. Blackberry Farm, https://www.blackberryfarm.com/about.

41. Blackberry Farm, https://www.blackberryfarm.com/about.

42. Blackberry Farm, https://www.blackberryfarm.com/about.

43. Martin, *Tourism*, 65.

44. Martin, *Tourism*, 66.

45. Martin, *Tourism*, xvii.

46. Martin, *Tourism*, 142.

47. Batteau, *Invention of Appalachia*, 12.

48. Presswood, *Digital Domestics*."

49. "About," Mountains of Music: Homecoming, https://mtnsofmusic.com/about/.

50. Bruce Ingram, "Meandering Around Main Street Marion, Virginia," *Smoky Mountain Living Magazine*, December 1, 2019, https://www.smliv.com/travel/.

51. The Floyd Country Store, https://www.floydcountrystore.com/.

52. Tim Thornton, "Mountains of Music Homecoming," *Virginia Living*, June 4, 2018, https://www.virginialiving.com/the-daily-post/.

53. Andrew Denson, *Monuments to Absence*, 64–65.

54. Martin, *Tourism*, 162.

55. Michael Beadle, "Scene Changes: Revised 'Unto these Hills' Garners Bigger Audiences and Mixed Reviews," *Smoky Mountain News*, September 6, 2006, https://smokymountainnews.com/archives/item/13126.

56. Jen Miller, "Frybread," *Smithsonian Magazine*, July 2008, https://www.smithsonianmag.com/arts-culture/frybread-79191.

57. Matt Peiken, "'Disruption is just the start of a shift in storytelling at the Museum of the Cherokee Indian," *Blue Ridge Public Radio*, September 13, 2022, https://www.bpr.org/arts-performance/2022-09-13/.

CHAPTER 5: COMMUNITY AND FOOD CARE RHETORIC

1. Lundy, "Crafting Asheville's Foodtopia," 224.

2. Terry, *Black Food*, 265; National Institute of Mental Health, "Caring for Your Mental Health," https://www.nimh.nih.gov/health/topics/.

3. Reese and Johnson, "We All We Got," 28; Terry, *Black Food*, 246.

4. Reese and Johnson, "We All We Got," 28.

5. Lundy, "Asheville's Foodtopia," 224.

6. Fletcher and Schumann, *Appalachia Revisited*.

7. Fletcher and Schumann, *Appalachia Revisited*; Fletcher, "(Re)introduction," 284.

8. Anglin, *Women, Power, and Dissent*; Duncan, *Worlds Apart*; Catte, *What You Are Getting Wrong*.

9. Catte, *What You Are Getting Wrong*; Fletcher and Schumann, *Appalachia Revisited*.

10. Vincent Gabrielle, "Appalachia was once the center of a multimillion-dollar international ginseng empire," *Commercial Appeal*, March 13, 2022; Ferris, *Edible North Carolina*.

11. Ferris, *Edible North Carolina*.

12. Monee Fields-White, "Leveraging Collaboration to tap into the Potential of Local Foods" *Sharable*, July 27, 2021, https://www.shareable.net/; Ferris, *Edible North Carolina*.

13. Ferris, *Edible North Carolina*, 331.

14. Ferris, *Edible North Carolina*, 261.

15. Schneider, "Good, Clean, Fair," 397.

16. Ferris, *Edible North Carolina*, 261, 329.

17. Garner, "Conflicting Messages," 2; Schneider, "Good, Clean, Fair."

18. Reese and Cooper, "Making Spaces," 451.

19. Gordon et al., "Food Justice," 302.

20. Singer et al., *Rooted Resistance*.

21. Singer et al., *Rooted Resistance*, 10.

22. Singer et al., *Rooted Resistance*, 4.

23. "New" refers to twentieth and twenty-first century interpretations that speak out against industrial agriculture and stress the need to overcome racism, sexism, and rural insularity in past agrarian discourses. See Singer et al., *Rooted Resistance*, 4.

24. Eckstein and Partlow-LeFevre, "Mythic Fragments," 215

25. Singer et al., *Rooted Resistance*, 6.

26. Vats, "Cooking Up Hashtag Activism;" Gordon et al., "Food Justice," 302.

27. Reese, *Black Food Geographies*, 134.

28. Reese, *Black Food Geographies*.

29. Singer et al., *Rooted Resistance*, 106; Zagacki, "Preserving Heritage."

30. Singer et al., *Rooted Resistance*, 108.

31. Vogler, *Scoff*.

32. Lynch and Stuckey, "This was His Georgia," 398; Newitz and Wray, *White Trash*; Hartigan, *Who Are These White People*.

33. Flynt, "Social Class," 1389.

34. DeGenaro, *Who Says?*

35. Patterson, "Alt-Country Rhetorics," 74.

36. Cloud, "Rhetoric of <Family Values>," 411.

37. Grano, "Cleansing the Superdome."

38. De Genaro, *Working Class Rhetoric*, 189.

39. Adair, "Branded with Infamy," 452.

40. Adair, "Branded with Infamy," 468.

41. Zarefsky, "President Johnson's War."

42. Zarefsky, "President Johnson's War."

43. Patterson, "Alt-Country Rhetorics," 66, 75.

44. Prody, "Call for Polycultural Arguments," 110.

45. Spoel and Derkatch, "Resilience and Self-Reliance," 13.

46. Spoel and Derkatch, "Resilience and Self-Reliance," 13, 14.

47. Spoel and Derkatch, "Resilience and Self-Reliance," 14.

48. Reese and Johnson, "We All We Got," 39.

49. McGreavy, "Resilience as Discourse," 177; Spoel and Derkatch, "Resilience and Self-Reliance," 17; Stormer and McGreavy, "Thinking Ecologically."

50. Scott, "Everyday Forms of Resistance"; White, *Freedom Farmers*.

51. White, *Freedom Farmers*.

52. Reese, "'We Will Not Perish,'" 4.

53. Young and Eckstein, "Topoi of the Lowcountry," 46, 111.

54. Prody, "Call for Polycultural Arguments," 108.

55. Young and Eckstein, "Topoi of the Lowcountry."

56. Young and Eckstein, "Topoi of the Lowcountry."

57. Schumann, "Introduction," 9.

58. Kathryn Trauth Taylor, "Naming Affrilachia: Toward Rhetorical Ecologies of Identity Performance in Appalachia," *Enculturation* 22, 2021, https://www.enculturation.net/.

59. Taylor, "Naming Affrilachia."

60. Taylor, "Naming Affrilachia."

61. Taylor, "Naming Affrilachia."

62. Taylor, "Naming Affrilachia," https://www.enculturation.net/; Calafell, "Rhetorics of Possibility."

63. Gray, "Race, Media, and the Cultivation of Concern;" Mack and McCann, "Recalling Persky," 375.

64. Mack and McCann, "Recalling Persky."

65. Mack and McCann, "Recalling Persky," 336–37.

66. Mack and McCann, "Recalling Persky," 337, 339.

67. Mack and McCann, "Recalling Persky," 342.

68. Reese and Johnson, "We All We Got," 32; Ahmed, "Affective Economies."

69. U.S. Bureau of Labor Statistics, https://www.bls.gov/opub/ted/2022/78-metropolitan-areas-had-jobless-rates-of-less-than-3-0-percent-in-june-2022.htm.

70. Marion County News, "Cornbread Festival: Where the Money is Being Used in the Community," *Marion County News*, January 22, 2020, https://www.mcnewstn.com/articles/.

71. National Cornbread Festival: A Video Memoir. https://nationalcornbread.com/about/history/.

72. National Cornbread: A Video Memoir.

73. National Cornbread: A Video Memoir.

74. National Cornbread: A Video Memoir.

75. VisitGreenvilleSC, "Research and Statistics," https://www.visitgreenvillesc.com/media/; Upstate Business Journal, https://upstatebusinessjournal.com/.

76. Mike McMillan, "Food Insecurity with Greenville County Remains a Challenge," *Greenville Journal*, https://greenvillejournal.com/; Manna Foodbank, "Children and Food Insecurity," https://www.mannafoodbank.org/.

77. Rob Cain, unpublished interview with Ashli Quesinberry Stokes and Wendy Atkins-Sayre, June 8, 2021.

78. Rob Cain, unpublished interview with Ashli Quesinberry Stokes and Wendy Atkins-Sayre, June 8, 2021.

79. Madi Holtzman, unpublished interview with Ashli Quesinberry Stokes, September 9, 2022.

80. Anonymous interviewee, unpublished interview with Ashli Quesinberry Stokes, September 11, 2022; quotation taken from sign in the Welcome Table dining area.

81. Quotation taken from sign in the Welcome Table dining area.

82. Heading quote from Tyson Sampson, unpublished interview with Ashli Quesinberry Stokes and Wendy Atkins-Sayre, May 10, 2021.

83. Ana Henry, "Cherokee Nation Heirloom Garden and Seed Bank," ArcGis Online, April 29, 2021, https://storymaps.arcigs.com/stories.

84. Christopher Flavelle and Kalen Goodluck, "Dispossessed, Again: Climate Change Hits Native Americans Especially Hard," *New York Times*, October 28, 2021, https://www.nytimes.com/2021/06/27/climate/.

85. Delle Chan, "Pioneer: How Chef Sean Sherman is Shining a Light on Native American Cuisine," *National Geographic*, August 2, 2021, https://www.nationalgeo graphic.co.uk/travel/2021/08/.

86. Lewis, "Native Food Sovereignty;" Justin Chang, "The Sioux Chef Uses Only Native Ingredients, https://www.wfdd.org/story/.

87. Ana Henry, "Cherokee Nation."

88. Nico Albert Williams, unpublished interview with Ashli Quesinberry Stokes, April 20, 2022.

89. Nico Albert Williams, unpublished interview with Ashli Quesinberry Stokes, April 20, 2022.

90. Nico Albert Williams, unpublished interview with Ashli Quesinberry Stokes, April 20, 2022.

91. Tyson Sampson, unpublished interview with Ashli Quesinberry Stokes and Wendy Atkins-Sayre, May 10, 2021.

92. Nico Albert Williams, unpublished interview with Ashli Quesinberry Stokes, April 20, 2022.

93. Nico Albert Williams, unpublished interview with Ashli Quesinberry Stokes, April 20, 2022.

94. Leading Fox, "Foreword," xi.

95. Lefler, *Under the Rattlesnake*, 5; Altman and Thomas Belt, "Cherokee Concept," 14.

96. Tyson Sampson, unpublished interview with Ashli Quesinberry Stokes and Wendy Atkins-Sayre, April 30, 2021.

97. Lundy, "Asheville's Foodtopia," 228.

98. Penniman, *Farming While Black*.

99. Penniman, *Farming While Black*, 3.

100. Coates, Ta-Nehisi, *Between the World and Me*, 5.

101. Penniman argues that 1% of farms are Black owned today. Penniman, *Farming While Black*, 7.

102. Terry, *Black Food*; Penniman, *Farming While Black*.

103. Malinda Russell, *A Domestic Cookbook, Containing a Careful Selection of Useful Receipts for the Kitchen*. Paw Paw, Michigan, 1866. Please note that this is an online resource for the first known cookbook of an African American. Please see: https://catalog.hathitrust.org/Record/005633422

104. Terry, *Black Food*, 3; Toni Tipton Martin, "The Mystery of Malinda Russell" (Lecture, Malinda Russell Dinner, Asheville, NC, September 10, 2022).

105. Penniman, *Farming While Black*, 3.

106. Ronni Lundy, "The Mystery of Malinda Russell" (Lecture, Malinda Russell Dinner, Asheville, NC, September 10, 2022).

107. Conley and Eckstein, *Cookery*, 13.

108. Hall, "Foodless Neighborhood," 126, 130.

109. Penniman, *Farming While Black*, 301.

110. Bryant Terry, *Black Food*.

111. Terry, *Black Food*, 240–41.

112. Penniman, *Farming While Black*, 181; Terry, *Black Food*, 245, 265.

113. Terry, *Black Food*, 247.

114. Ari Shapiro, "Some Compare Today's Political Divide to the Civil War. But What about the 1960s?" *All Things Considered*, National Public Radio, September 30, 2022, https://www.npr.org/2022/09/20/1124142684/; Michael Martin, "How Those Who Represent the Minority of Americans Hold Enough Power to Stop Policies," *All Things Considered*, September 25, 2022, https://www.npr.org/2022/09/25/1125024736/.

115. Flaccavento, *Building a Healthy Economy*, 237.

116. Tom Lee, "The Dreamingest, Wishingest Visionairies Ever," *Bitter Southerner*, December 1, 2020, https://bittersoutherner.com/feature/2020/.

117. Mack and McCann, "'Strictly an Act of Street Violence.'"

118. Cynthia Greenlee, "Cornbread and Contemplation: My Restaurant Reckoning in Asheville, North Carolina," *Charlotte (NC) Observer*, June 7, 2022, https://www.charlotteobserver.com/detour/article262175852.html.

119. Reese, "We Will Not Perish," 421.

120. Reese, "We Will Not Perish," 421.

121. Jodi Helmer, Black Farmers Markets Grow in North Carolina, *Carolina Public Press*, July 27, 2022, https://carolinapublicpress.org/55308/.

122. Kormann, "How Owamni Became the Best New Restaurant in the United States, *New Yorker*, September 12, 2022, https://www.newyorker.com/magazine/2022/09/19/.

123. Hanganu-Bresch, "Rhetoric of Food."

124. Tamia Dane, "Afrolachian Agriculture: Bringing People Closer to Food," Southern Appalachian Highlands Conservancy, https://appalachian.org/.

125. Hanganu-Bresch, "Rhetoric of Food."

126. Trozzo et al., "Forest Food;" Flora et al., *Rural Communities*.

127. Greden, "Farm and Food Tourism," 187.

128. Reese, Ashante, *Feeding the Crisis*," 143.

CHAPTER 6: DIGGING DEEPER INTO APPALACHIA'S STORIES OF RESILIENCE

1. Massey, "Rhetoric of the Real."

2. Wenrich and Lewis, *Sylvatus*.

3. Wenrich and Lewis, *Sylvatus*.

4. Hilliard, *Making Our Future*, 209.

5. Hilliard, *Making Our Future*.

6. Rae Johnson, "Two Months After Floods hit Eastern Kentucky, Appalachian Arts Festival is a Space to Heal," *Courier Journal*, September 29, 2022, https://www .courier-journal.com/.

7. Davis et al., "Decolonizing Regions."

8. North Carolina Humanities, *Mountain Legacies: Exploring Appalachia Culture* event. https://nchumanities.org/grantee-spotlight-transylvania-heritage-museum/.

9. Kevin West, "Discover Appalachian Cuisine, Craft Distilleries, and Music History on a Tennessee Road Trip," *Travel and Leisure*, August 20, 2022, https://www .travelandleisure.com/trip-ideas/road-trips/tennessee.

10. Shayla Martin, "36 Hours: Asheville," *New York Times*, May 4, 2023, https:// www.nytimes.com/interactive/2023/05/04/travel/.

11. Blake Becker, "Building Brotherhood for Black Asheville," *MountainXpress*, August 3, 2022, https://mountainx.com/food/.

12. Emily Hilliard, *Making Our Future*.

13. Emily Hilliard, *Making Our Future*, 216.

14. Emily Hilliard, *Making Our Future*, 13.

15. Maldonado, "Commemorative (Dis)Placement;" Middleton et al., "Articulating Rhetorical Field Methods."

16. Emily Hilliard, *Making Our Future*.

17. Emily Hilliard, *Making Our Future*, 12.

18. Emily Hilliard, *Making Our Future*.

19. Emily Hilliard, *Making Our Future*; Hilliard, 18.

20. Jennifer Bailey, unpublished interview with Ashli Quesinberry Stokes, December 3, 2020.

21. Woods et al., "Matter of Regionalism," 345.

22. Powell, *Critical Regionalism*, 34; Entrikin, *Betweenness of Place*, 40.

23. Powell, *Critical Regionalism*, 35.

24. Powell, *Critical Regionalism*.

25. Billings et al., *Confronting Appalachian Stereotypes*; Powell, *Critical Regionalism*, 61.

26. Powell, *Critical Regionalism*, 66.

27. David Weintraub, "Seeing the Future through the Eyes of the Past," *Blue Ridge Now*, July 26, 2013, https://www.blueridgenow.com/story/news/2013/07/28/.

28. Ella Adams, "Through Ella's Eyes: Boone Needs Sustainable Tourism," *Appalachian*, October 10, 2022, https://theappalachianonline.com/.

29. Here We Grow: Case Studies, "A Tourism Boost Through Placemaking and Partnerships in Western Carolina," Here We Grow NC, https://herewegrownc.org/case-studies/.

30. Flaccavento, *Building a Healthy Economy*, 86.

31. Terry, *Black Food*, 271.

32. Na'puti, "Speaking of Indigeneity."

33. Sherman et al., *Sioux Chef's Indigenous Kitchen*, 9.

34. Garringer, "Well, We're Fabulous." https://www.southerncultures.org/article/well-fabulous-appalachians-fabulachians/.

35. Here and Now, "Black Bluegrass Musician Arnold Schultz's Forgotten Legacy," *NPR*, September 27, 2022, https://www.npr.org/2022/09/27/1125400579/.

36. Alison Stine, "Appalachia's Front Porch Network is a Lifeline," *Resilience.org*, May 28, 2020, https://www.resilience.org/stories/2020-05-28/. Nic Paget-Clarke, "Health Wagon in the Appalachian Mountains," *In Motion Magazine*, November 16, 1997, https://www.inmotionmagazine.com/sbk.html.

37. Joseph Lamour, "Exclusive: Viral Country Fair Legend is Coming out with a Cookbook," *Today*, September 27, 2022, https://www.today.com/food/news/.

38. Sean Sherman, "Owamni Sweet Potatoes with Maple-Chile Crisp," *Food and Wine*, Oct. 18, 2022, https://www.foodandwine.com/recipes/.

39. United Nations Food and Agriculture Organization, "Young People Reconnecting to Ancestral Food Systems," United Nations Food and Agriculture Organization, February 10, 2022, https://www.fao.org/fao-stories/article/en/c/1471279/.

40. Sam Briger, "The Sioux Chef Uses Only Native Ingredients, but isn't Cooking Like it's 1491." *Fresh Air*, NPR.org, https://www.npr.org/2022/10/24/1130505141/.

41. Delia Jo Ramsey, "Step Inside Sean Brock's Artful and Ambitious New Dining Destination, Audrey," *Eater Nashville*, October 12, 2021, https://nashville.eater.com/2021/10/12/22721919/.

42. Staff Reports, "Maryville College Welcoming New Hospitality Major Focused on Southern Appalachia," *Daily Times*, June 5, 2022, https://www.thedailytimes.com/news.

43. Tony Rehagen, "Indigenous Brewers Tackle Hops and History with Native Craft Beer," *Bloomberg*, October 24, 2022, https://www.bloomberg.com/news/articles/2022-10-24/.

44. Entrikin, *Betweenness of Place*, 5; Powell, *Critical Regionalism*.

45. Emily Taylor, "Let's Imagine the South as a Place for Feminism," *Ms. Magazine*, October 13, 2022, https://msmagazine.com/2022/10/13/

WORKS CITED

Adair, Vivyan. "Branded with Infamy: Inscriptions of Poverty and Class in the United States." *Signs* 27, no. 2 (2002): 451–71. https://doi.org/10.1086/495693.

Ahmed, Sarah. "Affective Economies." *Social Text* 22, no. 2 (2004): 117–39. https://doi.org/10.1215/01642472-22-2_79–117.

Akhtar, Nadeem, Nohman Khan, Muhammad Mahroof Khan, Shagufta Ashraf, Muhammad Saim Hashmi, Muhammad Muddassar Khan, and Sanil S. Hishan. "Post-COVID 19 Tourism: Will Digital Tourism Replace Mass Tourism?" *Sustainability* 13, no. 10 (2021): 5352. https://doi.org/10.3390/su13105352.

Altman, Heidi, and Thomas Belt. "The Cherokee Concept of Well-Being." In *Under the Rattlesnake: Cherokee Health and Resiliency*, edited by Lisa Lefler, 9–22. Tuscaloosa: University of Alabama Press, 2009.

Anderson, Benedict. *Imagined Communities: Reflections on the Origin and Spread of Nationalism*. London: Verso, 2006.

Anglin, Mary K. *Women, Power, and Dissent in the Hills of Carolina*. Urbana: University of Illinois Press, 2002.

Antelmi, Donella. "Sustainable Tourism: A New Rhetoric in the Language of Tourism." In *Strategies of Adaptation in Tourist Communication*, edited by Gudrun Held, 95–119. Leiden: Brill, 2018.

Atkins-Sayre, Wendy, and Ashli Quesinberry Stokes, eds. *City Places, Country Spaces: Rhetorical Explorations of the Urban/Rural Divide*. New York: Peter Lang, 2020.

Austin, David. "Narratives of Power: Historical Mythologies in Contemporary Quebec and Canada." *Race & Class* 52, no. 1 (2010): 19–32. https://doi.org/10.1177/0306396810371759.

Balestier, Courtney. "Eating to Go." In *The Food We Eat, The Stories We Tell: Contemporary Appalachian Tables*, edited by Elizabeth S. D. Engelhardt, Lora E. Smith, and Ronni Lundy, 98–112. Athens: Ohio University Press, 2019.

Bates, Benjamin R. "Circulation of the World War II/Holocaust Analogy in the 1999 Kosovo Intervention: Articulating a Vocabulary for International Conflict." *Journal of Language and Politics* 8, no. 1 (2009): 28–51. https://doi 10.1075/jlp.8.1.03bat.

Batteau, Allen. *Invention of Appalachia*. Tucson: University of Arizona Press, 1990.

Bean, Hamilton, Lisa Keranen, and Margaret Durfy. "'This is London:' Cosmopolitan Nationalism and the Discourse of Resilience in the Case of the 7/7 Terrorist Attacks." *Rhetoric & Public Affairs* 14, no. 3 (2011): 427–64. https://doi.10.1353/rap.2011.0018.

Billings, Dwight. "Introduction." In *Confronting Appalachian Stereotypes: Back Talk from an American Region,* edited by Dwight B. Billings Norman Gurney, and Katherine Ledford, 3–20. Lexington: University of Kentucky Press, 1999.

Billings, Dwight B., Norman Gurney, and Katherine Ledford, eds. *Confronting Appalachian Stereotypes: Back Talk from an American Region.* Lexington: University of Kentucky Press, 1999.

Billings, Dwight B., and Ann E. Kingsolver, eds. *Appalachia in Regional Context: Place Matters.* Lexington: University Press of Kentucky, 2018.

Billings, Dwight B., Mary Beth Pudup, and Altina Laura Waller. "Introduction: Taking Exception with Exceptionalism." In *Appalachia in the Making: The Mountain South in the Nineteenth Century,* edited by Mary Beth Pudup, Dwight B. Billings, and Altina L. Waller, 1–24. Chapel Hill: University of North Carolina Press, 1995.

Black, Jason. "Native Authenticity, Rhetorical Circulation, and Neocolonial Decay: The Case of Chief Seattle's Controversial Speech." *Rhetoric and Public Affairs,* 15, no. 4 (2012): 635–45.

Blair, Carole, Greg Dickenson, and Brian L. Ott. "Introduction." In *Places of Public Memory: The Rhetoric of Museums and Memorials,* edited by Greg Dickinson, Carole Blair, and Brian L. Ott, 1–55. Tuscaloosa: University of Alabama Press, 2010.

Blethen, Tyler H., and Curtis W. Wood Jr. *From Ulster to Carolina: The Migration of the Scotch-Irish to Southwestern North Carolina.* Chapel Hill: University of North Carolina Press, 1998.

Bodnar, John. *Remaking America: Public Memory, Commemoration, and Patriotism in the Twentieth Century.* Princeton, NJ: Princeton University Press, 1992.

Boerboom, Samuel. *The Political Language of Food.* London: Lexington Books, 2015.

Bostdorff, Denise M. "Public Address Scholarship and the Effects of Rhetoric." *Western Journal of Communication* 84, no. 3 (2020): 349–64. https://doi:10.1080/10570314.2019.1702713.

Bowman, Michael S. "Tracing Mary Queen of Scots." In *Places of Public Memory: The Rhetoric of Museums and Memorials,* edited by Greg Dickinson, Carole Blair, and Brian L. Ott. 191–215. Tuscaloosa: University of Alabama Press, 2010.

Breathnach, Teresa. "Looking for the Real Me: Locating the Self in Heritage Tourism." *Journal of Heritage Tourism* 1, no 2 (2006):100–20. https://doi.org/10.2167/jht009.0.

Brown, Catherine. *Scottish Cookery.* Edinburgh: Birlinn Books, 2013.

Brown, Joyce Compton, and Les Brown. "Discourse of Food as Cultural Translation and Empowering Voice in Appalachian Women During the Outmigration Process." *Journal of Appalachian Studies* 7, no. 2 (2011): 315–29.

Bruce, Caitlin Frances. "Challenging National Borders and Local Genre Forms: Declaration of Immigration as Volatile Cultural Text." *Public Art Dialogue* 6, no. 2 (2016): 206–27. https://doi.org/10.1080/21502552.2016.1205398.

Buettner, Elizabeth. "'Going for an Indian': South Asian Restaurants and the Limits of Multiculturalism in Britain." *Journal of Modern History* 80, no. 4 (2008): 865–901. https://doi.org/10.1086/591113.

Burke, Kenneth. *Attitudes Toward History.* Los Altos, CA: Hermes Publications, 1959.

———. *Language as Symbolic Rhetoric.* Berkeley: University of California Press, 1966.

———. *Rhetoric of Motives.* Berkeley: University of California Press, 1950.

Burton, Monica, Osayi Endolyn, and Toni Tipton-Martin, "Legacy of Malinda Russell, the First African-American Cookbook Author," *Eater,* February 23, 2021, https://www.eater.com/22262716/malinda-russell-author-a-domestic-cookbook.

Buzzanell, Patrice. "Organizing Resilience as Adaptive-transformational Tensions." *Journal of Applied Communication Research* 46, no. 1 (2018): 14–18. https://doi.org/10.1080/00909882.2018.1426711.

Buzzanell, Patrice, and Lynn H. Turner. "Crafting Narratives for Family Crises: Communicative Behaviors Associated with Effectively Managing Job Loss." In *Communication for Families in Crisis: Theories, Methods, Strategies,* edited by Fran C. Dickson, and Lynne Webb, 281–306. Cresskill: Hampton Press, 2012.

Calafell, B. M. "Rhetorics of Possibility: Challenging the Textual Bias of Rhetoric through the Theory of the Flesh." In *Rhetorica in Motion: Feminist Rhetorical Methods and Methodologies,* edited by Ellen E. Schell and K. J. Dawson, 104–17. Pittsburgh: University of Pittsburgh Press, 2010.

Cambridge dictionary. https://dictionary.cambridge.org/us/.

Carstarphen, Meta G., et al. "Rhetoric, Race, and Resentment: Whiteness and the New Days of Rage." *Rhetoric Review* 36, no. 4 (2017): 255–347. https://doi.org/10.1080/07350198.2017.1355191.

Casey, Edward S. "Public Memory in Place and Time." In *Framing Public Memory,* edited by Kendall R. Phillips, 17–44. Tuscaloosa: University of Alabama Press, 2004.

Catte, Elizabeth. *What You Are Getting Wrong About Appalachia.* Cleveland, OH: Belt Publishing, 2018.

Charland, Maurice. "Constitutive Rhetoric: The Case of the Peuple Quebecois." *Quarterly Journal of Speech* 73, no. 2 (1987): 133–50. https://doi.org/10.1080/00335638709383799.

Chavez, Karma. *Queer Migration Politics.* Champaign: University of Illinois Press, 2013.

Cloud, Dana. "Rhetoric of <Family Values>: Scapegoating, Utopia, and the Privatization of Social Responsibility." *Western Journal of Communication* 62, no. 4 (1998): 387–419. https://doi.org/10.1080/10570319809374617.

Clukey, Amy. "White Troubles: The Southern Imaginary in Northern Ireland 2008–2016." *Arizona Quarterly: A Journal of American Literature, Culture, and Theory* 73, no. 4 (2017): 61–92. https://doi.org/10.1353/arq.2017.0021.

Conley, Donovan, and Justin Eckstein, eds. *Cookery: Food Rhetorics and Social Production.* Tuscaloosa: University of Alabama Press, 2020.

Cooley, Angela Jill. "Southern Food Studies: An Overview of Debates in the Field." *History Compass* 16, no. 10 (2018): e12490. https://doi.org/10.1111/hic3.12490.

———. *To Live and Die in Dixie: The Evolution of Urban Food Culture in the Jim Crow South.* Athens: University of Georgia Press, 2015.

Coomes, Steve. *Country Ham, A Southern Tradition of Hogs, Salt, and Smoke.* Mount Pleasant: History Press, 2014.

Cramer, Janet M., Carlnita Greene, and Lynn M. Walter, eds. *Food as Communication: Communication as Food*. New York: Peter Lang, 2011.

Cunningham, Rodger. *Apples on the Flood: Minority Discourse and Appalachia*. Knoxville: University of Tennessee Press, 1991.

———. "Writing on the Cusp: Double Alterity and Minority Discourse in Appalachia." In *Future of Southern Letters*, edited by Jefferson Humphries and John Lowe, 41–53. Oxford: Oxford University Press, 1996.

Dabney, Joseph Earl. *Mountain Spirits: A Chronicle of Corn Whiskey from King James' Ulster Plantation to America's Appalachians and the Moonshine Life*. New York: Charles Scribner's Sons, 1974.

Daniels, Shea. "Stay Here Anyway." *Journal of Appalachian Studies* 20, no. 2 (2014): 136–38. https://doi: 10.5406/jappastud.20.2.0136.

Davis, Patricia G. *Laying Claim: African American Cultural Memory and Southern Identity*. Tuscaloosa: University of Alabama Press, 2016.

Davis, Patricia, Brandon Inabinet, Christina L. Moss, and Carolyn B. Walcott. "Decolonizing Regions." *Rhetoric & Public Affairs* 24, no. 1–2 (2021): 349–64. https://doi.org/10.14321/rhetpublaffa.24.1–2.0349.

de Jong, Anna, and Peter Varley. "Food Tourism Policy: Deconstructing Boundaries of Taste and Class." *Tourism Management* 60 (2017): 212–22. https://doi.org/10.1016/j.tourman.2016.12.009.

Deathridge, Kristen Baldwin. "Heritage Spirits in Heritage Spaces." In *Modern Moonshine: The Revival of White Whiskey in the Twenty-first Century*, edited by Cameron D. Lippard and Bruce E. Stewart, 243–60. Morgantown: West Virginia University Press, 2019.

DeChaine, Robert. *Border Rhetorics: Citizenship and Identity on the US-Mexico Frontier*. Tuscaloosa: University of Alabama Press, 2012.

DeGenaro, William, ed. *Who Says? Working-Class Rhetoric, Class Consciousness, and Community*. Pittsburgh: University of Pittsburgh Press, 2007.

Denson, Andrew. *Monuments to Absence: Cherokee Removal and the Contest over Southern Memory*. Chapel Hill: University of North Carolina Press, 2017.

Depew, David. "Introduction to POROI 15.1: Special Issue on Resilience Rhetorics." *Poroi* 15, 1 (2020). https://doi.org/10.14321/rhetpublaffa.24.1–2.0349.

Diamond, Heather. "Beyond the Festival Afterglow." In *American Aloha: Cultural Tourism and the Negotiation of Tradition*, edited by Heather A. Diamond, 175–212. Honolulu: University of Hawai'i Press, 2008.

Dickinson, Greg. "Space, Place, and the Textures of Rhetorical Criticism." *Western Journal of Communication* 84, no. 3 (2020): 297–313. https://doi.org/10.1080/10570314.2019.1672886.

Drymon, M. M. *Scotch Irish Foodways in America: Recipes from History*. New York: Wythe Avenue Press, 2009.

Dubisar, Abby, and Kathleen Hunt. "Teaching Ethos from the Dumpster: Dive and

Food Waste Rhetoric." *Communication Teacher* 32, no. 2 (2017): 76–81. https://doi.org/10.1080/17404622.2017.1372597.

Duncan, Cynthia. *Worlds Apart: Why Poverty Persists in Rural America.* New Haven: Yale University Press, 1999.

Eckstein, Justin, and Sarah Partlow-LeFevre. "Mythic Fragments & Environmental Activists: Rhetorical and Mythic Justifications for the Locavore Movement." In *Proceedings of the Eleventh Biennial Conference on Communication and the Environment,* edited by Stacey Sowards, 205–17. Cincinnati: International Environmental Communication Association.

Edge, John T. *Potlikker Papers: A Food History of the Modern South.* New York: Penguin Press, 2017.

Edge, John T., Elizabeth S. D. Engelhardt, and Ted Ownby, eds. *Larder: Food Studies Methods from the American South.* Athens: University of Georgia Press, 2013.

Egerton, John. *Southern Food at Home and on the Road.* Chapel Hill: University of North Carolina Press, 1987.

Eller, Ronald D. "Foreword." In *Confronting Appalachian Stereotypes: Back Talk from an American Region,* edited by Dwight B. Billings, Gurney Norman, and Katherine Ledford, ix–xi. Lexington: University Press of Kentucky, 1999.

Engelhardt, Elizabeth S. D. "Beyond Grits and Gravy, Appalachian Chicken and Waffles: Countering Southern Food Fetishism." *Southern Cultures* 21, no. 2 (2015): 73–83. https://www.jstor.org/stable/e26220206.

———. "Gathering Wild Greens: Foodways Lessons from Appalachia's Past." In *Appalachia in Regional Context: Place Matters,* edited by Dwight Billings and Ann E. Kingsolver, 133–54. Lexington: University Press of Kentucky, 2018.

———. "Introduction. Redrawing the Grocery: Practices and Methods for Studying Southern Food." In *Larder: Food Studies Methods from the American South,* edited by John T. Edge, Elizabeth S. D. Engelhardt, and Ted Ownby, 1–6. Athens: University of Georgia Press, 2013.

———. *A Mess of Greens: Southern Gender and Southern Food.* Athens: University of Georgia Press, 2011.

———. *Tangled Roots of Feminism, Environmentalism, and Appalachian Literature.* Athens: Ohio University Press, 2003.

———. "Trying to Get Appalachia Less Wrong: A Modest Approach." *Southern Cultures* 23, no. 1 (2017): 4–9. https://doi.org/10.1353/scu.2017.0001.

Engelhardt, Elizabeth S. D., Lora E. Smith, and Ronni Lundy, eds. *Food We Eat, The Stories We Tell: Contemporary Appalachian Tables.* Athens: Ohio University Press, 2019.

Entrikin, J. Nicholas. *Betweenness of Place: Towards a Geography of Modernity.* Baltimore: John Hopkins University Press, 1991.

Everett, Holly J. "Vernacular Health Moralities and Culinary Tourism in Newfoundland and Labrador." *Journal of American Folklore* 122, no. 483 (2009): 28–52. https://doi.org/10.2307/20487645.

Everett, Sally. "Beyond the Visual Gaze? The Pursuit of an Embodied Experience through Food Tourism." *Tourist Studies* 8, no. 3 (2009): 337–58. https://doi.org/10.1177/1468797608100594.

Farley, Jill. "Political Rhetoric of Property and Natural Resource Ownership: A Mediation on Chance, Taxation, and Appalachia." *Society and Natural Resources* 25 (2012): 127–40. https://doi.org/10.1080/08941920.2011.611964.

Farmelo, Allen. "Another History of Bluegrass: The Segregation of Popular Music in the United States, 1820–1900." *Popular Music and Society* 25, no. 1–2 (2001): 179–203. https://doi.org/10.1080/03007760108591792.

Ferris, Marcie Cohen, ed. *Edible North Carolina: A Journey Across the State of Flavor.* Chapel Hill: The University of North Carolina Press.

Ferris, Marcie Cohen. *Edible South: The Power of Food and the Making of an American Region.* Chapel Hill: University of North Carolina Press, 2014.

———. "'Stuff' of Southern Food: Food and Material Culture in the American South." In *Larder: Food Studies Methods from the American South,* edited by John T. Edge, Elizabeth S. D. Engelhardt, and Ted Ownby, 276–311. Athens: University of Georgia Press, 2013.

Flaccavento, Anthony. *Building a Healthy Economy from the Ground Up: Harnessing Real-World Experience for Transformative Change.* Lexington: University Press of Kentucky, 2016.

Fletcher, Rebecca Adkins. "(Re)introduction: The Global Neighborhoods of Appalachian Studies." In *Appalachia Revisited: New Perspectives on Place, Tradition, and Progress,* edited by William Schumann and Rebecca Adkins Fletcher, 275–90. Lexington: University Press of Kentucky, 2016.

Fletcher, Rebecca Adkins, and William Schumann, eds. *Appalachia Revisited: New Perspectives on Place, Tradition, and Progress.* Lexington: University Press of Kentucky, 2016.

Flora, Cornelia Butler, Jan Flora, and Stephen Gasteyer, eds. *Rural Communities: Legacy and Change.* New York: Routledge, 2016.

Flores, Lisa A. "Constructing Rhetorical Borders: Peons, Illegal Aliens, and Competing Narratives of Immigration." *Critical Studies in Media Communication* 20, no. 4 (2003): 362–87. https://doi.org/10.1080/0739318032000142025.

Flynt, J. Wayne. "Social Class." In *Encyclopedia of Southern Culture,* edited by Charles Reagan Wilson and William Ferris, 1383–430. Chapel Hill: University of North Carolina Press, 1989.

Frye, Joshua, and Michael Bruner. *Rhetoric of Food: Discourse, Materiality, and Power.* New York: Routledge, 2012.

Garner, Benjamin. "Conflicting Messages: The Visual Rhetoric of Slow Food." *Communication Today* 6, no. 2 (2015): 112–19.

Garringer, Rachel. "Well, We're Fabulous and We're Appalachians, so We're Fabulachians." *Southern Cultures* 23, no. 1 (2017): 79–91. https://doi.org/10.1353/scu.2017.0006.

Gatchet, Roger Davis, and Stephen A. King, "'I Call Him Father of us All': Vicarious

Transcendence at the B. B. King Museum and Delta Interpretive Center." *Communication and Critical/Cultural Studies* 15, no. 1 (2018): 53–69. https://doi.org/10.1080/14791420.2018.1434315.

German, Kieran, and Gregor Adamson. "Distilling in the Cabrach, c. 1800–1850: The Illicit Origins of the Scotch Whisky Industry." *Journal of Scottish Historical Studies* 39, no. 2 (2019): 146–65.

Goldthwaite, Melissa A. *Food, Feminisms, Rhetorics.* Carbondale: Southern Illinois University Press, 2017.

Goldzwig, Steven R. "LBJ, the Rhetoric of Transcendence, and the Civil Rights Act." *Rhetoric & Public Affairs* 6, no. 1(2003): 25–53. https://www.jstor.org/stable/41939808.

Gordon, Constance, Phaedra C. Pezzullo, and Michelle Gabrieloff-Parish. "Food Justice Advocacy Tours: Remapping Rooted, Regenerative Relationships through Denver's 'Planting Just Seeds." In *Rhetoric of Social Movements: Networks, Power, and New Media,* edited by Nathan Crick, 299–316. New York: Routledge, 2020.

Grano, Daniel. "Cleansing the Superdome: The Paradox of Purity and Post-Katrina Guilt." *Quarterly Journal of Speech* 97, no. 2 (2011): 201–23. https://doi.org/10.1080/00335630.2011.560175.

Gray, Herman. "Race, Media, and the Cultivation of Concern." *Communication and Critical/Cultural Studies* 10, no. 2–3 (2013): 253–58. https://doi:10.1080/14791420.2013.821641.

Greden, Matthews. "Farm and Food Tourism as a Strategy for Linking Rural and Urban Land, People, and Place: The Case of Western North Carolina." In *Linking Urban and Rural Tourism: Strategies in Sustainability,* edited by Susan L. Slocum and Carol L. Kline, 187–201. Wallingford: CAB International, 2017.

Green, Rayna. "Mother Corn and the Dixie Pig: Native Food in the Native South." In *Larder: Food Studies Methods from the American South,* edited by John T. Edge, Elizabeth S. D. Engelhardt, and Ted Ownby, 155–65. Athens: University of Georgia University Press, 2013.

Grey, Stephanie Houston. "American Food Rhetoric." In *Encyclopedia of Food and Agricultural Ethics,* edited by Paul B. Thompson, 129–34. Dordrecht: Springer Press, 2014.

———. "A Growing Appetite: The Emerging Critical Rhetoric of Food Politics." *Rhetoric & Public Affairs* 19, no. 2 (2016): 307–20. https://doi.org/10.14321/rhetpublaffa.19.2.0307.

Gupta, Akhil. "A Different History of the Present." In *Curried Cultures: Globalization, Food and South Asia,* edited by Krishnendu Ray and Tulasi Srinivas, 29–46. Berkeley: University of California Press, 2012.

Hall, John Whitling. "Toward a Culture History of Whiskey." *North American Culture* 2, no. 1 (1985): 49–54.

Hall, Nina Flager. "A Foodless Neighborhood in a 'Foodie' Town: Tracing Scarcity in Asheville's East End Neighborhood." *Southern Cultures* 23, no. 2 (2017): 113–33. https://doi.org/10.1353/scu.2017.0017.

Hanganu-Bresh, Cristina. "Rhetoric of Food as Medicine: Introduction to the Special Issue on the Rhetoric of Food and Health." *Rhetoric of Health & Medicine* 4, no. 2 (2022): 111–25. https://doi.org/10.5744/10.5744/rhm.2021.2001.

Hariman, Robert, and John Louis Lucaites. "Performing Civic Identity: The Iconic Photograph of the Flag Raising on Iwo Jima." *Quarterly Journal of Speech* 88, no. 4 (2002): 363–92. https://doi.org/10.1080/00335630209384385.

Harkins, Anthony. *Hillbilly: A Cultural History of an American Icon.* Oxford: Oxford University Press, 2003.

Harkins, Anthony, and Meredith McCarroll. *Appalachian Reckoning: A Region Responds to Hillbilly Elegy.* Morgantown: West Virginia Press, 2019.

Harris, Jessica. *High on the Hog: A Culinary Journey from Africa to America.* New York: Bloomsbury Press, 2011.

Hartigan, John Jr., "Who Are These White People?: 'Rednecks,' 'Hillbillies,' and 'White Trash' as Marked Racial Subjects." In *White Out: The Continuing Significance of Racism,* edited by Ashley W. Doane and Eduardo Bonilla-Silva. New York: Routledge, 2003.

Hauser, Gerard A. "Attending the Vernacular: A Plea for an Ethnographical Rhetoric." In *Readings in Rhetorical Fieldwork,* edited by Samantha Senda-Cook et al., 157–72. New York: Routledge, 2018.

Herrman, Helen., Donna E. Stewart, Natalia Diaz-Granados, Elena L. Berger, Beth Jackson, and Tracy Yuen. "What is Resilience?" *Canadian Journal of Psychiatry* 56, no. 5 (2011): 258–65.

Hess, Aaron. "Critical-Rhetorical Ethnography: Rethinking the Place and Process of Rhetoric." In *Readings in Rhetorical Fieldwork,* edited by Samantha Senda-Cook et al., 56–77. New York: Routledge, 2019.

Heuman, Amy, and Catherine Langford. "Tradition and Southern Confederate Culture: Manifesting Whiteness through Public Memory at Texas A&M University." In *Public Memory, Race, and Ethnicity,* edited by G. Mitchell Reyes, 120–44. Newcastle: Cambridge Scholars Publishing, 2010.

Hilliard, Emily. "Foreword." In *West Virginia Pepperoni Roll,* edited by Candace Nelson. Morgantown: West Virginia University Press, 2017.

———. *Making Our Future: Visionary Folklore and Everyday Culture in Appalachia.* Chapel Hill: University of North Carolina Press, 2022.

Himes, Audra, and Charles F. Moore. "Hillbilly." In *Encyclopedia of Appalachia,* edited by Rudy Abramson and Jean Haskell, 260. Knoxville: University of Tennessee Press, 2006.

Hoerl, Kristen. "Selective Amnesia and Racial Transcendence in News Coverage of President Obama's Inauguration." *Quarterly Journal of Speech* 98, no. 2 (2012): 178–202. https://doi.org/10.1080/00335630.2012.663499.

Hsiung, David C. *Two Worlds in the Tennessee Mountains: Exploring the Origins of Appalachian Stereotypes.* Lexington: University Press of Kentucky, 2014.

Huber, Patrick. "Riddle of the Horny Hillbilly." In *Dixie Emporium: Tourism, Foodways, and Consumer Culture in the American South,* edited by Anthony J. Stanonis, 69–88. Athens: University of Georgia Press, 2008.

Ishii, Izumi. "Alcohol and Politics in the Cherokee Nation Before Removal." *Ethnohistory* 50, no. 4 (2003): 671–95.

James, Robin. *Resilience & Melancholy: Pop Music, Feminism, Neoliberalism.* New Alresford: John Hunt Publishing, 2015.

Jasinski, James. *Sourcebook on Rhetoric.* Thousand Oaks: Sage Publications, 2001.

Jasinski, James, and Jennifer R. Mercieca. "Analyzing Constitutive Rhetorics: Virginia and Kentucky Resolutions and the 'Principles of '98.'" In *Handbook of Rhetoric and Public Address,* edited by Shawn J. Parry-Giles and J. Michael Hogan, 313–41. Hoboken: Wiley-Blackwell, 2010.

Jenkins, Eric S. "Modes of Visual Rhetoric: Circulating Memes as Expressions." *Quarterly Journal of Speech* 100, no. 4 (2014): 442–66. https://doi.org/10.1080/00335630.2014.989258.

Johnson, Judith. "Resilience: The Bi-dimensional Framework." In *Wiley Handbook of Positive Clinical Psychology,* edited by Alex M. Wood and Judith Johnson, 73–88. Hoboken: Wiley Publications, 2016.

Jones, Bradley M. "Producing Heritage: Politics, Patrimony, and Palatability in the Reinvention of Lowcountry Cuisine." *Food, Culture, and Society* 20, no. 2 (2017): 217–36. https://doi:10.1080/15528014.2017.1305826.

Kant-Byers, Kristin. "Revisiting Appalachian Icons in the Production and Consumption of Tourist Art." In *Appalachia Revisited: New Perspectives on Place, Tradition, and Progress,* edited by William Schumann and Rebecca Adkins Fletcher, 155–70. Lexington: University Press of Kentucky, 2016.

Kelly, Casey Ryan. *Food Television and Otherness in the Age of Globalization.* London: Lexington Books, 2017.

Kelting, Lily. "Entanglement of Nostalgia and Utopia in Contemporary Southern Food Cookbooks." *Food, Culture, & Society* 19, no. 2 (2016): 361–87. https://doi.org/10.1080/15528014.2016.1178549.

Knight, Christine. "Negative Stereotypes of the Scottish Diet: A Qualitative Analysis of Deep-fried Mars Bar References in Best Selling Newspapers in Scotland, 2011–14." *Appetite* 103 (2016): 369–76.

Knight, Christine, and Jessica Shipman. "Food in Contemporary Migration Experiences between Britain and Australia: A Duoethnographic Exploration." *Nutrition & Dietetics* 63, no. 2 (2006): 91–102. https://doi.org/10.1080/07409710.2021.1860328.

Kosar, Kevin R. *Moonshine: A Global History.* London: Reaktion Books, 2017.

Leading Fox, Susan. "Foreword." In *Under the Rattlesnake: Cherokee Health and Resiliency,* edited by Lisa J. Lefler, xi-xiii. Tuscaloosa: University of Alabama Press, 2009.

LeBesco, Kathleen, and Peter Naccarato, eds. *Edible Ideologies: Representing Food and Meaning.* Albany: State University of New York Press, 2008.

Lechuga, Michael, and Antonio Tomas de la Garza. "Forum: Border Rhetorics." *Communication and Critical/Cultural Studies* 18, no. 1 (2021): 30–40. https://doi.org/10.1080/14791420.2021.1898008.

Ledford, Katherine, Norman Gurney, and Dwight Billings. *Back Talk from Appalachia: Confronting Stereotypes.* Lexington: University Press of Kentucky, 2001.

Lee, Benjamin, and Edward LiPuma. "Cultures of Circulation: The Imaginations of Modernity." *Public Culture* 14, no. 1 (2002): 191–213. https://doi.org/10.1215/08992363-14-1-191.

Lefler, Lisa J., ed. *Under the Rattlesnake: Cherokee Health and Resiliency.* Tuscaloosa: University of Alabama Press, 2009.

Lewis, Courtney. "Native Food Sovereignty." In *Edible North Carolina: A Journey Across a State of Flavor,* edited by Marcie Ferris. Chapel Hill: University of North Carolina Press, 2022.

Licensed Beverage Industries. *Incredible Moonshine Menace.* New York: Licensed Beverage Industries, Inc., December 1967.

Lindenfeld, Laura. "Visiting the Mexican American Family: Tortilla Soup as Culinary Tourism." *Communication and Critical/Cultural Studies* 4, no. 3 (2007): 303–20. https://doi.org/10.1080/14791420701459723.

Lockhart, G. W. and William Lockhart. *Scots and Their Oats.* Edinburgh: Birlinn Publishers, 1998.

Locklear, Erica Abrams. *Appalachia on the Table: Representing Mountain Food and People.* Athens: University of Georgia Press, 2023.

———. "'A Comfort During a Hard Time': Food in Ron Rash's Poems, Stories, and Novels." In *Summoning the Dead: Critical Essays on Ron Rash,* edited by Randall Wilhelm and Zackary Vernon, 66–79. Columbia: University of South Carolina Press, 2018.

———. "Fragrant Memories: They'll Get Your Attention." *North Carolina Folklore Journal* 54, no. 1 (2007): 12–17.

———. "A Matter of Taste: Reading Food and Class in Appalachian Literature." In *Writing in the Kitchen: Essays on Southern Literature and Foodways,* edited by David A. Davis and Tara Powell, 124–42. Oxford: University of Mississippi Press, 2014.

———. "Setting Tobacco, Banquet Style." In *Food We Eat, The Stories We Tell: Contemporary Appalachian Tables,* edited by Elizabeth Engelhardt, Lora E. Smith, and Ronni Lundy, 24–45. Athens: Ohio University Press, 2019.

Long, Lucy M., ed. *Culinary Tourism.* Lexington: University Press of Kentucky, 2004.

———. "Culinary Tourism: A Folkloristic Perspective on Eating and Otherness." *Southern Folklore* 55, no. 3 (1998): 181–204.

———. "Culinary Tourism and the Emergence of an Appalachian Cuisine: Exploring the 'Foodscape' of North Carolina." *North Carolina Folklore Journal* 57, no. 1 (2010): 4–19.

———. "Cultural Politics in Culinary Tourism with Ethnic Foods." *Revista de Administração de Empresas* 58 (2018): 316–24. https://doi.org/10.1590/s0034-759020180313.

———. "Introduction." In *Culinary Tourism,* edited by Lucy M. Long, 1–19. Lexington: University Press of Kentucky, 2004.

Lundy, Ronni. "Crafting Asheville's Foodtopia: Two Decades in the Mountain South." In *Edible North Carolina: A Journey Across a State of Flavor,* edited by Marcie Ferris, 212–20. Chapel Hill: University of North Carolina Press, 2022.

———. *Sorghum's Savor.* Gainesville: University Press of Florida, 2015.

———. *Victuals: An Appalachian Journey, With Recipes.* New York: Clarkson Potter, 2016.

Lynch, John, and Mary Stuckey. "'This was His Georgia': Polio, Poverty, and Public Memory at FDR's Little White House." *Howard Journal of Communications* 28, no. 4 (2017): 390–404. https://doi.org/10.1080/10646175.2017.1315689.

Mack, Ashley Noel, and Bryan J. McCann, "Recalling Persky: White Rage and Intimate Publicity After Brock Turner." *Journal of Communication Inquiry* 43, no. 4 (2019): 372–93. https://doi.org/10.1177/0196859919867265.

Mack, Ashley Noel, and Bryan J. McCann, "'Strictly an Act of Street Violence': Intimate Publicity and Affective Divestment in the New Orleans Mother's Day Shooting." *Communication and Critical/Cultural Studies* 14, no. 4 (2017): 334–350.

Maldonado, Chandra Ann. "Commemorative (Dis)Placement: On the Limits of Textual Adaptability and the Future of Public Memory Scholarship." *Rhetoric & Public Affairs* 24, no. 1–2 (2021): 239–52. https://doi.org/10.14321/rhetpublaffa.24.1–2.0239.

Martin, C. Brenden. *Tourism in the Mountain South: A Double-Edged Sword.* Knoxville: University of Tennessee Press, 2007.

Massey, Carissa. "Rhetoric of the Real: Stereotypes of Rural Youth in American Reality Television and Stock Photography." *Discourse: Studies in the Cultural Politics of Education* 38, no. 3 (2017): 365–76. https://dx.doi.org/10.1080/01596306.2017.1306982.

McGreavy, Bridie. "'It's just a cycle': Resilience, Poetics, and Intimate Disruptions." *Poroi* 15, no. 1 (2020). https://pubs.lib.uiowa.edu/poroi/article/id/3344/.

———. "Resilience as Discourse." *Environmental Communication* 10, no. 1 (2016): 104–21. https://doi:10.1080/17524032.2015.1014390.

McKeithan, Seán S. "Every Ounce a Man's Whiskey? Bourbon in the White Masculine South." *Southern Cultures* 18, no. 1 (Spring 2012): 5–20.

McKinnon, Sara L., Robert Asen, Karma R. Chavez, and Robert Glenn Howard., eds. *Text + Field: Innovations in Rhetorical Method.* University Park: Pennsylvania State University Press, 2016.

McMurry, Andrew. "Rhetoric of Resilience." *Alternatives Journal* 36, no. 2 (2010): 20–2. https://www.jstor.org/stable/i40214267.

Middleton, Michael K., Samantha Senda-Cook, and Danielle Endres. "Articulating Rhetorical Field Methods: Challenges and Tensions," In *Readings in Rhetorical Fieldwork,* edited by Samantha Senda-Cook, et al., 35–58. New York: Routledge, 2019.

Miller, Adrian. *Soul Food: The Surprising Story of an American Cuisine One Plate at a Time.* Chapel Hill: University of North Carolina Press, 2017.

Moss, Christina L., and Brandon Inabinet. "Introduction: Reconstructing Southern Rhetoric." In *Reconstructing Southern Rhetoric,* edited by Christina L. Moss and Brandon Inabinet, 3–19. Jackson: University Press of Mississippi, 2021.

———, eds. *Reconstructing Southern Rhetoric.* Jackson: University Press of Mississippi, 2021.

Murdy, Samantha, Matthew Alexander, and Derek Bryce. "Role Conflict and Changing Heritage Practice: Ancestral Tourism in Scotland." *Journal of Marketing Management* 32, (2016): 1494–512. https://doi.org/10.1080/0267257X.2016.1181668.

Myres, Jason D. "Five Formations of Publicity: Constitutive Rhetoric From its Other Side." *Quarterly Journal of Speech* 104, no. 2 (2018): 189–212. https://doi: 10.1080/00335630.2018.1447140.

Na'puti, Tiara R. "Speaking of Indigeneity: Navigating Genealogies Against Erasure and #RhetoricSoWhite." *Quarterly Journal of Speech* 105, no. 4 (2019): 495–501. https://doi.org/10.1080/00335630.2019.1669895.

Nelson, Kay Shaw. *Art of Scottish-American Cooking.* New Orleans: Pelican Publishing, 2007.

Newitz, Annalee, and Matt Wray., eds. *White Trash: Race and Class in America.* New York: Routledge, 1996.

Newman, Joshua. "Appalachian Appellations: Tourist Geographies, Cultural Embodiment, and the Neoliberal 'Hillbilly." *International Review of Qualitative Research* 7, no. 3 (2014): 359–86. https://doi.org/10.1525/irqr.2014.7.3.359.

Obermiller, Philip J., and Michael E. Maloney. "Uses and Misuses of Appalachian Culture." *Journal of Appalachian Studies* 22, no. 1 (2016): 103–22. https://doi.org/10.5406/jappastud.22.1.0103.

Okamoto, Kristen E. "'As Resilient as an Ironweed': Narrative Resilience in Nonprofit Organizing." *Journal of Applied Communication Research* 48, no. 5 (2020): 618–36. https://doi:10.1080/00909882.2020.1820552.

Olson, Ted. "Agricultural Themes in Appalachian Folk Songs: The Farmer is the Man Who Feeds Them All." *Journal of the Appalachian Studies Association* 4 (1992): 59–68.

Ono, Kent A., and John M. Sloop. *Shifting Borders: Rhetoric, Immigration, and California's Proposition 187.* Philadelphia: Temple University Press, 2002.

Paliewicz, Nicholas S. "Bent but Not Broken: Remembering Vulnerability and Resiliency at the National September 11 Memorial Museum." *Southern Communication Journal* 82, no. 1 (2017): 1–14. https://doi.org/10.1080/1041794X.2016.1252422.

Patterson, G. "Alt-Country Rhetorics: Relearning (Trans) Activism in Rural Indiana." In *Activism and Rhetoric: Theories and Contexts for Political Engagement,* edited by Seth Kahn and Jonghwa Lee, 65–77. New York: Routledge, 2020.

Peine, Emily K., and Kai A. Schafft. "Moonshine, Mountaineers, and Modernity: Distilling Cultural History in the Southern Appalachian Mountains." *Journal of Appalachian Studies* 18, no. 2 (Spring/Fall 2012): 93–112. https://www.jstor.org/stable/23337709.

Penman, Will. "A Field-based Rhetorical Critique of Ethical Accountability." *Quarterly*

Journal of Speech 104, no. 3 (2018): 307–28. https://doi.org/10.1080/00335630.2018.14 86032.

Penniman, Leah. *Farming While Black: Soul Fire Farm's Practical Guide to Liberation on the Land.* London: Chelsea Green Publishing Company, 2018.

Pezzullo, Phaedra C. "Contaminated Children: Debating the Banality, Precarity, and Futurity of Chemical Safety." *Resilience: A Journal of the Environmental Humanities* 1, no. 2 (2014). http://muse.jhu.edu/article/565698.

———. "Resisting 'National Breast Cancer Awareness Month': The Rhetoric of Counterpublics and Their Cultural Performance." In *Readings in Rhetorical Fieldwork,* edited by Samantha Senda-Cook et al., 189–210. New York: Routledge, 2019.

———. *Toxic Tourism: Rhetorics of Pollution, Travel, and Environmental Justice.* Tuscaloosa: University of Alabama Press, 2009.

Phillips, Kendall R. "Introduction." In *Framing Public Memory,* edited by Kendall R. Phillips, 1–14. Tuscaloosa: University of Alabama Press, 2004.

Pierce, Daniel S., ed. *Corn from a Jar: Moonshining in the Great Smoky Mountains.* Gatlinburg: Great Smoky Mountains Association, 2013.

———. "Jim Tom Hedrick, Popcorn Sutton, and the Rise of the Postmodern Moonshiner." In *Modern Moonshine: The Revival of White Whiskey in the Twenty-first Century,* edited by Cameron D. Lippard and Bruce E. Stewart, 50–66. Morgantown: West Virginia University Press, 2019.

Poirot, Kristan, and Shevaun E. Watson. "Memories of Freedom and White Resilience: Place, Tourism, and Urban Slavery." *Rhetoric Society Quarterly* 45, no. 2 (2015): 91–116. https://doi.org/10.1080/02773945.2014.991879.

Powell, Douglas R. *Critical Regionalism.* Chapel Hill: University of North Carolina Press, 2007.

Presswood, Alane. *Digital Domestics: Food Blogs, Postfeminism, and the Communication of Expertise.* Lanham: Lexington Books, 2020.

Prody, Jessica M. "A Call for Polycultural Arguments: Critiquing the Monoculture Rhetoric of the Local Food Movement." *Argumentation and Advocacy* 50, no. 2 (2013): 104–19. https://doi.org/10.1080/00028533.2013.11821813.

Pudup, Mary Beth, Dwight B. Billings, and Altina L. Waller, eds. *Appalachia in the Making: The Mountain South in the Nineteenth Century.* Chapel Hill: University of North Carolina Press, 1995.

Rai, Candace, and Caroline Gottschalk Druschke, eds. *Field Rhetoric: Ethnography, Ecology and Engagement in the Places of Persuasion.* Tuscaloosa: University of Alabama Press, 2018.

Randolph, Justin. "Making of Appalachian Mississippi." *Southern Cultures* 26, no. 4 (2020): 91–109. https://doi.org/10.1353/scu.2020.0057.

Rappas, Ipek, and Stefano Baschiera. "Fabricating 'Cool' Heritage for Northern Ireland: Game of Thrones Tourism." *Journal of Popular Culture* 53, no 3 (2020): 648–66. https://doi.org/10.1111/jpcu.12926.

Ray, Celeste. "Europeans," In *New Encyclopedia of Southern Culture,* edited by Celeste Ray, 41–56. Chapel Hill: University of North Carolina Press, 2007.

———. *Highland Heritage: Scottish Americans in the American South.* Chapel Hill: University of North Carolina Press, 2015.

———. "'Thigibh' Means 'Y'all Come!': Renegotiating Regional Memories through Scottish Heritage Celebration." In *Southern Heritage on Display: Public Ritual and Ethnic Diversity within Southern Regionalism,* edited by Celeste Ray, 251–82. Tuscaloosa: University of Alabama Press, 2003.

Ray, Krishendu. "Migration, Transnational Cuisines, and Invisible Ethics." In *Food in Time and Place: The American Historical Association Companion to Food History,* edited by Paul Freedman, Joyce E. Chaplin, and Ken Abala, 209–32. Berkeley: University of California Press, 2014.

Ray, Nina M., and Gary McCain. "Personal Identity and Nostalgia for the Distant Land of Past: Legacy Tourism." *International Business & Economics Research Journal (IBER)* 11, no. 9 (2012): 977–90. https://doi.org/10.19030/iber.v11i9.7181.

Reese, Ashanté M. *Black Food Geographies: Race, Self-Reliance, and Food Access in Washington, D.C.* Chapel Hill: University of North Carolina Press, 2019.

———. "Review of *Feeding the Crisis: Care and Abandonment in America's Food Safety Net,* by Maggie Dickinson." *Food and Foodways* 30, no. 1–2 (2022): 142–44. https://doi.org/10.1080/14649365.2022.2048537.

———. "'We Will Not Perish; We're Going to Keep Flourishing': Race, Food Access, and Geographies of Self-Reliance." *Antipode* 50, no. 2 (2018): 407–24.

Reese, Ashanté M., and Dara Cooper. "Making Spaces Something Like Freedom: Black Feminist Praxis in the Re/Imagining of a Just Food System." *ACME: An International Journal for Critical Geographies* 20, no. 4 (2021): 450–59.

Reese, Ashanté M., and Symone Johnson. "We All We Got: Urban Black Ecologies of Care and Mutual Aid." *Environment and Society* 13, no. 1 (2022): 27–42.

Reyes, G. Mitchell. "Introduction: Public Memory, Race, and Ethnicity." In *Public Memory, Race, and Ethnicity,* edited by G. Mitchell Reyes, 1–14. Newcastle: Cambridge Scholars Publishing, 2010.

Rice, Jenny. "From Architectonic to Tectonics: Introducing Regional Rhetorics." *Rhetoric Society Quarterly* 42, no. 3 (2012): 201–13. https://doi.org/10.1080/02773945.2012.682831.

———. *Regional Rhetorics: Real and Imagined Places.* New York: Routledge Press, 2014.

Roberts, Mark A. "Performing Hillbilly: Redeeming Acts of a Regional Stereotype." *Appalachian Journal* 30, no. 1 (Fall 2010): 78–90.

Robertson, Sarah. *Poverty Politics: Poor Whites in Contemporary Southern Writing.* Jackson: University Press of Mississippi, 2019.

Rodriguez, Eric, and Dawn Opel. "Addressing the Social Determinants of Health: 'Vulnerable' Populations and the Presentation of Healthy People 2020." *Poroi* 15, no. 1 (2020). https://pubs.lib.uiowa.edu/poroi/article/id/3341/.

Romine, Scott. "God and the Moonpie: Consumption, Disenchantment, and the Reliably Lost Cause." In *Creating and Consuming the American South,* edited by Martyn Bone, Brian Ward, and William A. Link, 49–71. Gainesville: University Press of Florida, 2015.

Rosko, Helen M. "Distilling a Commercial Moonshine in East Tennessee: Mashing a New Type of Tourism." In *Modern Moonshine: The Revival of White Whiskey in the Twenty-first Century,* edited by Cameron D. Lippard and Bruce E. Stewart, 219–42. Morgantown: West Virginia University Press, 2019.

———. "Drinking and (re) making Place: Commercial Moonshine as Place-making in East Tennessee." *Southeastern Geographer* 57, no. 4 (2017): 351–70.

Russell, Malinda. *A Domestic Cookbook, Containing a Careful Selection of Useful Receipts for the Kitchen.* Paw Paw, Michigan, 1866. https://catalog.hathitrust.org /Record/005633422.

Ryan, Simon, Louise Edwards, and Stefano Occhipinti. "'Must Have Been the Chinese I Ate:' Food Poisoning, Migration and National Indigestion." *Continuum: Journal of Media & Cultural Studies* 13, no. 3 (1999): 315–23. https://doi.org/10.1080 /10304319909365803.

Satterwhite, Emily. *Dear Appalachia: Readers, Identity, and Popular Fiction since 1878.* Lexington: University Press of Kentucky, 2011.

———. "'That's What They're Singing About': Appalachian Heritage, Celtic Pride, and American Nationalism at the 2003 Smithsonian Folklife Festival." *Appalachian Journal* 32, no. 3 (2005): 302–38.

Sauceman, Fred. *Buttermilk and Bible Burgers: More Stories from the Kitchens of Appalachia.* Macon: Mercer University Press, 2014.

Scharp, Kristina M., Devon E. Geary, Brooke H. Wolfe, Tiffany R. Wang, and Margaret A. Fesenmaier. "Understanding the Triggers and Communicative Processes that Constitute Resilience in the Context of Migration to the United States." *Communication Monographs* 88, no. 4 (2021): 395–417. https:// doi:10.1080/03637751.2020.1856 395.

Scharp, Kristina M., Tiffany Wang, and Brooke H. Wolfe. "Communicative Resilience of First-Generation College Students During the COVID-19 Pandemic." *Human Communication Research* 48, no. 9 (2021): 1–30. https:// doi:10.1080/03637751.2020 .1856395.

Schneider, Stephen. "Good, Clean, Fair: The Rhetoric of the Slow Food Movement." *College English* 70, no. 4 (2008): 384–402.

Schumann, William. "Introduction: Place and Place-Making in Appalachia." In *Appalachia Revisited: New Perspectives on Place, Tradition, and Progress,* edited by William Schumann and Rebecca Adkins Fletcher, 1–26. Lexington: University Press of Kentucky, 2016.

Scott, James C. "Everyday Forms of Resistance." *Copenhagen Journal of Asian Studies* 4, no. 1(1989): 33–62.

Senda-Cook, Samantha, Aaron Hess, Michael K. Middleton, and Danielle Endres, eds. *Readings in Rhetorical Fieldwork.* New York: Routledge, 2019.

Shapiro, Henry D. *Appalachia on Our Mind: The Southern Mountains and Mountaineers in the American Consciousness, 1870–1920.* Chapel Hill: University of North Carolina Press, 1978.

Sharpless, Rebecca. *Grain and Fire: A History of Baking in the American South.* Chapel Hill: University of North Carolina Press, 2022.

Sheldon, Zachary. "Public Memory and Popular Culture: Biopics, #MeToo, and David Foster Wallace." *Atlantic Journal of Communication* 29, no. 2 (2021): 65–78. https://doi.org/10.1080/15456870.2020.1712603.

Sherman, Sean, and Beth Dooley. *Sioux Chef's Indigenous Kitchen.* Minneapolis: University of Minnesota Press, 2017.

Shields, David. *Southern Provisions: The Creation and Revival of a Cuisine.* Chicago: University of Chicago Press, 2015.

Singer, Ross, Stephanie Houston Grey, and Jeff Motter, eds. *Rooted Resistance: Agrarian Myth in Modern America.* Fayetteville: University of Arkansas Press, 2020.

Smith, Barbara Ellen, Stephen Fisher, Phillip Obermiller, David Whisnant, Emily Satterwhite, and Rodger Cunningham. "Appalachian Identity: A Roundtable Discussion." *Appalachian Journal* 38, no. 1 (2010): 56–76. https://www.jstor.org/stable/41320248.

Sohn, Mark F. *Appalachian Home Cooking: History, Culture, and Recipes.* Lexington: University of Kentucky Press, 2005.

Spoel, Philippa, and Colleen Derkatch. "Resilience and Self-reliance in Canadian Food Charter Discourse." *Poroi* 15, no. 1 (2020). https://10.13008/2151-2957.1298.

Spurlock, Cindy M. "Performing and Sustaining (Agri)Culture and Place: The Cultivation of Environmental Subjectivity on the Piedmont Farm Tour." In *Readings in Rhetorical Fieldwork,* edited by Samantha Senda-Cook et al., 114–27. New York: Routledge, 2019.

Staley, Kathryn L. "Identity in a Mountain Family." *Journal of Appalachian Studies* 4, no. 2 (1998): 239–53.

Stewart, Bruce. *Moonshiners and Prohibitionists.* Lexington: University Press of Kentucky, 2011.

Stewart, Bruce E., and Cameron D. Lippard. "Revival of Moonshine in Southern Appalachia and the United States." In *Modern Moonshine: The Revival of White Whiskey in the Twenty-first Century,* edited by Cameron D. Lippard and Bruce E. Stewart, 1–24. Morgantown: West Virginia University Press, 2019.

Stewart, Charles J., Craig Allen Smith, and Robert E. Denton, Jr., eds. *Persuasion and Social Movements.* Long Grove: Waveland Press, 2021.

Stokes, Ashli Quesinberry. "You Are What You Eat: Slow Food USA's Constitutive Public Relations." *Journal of Public Relations Research* 25, no. 1: (2013): 68–90. https://doi.org/10.1080/1062726X.2013.739102.

Stokes, Ashli Quesinberry, and Wendy Atkins-Sayre. *Consuming Identity: The Role of Food in Redefining the South.* Oxford: University Press of Mississippi, 2016.

———. "Southern Skillet: Creating Relational Identity to a Changing South through Food." In *Reconstructing Southern Rhetoric,* edited by Christi L. Moss and Brandon Inabinet, 230–53. Oxford: University of Mississippi Press, 2021.

Stormer, Nathan, and Bridie McGreavy. "Thinking Ecologically About Rhetoric's Ontology: Capacity, Vulnerability, and Resilience." *Philosophy & Rhetoric* 50, no. 1 (2017): 1–25. https://doi.org/10.5325/philrhet.50.1.0001.

Stuckey, Mary E. "On Rhetorical Circulation," *Rhetoric & Public Affairs* 15, no. 4 (2012): 609–12. https://doi.org/10.1353/rap.2012.0049.

Taylor, Kathryn Trauth. "Naming Affrilachia: Toward Rhetorical Ecologies of Identity Performance in Appalachia." *Enculturation* 10 (2011). https://enculturation.net/naming-affrilachia.

Terry, Bryant. *Black Food: Stories, Art, and Recipes from Across the African Diaspora [A Cookbook].* Berkeley: 4 Color Books, 2019.

Thompson, Charles D. *Spirits of Just Men: Mountaineers, Liquor Bosses, and Lawmen in the Moonshine Capital of the World.* Chicago: University of Illinois Press, 2011.

Thompson, Deborah J. "Searching for Silenced Voices in Appalachian Music." *GeoJournal* 65, no.1–2 (2006): 67–78. https://doi:10.1007/s10708-006-7055.

Timothy, Dallen J., and S. Ron Amos. "Understanding Heritage Cuisines and Tourism: Identity, Image, Authenticity, and Change." *Journal of Heritage Tourism* 8, no. 2–3 (2013): 99–104. https://doi.org/10.1080/1743873X.2013.767818.

Tippen, Carrie. *Inventing Authenticity: How Cookbook Writers Define Authenticity.* Fayetteville: University of Arkansas Press, 2018.

Trozzo, Katie, John Munsell, Kim Niewolny, and James L. Chamberlain. "Forest Food and Medicine in Contemporary Appalachia." *Southeastern Geographer* 59, no. 1 (2019): 52–76. https://doi.org/10.1353/sgo.2019.0005.

Twitty, Michael. *Cooking Gene.* New York: Harper Collins, 2017.

Urry, John. *Tourist Gaze.* Thousand Oaks: Sage Publications, 2002.

Van Wagenen, Jared. *Golden Age of Homespun.* New York: Farrar, Straus, & Giroux, 1960.

Vats, Anjali. "Cooking Up Hashtag Activism: #PaulasBestDishes and Counternarratives of Southern Food." *Communication and Critical/Cultural Studies* 12, no. 2 (2015): 209–14. https://doi: 10.1080/14791420.2015.1014184.

———. "Racechange is the New Black: Racial Accessorizing and Racial Tourism in High Fashion as Constraints on Rhetorical Agency." *Communication, Culture & Critique* 7, no.1 (2014): 112–35. https://doi.org/10.1111/cccr.12037.

Vogler, Pen. *Scoff: A History of Food and Class in Britain.* London: Atlantic Books, 2020.

Walden, Sarah. *Tasteful Domesticity: Women's Rhetoric and the American Cookbook 1790–1940.* Pittsburgh: University of Pittsburgh Press, 2018.

Wallace, Eric C. "Chef Restoring Appalachia's World-Class Food Culture," *Atlas*

Obscura, January 10, 2020, https://www.atlasobscura.com/articles/what-is-appalachian-food.

Wallach, Jennifer Jensen. *Dethroning the Deceitful Pork Chop: Rethinking African American Foodways from Slavery to Obama.* Fayetteville: University of Arkansas Press, 2015.

———. *Every Nation Has Its Dish: Black Bodies & Black Food in the Twentieth-Century America.* Chapel Hill: University of North Carolina Press, 2019.

Walker, Kenneth, and Lauren E. Cagle. "Resilience Rhetorics in Science, Technology, and Medicine." *Poroi* 15, no. (1) (2020). https://doi.org/10.13008/2151–2957.1303.

Wanzer-Serrano, Darrel. "Rhetoric's Race(ist) Problems." *Quarterly Journal of Speech* 105, no. 4 (2019): 465–76. https://doi.org/10.1080/00335630.2019.1669068.

Warner, Michael. "Publics and Counterpublics." *Public Culture* 14, no. 1 (2002): 44–90. https://doi.org/10.1215/08992363–14–1–49.

Webb-Sunderhaus, Sarah. "Keep the Appalachian, Drop the Redneck: Tellable Student Narratives of Appalachian Identity." *College English* 79, no. 1 (2016): 11–33.

Wenrich, John, and Jack Lewis. *Sylvatus: A History.* Sylvatus, VA: Sylvatus Ruritan Club, 1985.

Whisnant, David. *Modernizing the Mountaineer: People, Power, and Planning in Appalachia.* Knoxville: University of Tennessee Press, 1994.

White, Monica. *Freedom Farmers: Agricultural Resistance and the Black Freedom Movement.* Chapel Hill: University of North Carolina Press, 2018.

Wiggington, Eliot. *Foxfire Book.* New York: Doubleday, 1972.

Wilkerson, Jessica. *To Live Here You Have to Fight: How Women Led Appalachian Movements for Social Justice.* Champaign: University of Illinois Press, 2018.

Williams-Forson, Psyche A. *Building Houses Out of Chicken Legs: Black Women, Food, and Power.* Chapel Hill: University of North Carolina Press, 2006.

Williamson, J. W. *Hillbillyland: What the Movies Did to the Mountains and What the Mountains Did to the Movies.* Chapel Hill: University of North Carolina Press, 1995.

Wilson, Geoff A., Zhanping Hu, and Sanzidur Rahman. "Community Resilience in Rural China: The Case of Hu Village, Sichuan Province." *Journal of Rural Studies* 60 (2018): 130–40. https://doi.org/10.1016/j.jrurstud.2018.03.016.

Wilson, Kathleen Curtis. "Material Culture: The Opportunity to Study the Blending of Ethnic Traditions." *Journal of Scotch-Irish Studies* 1, no. 2 (2001): 66–85.

Witt, Doris. *Black Hunger.* Minneapolis: University Press of Minnesota, 2004.

Wood, Sara, and Malinda Maynor Lowery. "As We Cooked, As We Lived: Lumbee Foodways." *Southern Cultures* 21, no. 1 (2015): 84–91.

Woods, Karly, Joshua P. Ewalt, and Sara J. Baker. "A Matter of Regionalism: Remembering Brandon Teena and Willa Cather at the Nebraska History Museum." *Quarterly Journal of Speech* 99, no. 3 (2013): 341–63.

Young, Anna Marjorie, and Justin Eckstein. "Terroir and Topoi of the Lowcountry." In *Cookery: Food Rhetorics and Social Production,* edited by Donovan Conley, Justin Eckstein, 43–60. Tuscaloosa: University of Alabama Press, 2020.

Zafar, Rafia. *Recipes for Respect: African American Meals and Meaning.* Athens: University of Georgia Press, 2019.

Zagacki, Kenneth. "Preserving Heritage and Nature During the 'War on Terrorism': The North Carolina Outlying Landing Field ("OLF") Controversy." *Southern Communication Journal* 73, no. 4 (2008): 261–79. https://doi.org/10.1080/10417940802418775.

Zappen, James P. "Kenneth Burke on Dialectical-Rhetorical Transcendence." *Philosophy & Rhetoric* 42, no. 3 (2009): 279–301. https://doi.org/10.1353/par.0.0039.

Zarefsky, David. "President Johnson's War on Poverty: The Rhetoric of Three 'Establishment' Movements." *Communication Monographs* 44, no. 4 (1977): 352–73. https://doi.org/10.1080/03637757709390146.

INDEX

Italicized page numbers indicate illustrations.